Rabbi Leo Baeck

JEWISH CULTURE AND CONTEXTS

Published in association with
the Herbert D. Katz Center for Advanced Judaic Studies
of the University of Pennsylvania

Series Editors: Shaul Magid, Francesca Trivellato, Steven Weitzman

A complete list of books in the series
is available from the publisher.

RABBI LEO BAECK

Living a
Religious Imperative
in Troubled Times

Michael A. Meyer

PENN

UNIVERSITY OF PENNSYLVANIA PRESS

PHILADELPHIA

Publication of this volume was assisted by a grant from the Herbert D. Katz Publications Fund of the Center for Advanced Judaic Studies.

Published by
University of Pennsylvania Press
Philadelphia, Pennsylvania 19104-4112
www.upenn.edu/pennpress

Printed in the United States of America on acid-free paper
1 3 5 7 9 10 8 6 4 2

Library of Congress Cataloging-in-Publication Control Number: 2020004168

ISBN 978-0-8122-5256-9

To my friends
at the Leo Baeck Institute in Jerusalem,
London, New York, and Berlin

Contents

Preface

By August 1939, the German Jews' situation had become desperate. Since Hitler's rise to power six years earlier, the civic equality they had so laboriously gained in the preceding century was being eroded bit by bit. In 1933, they were removed from all positions of power or influence in German society; two years later, with the Nuremberg Laws, they were reduced from the status of citizens to mere subjects of the state. Simultaneously, the Nazi regime, by taking over their property, was imposing a steadily worsening impoverishment. In November 1938, legal discrimination burst into a massive outbreak of violence as Jewish lives, synagogues, and private property were destroyed in a pogrom known as Kristallnacht (night of broken glass). Jews were now singled out by the names they were forced to take: "Israel" for men and boys; "Sarah" for women and girls. Initially, most German Jews tried to ride out the storm. Some were descendants of a long line of ancestors in the country, and they had chosen the familiar over the foreign. But now, almost everyone was looking for any avenue of escape, their efforts frustrated as countries that might have accepted persecuted Jews severely limited their immigration. Among those fortunate to find a refuge outside Germany were communal leaders and rabbis, who, understandably, chose to save their own lives and those of their families.

In 1939, Leo Baeck—rabbi, scholar, and leader of the organized German Jewish community—was engaged in multiple efforts to facilitate emigration, especially for the young. That August, on the eve of World War II, he visited close relatives who had received permission to settle in England. While in England, he was urged to accept offers allowing him to remain, joining his daughter and her family. A British university offered the scholarly rabbi an academic position, and the German Jewish refugee community was eager for his rabbinical leadership. But Baeck steadfastly refused the opportunity. Nor was it the only time that he was offered a position in Great Britain or the United States. In each instance, he demurred, for he believed that it was his responsibility to be "the last Jew out of Germany." Despite the dangers, he would remain, attempting to do what he could to expedite the emigration as long as any Jews were still permitted to leave Germany and until the deportations to the East began. From then on, his principal task shifted to upholding morale and alleviating the suffering of those who no longer had any choice but to remain, while assisting those who went into hiding. In January 1943, Baeck was deported to the concentration-camp-like ghetto of Theresienstadt, where he continued to serve the emotional, spiritual, and intellectual needs of fellow Jews, along with some persecuted non-Jews, all of them confined in a way station on the road to death.

This same Leo Baeck was not only a tenacious keeper of his flock but also one of the most significant Jewish thinkers of the twentieth century, comparable with such better-known figures as Martin Buber, Franz Rosenzweig, and Abraham Joshua Heschel. Today, it is his career as a courageous leader of his community in darkest times that is best known, though he has also received some attention as a religious thinker. What has been lacking is a study of Baeck that not only combines these two aspects of his life but explores how they interacted with each other in his own consciousness and his changing environment. The combination of active leadership with profound thought is rare; perhaps even more remarkable is a personal philosophy that so completely harmonizes public and private action. Unlike numerous prominent personalities in the humanities and the arts, whose personal lives do not reflect the essence of their accomplishments, Baeck integrated what he believed in with what he did. His faith in God implied the ineluctable acceptance of moral obligation in all areas of life. Fulfilling that obligation was, in his eyes, no less a requirement in difficult times than it was in calmer ones, even if the cost should be far greater. Admired by many, Baeck also had his detractors: although many lent him support, some sought to undermine his work. His decisions involving life and death were controversial both in his time and down to the present.

To fully understand Leo Baeck requires probing not only his thought and public activity but also his personality—a difficult endeavor, since Baeck rarely dwelled on himself. Though he was usually formal and restrained on the outside, his engagement with events could not fail to stir his inner life. Generally described as gentle and kind, when necessary he could also be combative. A streak of puritanism and an outsize veneration for martyrdom ran through his psychological makeup. This personal element must receive its due if one is to understand Leo Baeck. The integration of these perspectives is the task of this volume. Drawing upon a broad variety of sources (some coming to light only in recent years) and especially turning to his own writings, I attempt a more complex and nuanced image of one of the most noteworthy personalities in the Jewish history of our age.

For convenience in locating references to the Baeck publications mentioned in the notes, I have listed individual items (in italics for books; in quotation marks for articles) by date of original publication followed by their location in *Werke*, the six-volume edition of Leo Baeck's works: Albert H. Friedlander et al., eds., *Leo Baeck Werke* (Gütersloh: Gütersloher Verlagshaus, 1996–2003). At various points, especially for a portion of Chapter 2, I have drawn upon my essay "Jewish Scholarship and Religious Commitment: Their Relative Roles in the Writings of Rabbi Leo Baeck," *Daat: A Journal of Jewish Philosophy & Kabbalah* 88 (2019): 127–143.

Chapter 1

An Unconventional Student and Rabbi

The Background

During medieval times, Jews in Western and Eastern Europe, though their religious customs differed, were almost uniformly observant in their religious practice. They lived in tightly knit communities, their social and spiritual lives focused inward toward their coreligionists. Regardless of the kingdom or duchy in which they dwelled, they were first and foremost Jews—not German, French, English, or Polish. That situation began to change in the late eighteenth century, as Jews in the West increasingly identified with the surrounding non-Jewish culture, which—in some places and among some individuals—was, to some extent, willing to include them. New vistas opened outside Judaism; identities, now comprising Jewish and non-Jewish components, began to split in two as a process of acculturation gained momentum to the west of the Elbe River, separating Western from Eastern Ashkenazi Jews. But within the immense Jewry of Poland, to a much greater extent than in Germany, traditional Jewish life hung on.

Between these two realms, on the border, lay the province of Posen (today, Poznan) with its capital of the same name. In 1793, at the Second Partition of Poland, Posen fell to Prussia, only to return to Poland after World War I. Initally, the political transfer had little effect on Posen's traditional Jewish life, which remained vibrant in the nineteenth century. The Jewish community had a traditional rabbinical academy (yeshiva), founded by the outstanding Talmud scholar Rabbi Akiba Eger, who had arrived there in 1815. Gradually, however, in the course of the nineteenth century, Western influences began to be felt. The Jewish Enlightenment (Haskalah), born in Königsberg and Berlin, gained a foothold in Posen: an increasing number of

Jews, who had exclusively focused inward under Polish rule, became Germanized and Europeanized, creating an interaction between the old and the new that spawned religious and intellectual ferment. Major figures in Jewish thought who mingled tradition with modernity emerged from this borderland. They included the proto-Zionist rabbi Zvi Hirsch Kalischer, as well as the popular historian of the Jews Heinrich Graetz. From the province of Posen came a son whose fame would spread far beyond the Jewish community and beyond the ocean: Haym Salomon, a close associate of George Washington and a major financier of the American Revolution.

It was in the small Posen town of Lissa (today, Leszno), with little more than a thousand Jews, that Leo Baeck was born on May 23, 1873, and given the Hebrew name Uri, followed by the Yiddish Lipmann. His surname, Baeck, was said to be an abbreviation for *ben kedoshim*, literally "an offspring of holy ones," but specifically referring to Jews who had undertaken the ultimate sanctification of God's name by preferring to die rather than give up their Jewish faith. There was a tradition in the Baeck family that an ancestor in medieval times was such a martyr, and this knowledge may well have played a role in the emphasis on martyrdom in Baeck's writings.

Leo Baeck was one of eleven children, the only one among them to become a rabbi. Growing up in Lissa, he was touched by both the traditional and modern spheres—the inner Jewish world but also the non-Jewish world beyond. Throughout his life, he would strive to integrate a profound sense of Jewish heritage with a striving to harmonize Jewish teaching with universal values. Though not an advocate of Jewish Orthodoxy, he refrained from criticizing expressions of Judaism that were more traditional than his own, just as he respected competing views of Jewish life in modernity. He valued and personally practiced Jewish ritual but did not seek to impose it on others. Baeck's lifelong desire and ability to mediate among Jewish factions was surely related to the milieu of the place on the border where he was born and grew up. The value he learned to place on the sense of community that reigned in a small town like Lissa would find repeated expression as he moved on to ever larger centers of activity.

The Student

Leo Baeck was the descendant of prominent rabbis on both sides of his family. His father, Rabbi Samuel Bäck (as the name was originally spelled), was a learned Talmudist who held a doctoral degree from the University of Leipzig. Samuel's interest in Jewish history, uncommon among traditional Jewish scholars, was employed for his contributions to the *Jewish Encyclopedia*—remarkably, produced in the United States—the publication that long held the field as the most important work of Jewish reference. In 1878, the elder Baeck published a history of the Jewish people and its literature, which was sufficiently popular to achieve three printings. As would be true of his son, who made additions and corrections to the third edition of 1906, the father sought to avoid sectarianism. Bäck presented all religious streams in Judaism as legitimate and bound in a common antagonism to indifferentism and materialism. He recognized the Zionist movement as a positive development in that it reawakened a diminishing sense of Jewish unity.[1] Yet, unlike his son, he eschewed biblical criticism, avoiding the subject by beginning his history with the Babylonian Exile.

Samuel Bäck provided Leo with a thorough education in Jewish sources, in part as his private tutor. Thus for the son, love of his father became entwined with a love for Jewish tradition. Like his father, the young Leo Baeck combined regular Talmud study with a thorough grounding in non-Jewish fields of knowledge. Despite its small-town milieu, Lissa boasted a first-rate academic high school, named after the Czech educational innovator John Amos Comenius. It welcomed Jewish students, who numbered more than sixty by the last decades of the nineteenth century.[2] Here Leo could lay the foundation for the extensive knowledge of classical languages that he would later display in his scholarly work. He did well there, finishing first in his class and thereby receiving the privilege, no doubt extraordinary for a Jewish student, of delivering the graduation address. The high school also gave young Baeck an early and pleasant contact with non-Jews, which may well have influenced his lifelong disdain for any form of Jewish—or non-Jewish—chauvinism. The living arrangements of the Bäck family may also have been an influence in this regard. Lissa had a small Calvinist community whose pastor owned the Bäck home; out of consideration for the relative poverty of his Jewish tenants, he charged only a minimal rent. It may well have been this early experience with a tolerant and merciful Calvinist pastor that set Baeck on a path of lifelong intellectual respect for the good works–oriented Calvinist form of Protestantism, as opposed to the personal faith–centered Lutheranism that he would encounter in his scholarship.

Many years later, after the destruction of German Jewry, Baeck nostalgically recalled his youth in Lissa. To a fellow survivor from his place of birth, he wrote in 1948: "I think back with deep appreciation of the town of my childhood and youth and of some of the people there, young and old; not least [I think] of the high school and its teachers and students. It is a lost world, but it was indeed a world. Alas, that it will never return."[3] Baeck was seventeen when he left Lissa, determined to become a rabbi, like his father.

Initially, Leo Baeck chose to obtain his rabbinical training at the Jewish Theological Seminary in Breslau (today, Polish Wrocław), in Silesia. Of the three modern rabbinical seminaries in Germany at the time, Breslau's was middle of the road. As in a typical yeshiva, its students devoted the largest portion of their time to Jewish law as it was anchored in the traditional texts of Judaism. Its founding director, Rabbi Zacharias Frankel, favored the more cloistered environment of a Jewish institution, as opposed to the establishment of Jewish studies within a university, for which more radical rabbinical colleagues had argued. Students prayed together regularly and, like their teachers, were expected to observe the ritual commandments. Although the school published an important scholarly journal, modern biblical criticism was decidedly excluded from its pages. Yet the curriculum included Jewish history and the practical skills that a rabbi would require in a modern congregation, especially the ability to present edifying sermons. The school's intellectual approach was that Judaism evolved within history and that modern scholarship could reveal that development, especially for the first centuries of the common era, the period of the early Rabbis. Religious reform was therefore precedented and indigenous to Jewish history. But the only form of change held legitimate was the one that occurred within the framework of Jewish tradition, not through an arbitrary advance beyond what Frankel had deemed the "collective will" of the contemporary community.

Leo Baeck entered the Breslau seminary in May 1891, when he was almost eighteen. There, he was among the last students taught Jewish history by the widely read Heinrich Graetz. Like his fellow rabbinical students, he began taking courses simultaneously at the University of Breslau, where he chose philosophy as his major academic field. Surprisingly, he remained in Breslau for less than two years, completing neither his rabbinical education nor his secular studies there. Why he undertook this unconventional move, of which his father seems to have disapproved, has remained unclear.

There are at least three possible explanations, each of which may bear some truth. The first relates to the Breslau seminary itself, where Baeck may have felt constrained by the restrictive atmosphere. This unhappiness may have been conjoined with the wish for a broader exposure to Jewish scholars and a freer academic atmosphere, such as reigned at the Liberal seminary in Berlin, where he now decided to continue his studies for the rabbinate. The Lehranstalt für die Wissenschaft des Judentums (Educational Institution for the Scientific Study of Judaism), as it was then called,[4] was devoted to the unfettered and uncompromising study of Jewish texts, including the Bible, while boasting a faculty committed to diverse theologies and varying ritual practice. It saw itself as serving both as a rabbinical seminary for students on the liberal side of the religious spectrum and as an academic institution for incipient Jewish scholars, who would not necessarily become rabbis. Although the Lehranstalt was doubtless attractive to Baeck, another very likely reason for his transfer is that he also wanted to study at the leading university in Germany, which was not that of Breslau but rather the prestigious University of Berlin. Finally, as would become characteristic of Baeck, he may have chosen to attend more than a single seminary, since he did not want his approach to Judaism to rest within but one of the channels in which Judaism then flowed in Germany. We know that while a student in Berlin, he supplemented his studies at the Lehranstalt with courses at a yeshiva run by a local Orthodox rabbi. He was clearly intent on not excluding any of the three branches of modern Judaism from his consciousness as a Jew.

When Leo Baeck came to Berlin in 1893, the wave of antisemitism that had shaken German Jews in the preceding decade and a half was about to evoke the establishment of a major Jewish defense organization, but Jews in the capital widely believed that the hatred had passed its apogee and that a comfortable future for them in Germany was not in doubt. The major challenge in the eyes of the religious leadership was not so much the enmity of non-Jews but the materialism that went along with the rising economic status of a Jewry that was now dominantly urban. In this atmosphere and with no German university open to Jewish studies, the Lehranstalt—among whose first teachers following its founding in 1872 had been Abraham Geiger, the radical Liberal scholar and rabbi, but whose faculty also included teachers of a more traditional persuasion—sought to serve as a center of both serious Jewish research and spiritual guidance. Yet Jewish support for the institution, which received no assistance from the government, was stingy, and its students, mostly from poor backgrounds, were forced to live in poverty. Baeck could earn very modest sums by teaching Judaism to young people but was sometimes forced to feed himself from leftover scraps of bread or rolls from Berlin restaurants, where he also gathered candle stubs for illumination. It was surely an unpleasant regimen but one that prepared him for the severities that would come later in life. Yet despite his privations, Baeck displayed a sense of humor, to which later acquaintances would frequently attest. There is evidence that at this time, he contributed his first published article to a popular satirical weekly, *Simplicissimus*, whose writers included such leading German literary figures as Thomas Mann, Rainer Maria Rilke, and Hermann Hesse.[5]

The increasing but incomplete secularization among Berlin Jews meant that whereas few attended religious services regularly, large numbers came to worship at the Jewish High Holidays, more than the synagogues could contain and more than the regularly employed rabbis of the community were able to serve. Consequently, additional religious services were arranged in public facilities, and rabbinical students were assigned to lead them. For three years, from 1894 through 1896, Leo Baeck was called upon to participate in this program. When, in May 1897, around his twenty-fourth birthday and after six years as a rabbinical student, he successfully passed a comprehensive examination at the Lehranstalt, he was certified as a full-fledged rabbi.

Baeck's progress at the University of Berlin was more rapid. In 1894, he passed a comprehensive doctoral examination in philosophy; a year later, he successfully defended a heavily footnoted dissertation on Benedict Spinoza's early influence in Germany. Published that same year, this exceedingly erudite work, which draws upon the original Latin versions of Spinoza's writings, is more historical than philosophical in nature. Although Baeck was a student of philosophy, his later writing would avoid philosophical systems in favor of historical research. He was attracted to Spinoza not so much for his philosophy as for his historical role and influence, perhaps also because, among philosophers of Jewish origin, Spinoza was the best known outside the Jewish sphere. Baeck implicitly sympathized with those who defended this Jew expelled from Amsterdam Jewry in an early modern Germany that was intolerant of his ideas. Proponents of Spinozism in Holland, he noted, could propagate his ideas freely, while crypto-Spinozists in Germany were forced to do so surreptitiously. Baeck was able to show how, without explicit reference to Spinoza, they drew freely upon his ideas. Whereas many, if not most, rabbinical students, who were required by the state to complete an advanced university education, chose to write on strictly Jewish subjects, Baeck, in selecting to write on Spinoza, thereby indicated an unconventional desire to expand his knowledge beyond the Jewish sphere and thus more fully complement his rabbinical studies.

Yet Baeck was never a Spinozist. In a later analysis of Spinoza, he severely criticized him for what his theology left out: he had allowed "history and community to disappear in the face of the absolute."[6] Baeck's own theology, as it developed over time, leaned away from Spinoza and rather in the direction of Immanuel Kant, whom he continued to admire throughout his life. For Baeck, Kant represented German thought at its most elevated. What he admired was not Kantian philosophy per se; rather, he strove to embody what he would later call "the Kantian personality, which stands as the bearer of the moral law, and in loyalty to the commandment finds itself and thereby its freedom."[7] What distinguishes his Jewish admirer from Kant is that for Baeck the Kantian sense of duty has its origins in the moral commandment emanating from God, and not in human reason alone. Kant's ethics fiercely rejected the notion of divine command, arguing instead for the autonomous will of the individual. In sharp contrast, as a believing Jew, Baeck insisted upon the sense of obligation issuing from a transcendent God. "God does not reveal Himself," Baeck later wrote of God, "but He reveals commandment and grace."[8] Like Kant, Baeck found the source of his faith both in nature and in morality—but for him, it was morality that mattered most in religion. With obvious reference to Kant's famous statement regarding the two sources of inspiration, the starry heavens above and the moral law within, Baeck later wrote: "There is a grandeur in fulfillment of the commandment that is higher than the inspiring world of stars. Or, in other words: the moral law within us means yet more than the starry heavens above us."[9]

Kantianism was transmitted to Baeck in its later form, neo-Kantianism, as that form was propagated by Hermann Cohen, the Jewish thinker who was more influential for Baeck's own thought than any other. Baeck did not study personally with Cohen, who, at that time, was not yet teaching at the Lehranstalt in Berlin. He met Cohen only later, in 1912, when Baeck assumed a rabbinate in Berlin.[10] But clearly, he read Cohen's work, if not during his student days, then certainly thereafter. Cohen was a severe critic of Spinoza on account of the earlier philosopher's conception of an immanent God who was virtually equivalent to nature. A Spinozistic theology did not allow for the ethical imperative of a transcendent God directed to the free will of human beings. Only such a God, according to Cohen, could create a moral tension within the human spirit and point toward a messianic future in whose establishment human beings played a role. Baeck found Cohen's message exceedingly appealing and very much in harmony with the emphasis upon the moral imperative that he believed to be firmly embedded in Jewish tradition. Cohen had noted that the confession in the liturgy of the Day of Atonement referred only to moral, not to ritual transgressions, a position fully in accord with Baeck's thought.[11] If Baeck regarded Cohen as his mentor, Cohen, for his part, apparently felt that Baeck would carry on in his footsteps. Shortly before he died in 1918, Cohen is alleged to have consoled some of his friends with the words: "Be of good cheer; when I go, Leo Baeck will still be with you."[12]

Cohen's influence was indirect, but Wilhelm Dilthey, one of Baeck's teachers at the University of Berlin and the supervisor of his dissertation, made a personal as well as an intellectual impact that would be evident throughout Baeck's writings. Influential in his time and down to the present, Dilthey was a multifaceted scholar: an intellectual historian, a psychologist, and a philosopher without adhering to any philosophical system. His approach to historical research seems to be what most impressed Baeck. Dilthey famously distinguished the study of the humanities (including history) from the natural sciences, insisting that each required its own scholarly approach. Historians were obligated to go beyond the externals of their subject, to seek psychological insights. Their work required not only knowledge but also understanding (*Verstehen*), which could be gained only by pressing to the interior of a subject. Without abandoning their objectivity, historians were called upon to develop sympathy with their subjects (*Mitfühlen*) in order to understand how human beings related to one another, even as they interacted within the framework of nature and the current of events.[13] As we shall see, Baeck was soon to apply a Diltheyan critique in his own writings.

Rabbi in Oppeln

Armed with advanced rabbinical studies as well as a secular education, Leo Baeck sought a position as a community rabbi. He first applied for one in the Prussian city of Königsberg (today, Kaliningrad in Russia), once the home of the great Immanuel Kant. But the community chose the slightly older Hermann Vogelstein, who had the advantage of previous experience as a rabbi in the small Jewish community of Oppeln, to the southeast of Breslau. That same Oppeln community now accepted Baeck as Vogelstein's successor.[14] The novice rabbi would spend a full decade there.

At the end of the nineteenth century, Oppeln in Prussian Silesia (today, Opole in Poland) had grown to nearly 30,000 inhabitants, most of them German speakers. When Baeck arrived, the little country town had become a center of industry and commerce. The Jewish community was quite new. In

1565, Jews were expelled from the town, which in the eighteenth century still had the right not to tolerate them. It was only after the Prussian takeover in 1742 that a small Jewish community began to take shape and gradually grow in size; by the end of the nineteenth century, there were about 750 Jews. Such a middle-size Jewish community, Baeck believed, was ideal: unlike a very small one, it was not plagued by an inadequacy of resources that hindered carrying out religious life; and unlike a large one, it was not as subject to anomie and large-scale assimilation. When Jews exceeded a certain number, Baeck noted in 1905, city Jews ceased to be closely tied to one another. By contrast, in Oppeln everyone had a sense of mutual responsibility and a larger measure of willingness to sacrifice for the common good. Yet, ironically, Baeck would eventually spend the bulk of his career in Berlin, which, he believed, was the very epitome of a Jewish non-community.[15]

Despite the town's history of not tolerating Jews and the likely continuation of at least limited anti-Jewish feelings, Oppeln Jews were fortunate in that relations between them and non-Jews had become quite friendly by the time the new rabbi arrived, just as had been true in Lissa, the town of Baeck's birth. Rabbi Joachim Prinz, who spent his childhood in Oppeln and whose parents were married there by Rabbi Baeck, recorded in his memoirs that he had never heard an unfriendly word spoken against Jews there. Whenever a funeral procession, Jewish or Gentile, passed through the streets, men and women of both religious groups paid their respects. Jews and Christians lived intermingled in the town, and, according to Prinz, most Jews were economically well off; they owned the largest stores, and the professionals among them, doctors and lawyers, were well respected.[16] As a relatively affluent community, Oppeln helped support smaller Jewish settlements that, having suffered from an outflow of their members to larger communities, consequently had difficulty maintaining their institutions. From the mid-nineteenth century, a succession of Liberal rabbis made Oppeln the center of Jewish religious reform in Upper Silesia. When the first synagogue was built in 1842, the religious reformer Rabbi Abraham Geiger was chosen to deliver the dedicatory address.

On June 1, 1897, the community of Oppeln dedicated a new synagogue. Resting on a small hill overlooking the Oder River, it boasted a dome, crowned by a Star of David visible in a large portion of the town. In the tradition of Liberal Judaism, the structure was enhanced by a pipe organ, and religious services were musically embellished by a choir that included both sexes. However, in the traditional manner of all German synagogues at that time, Orthodox or Liberal, men and women sat separately, although there was no barrier between them. Having arrived in Oppeln scarcely three weeks earlier, Baeck was called upon to inaugurate the newly completed synagogue by kindling its Eternal Light.

As rabbi of the community, Baeck enjoyed no less respect than the Christian clergy. When he entered a room, it was customary for everyone to rise and wait until he began to speak. However, in his rabbinical role, Baeck did not sparkle. He was not a dynamic preacher: his sermons lacked the sentimentality that worshipers expected; and, with his soft voice vibrating disconcertingly, he eschewed every popular rhetorical device. But his message reached at least some of his listeners. In one family, his sermons often provided the chosen topic of discussion around the table, following services.[17]

As in other communities, the rabbi, in addition to his duties as pastor and preacher, was expected to give the religion course for Jewish students in the municipal high school. Although teaching children was not Baeck's forte, his students appreciated the patient interest he showed in their own thinking and his concern for their welfare. Other teachers at the time, and long thereafter, stood over their classes, giving pupils little opportunity to express personal opinions. Later, in Düsseldorf, a grateful student recalled how Baeck treated pupils in his classes as if they were adults, encouraging them to ask critical questions. "With real enthusiasm, we welcomed these novelties," one student recalled.[18] In Oppeln Baeck's experience was unusual in that he was considered a regular member of the high school's faculty. When colleagues were absent, he was called upon to teach secular subjects such as mathematics and spelling. Years later, in difficult times, he would attempt mathematical puzzles as a distraction from more serious matters.

It was in Oppeln, not long after his arrival, that Baeck met and married Natalie Hamburger, granddaughter of the radical religious reformer Rabbi Adolf Wiener, who had served the Jewish community of Oppeln until his death in 1895. She was an attractive woman with dark hair, often mistaken for a Gentile. According to a story that Baeck loved to tell, he was once out walking with his bride-to-be when a friend, encountering them, quickly crossed the street and judiciously looked away. It seems the friend thought that the rabbi was having an illicit affair with a non-Jewish woman. "Here you are, engaged to a girl from one of the finest Jewish families in Germany, and you're out in public with a shikse!"[19] According to one contemporary source, Natalie was indeed the loveliest woman in all of Oppeln.[20] Leo and Natalie had a daughter, Ruth, in 1900, and suffered the anguish of a still-

Figure 1. Leo Baeck with his fiancée, Natalie Hamburger, in 1898.
Courtesy of Leo Baeck Institute, New York.

born son six years later. There would be no further children. In keeping with the customs of the time, Natalie was the helpmate of her husband, without a profession of her own except to be the proper wife of a rabbi. Her early death in 1937 left Baeck a widower at the age of sixty-three. It came at a difficult time in his public life, when he must have needed her love and moral support more than ever.

Near the conclusion of his first year in Oppeln, Baeck, then a fledgling rabbi, dared to espouse two views in open opposition to those of his older colleagues. He first did so at a meeting of the General German Rabbinical Association, which had convened nearly a hundred German rabbis, all but the most extreme orthodox. Baeck attended the meeting, held in Berlin—along with his father, who represented the rabbinate of Lissa—in early June 1898, a year after the First Zionist Congress. Members of the rabbinical organization's executive committee had protested the convening of the congress, which led

Theodor Herzl, founder of political Zionism and organizer of the congress, to brand them "protest rabbis." Their objections forced Herzl to move the congress from Munich to Basel—from Germany to Switzerland. The rabbinical executive committee was now looking for a more broad-based condemnation of this alleged offense against the patriotism and loyalty of German Jewry. When the vote was taken, virtually all the assembled rabbis, Liberal and Orthodox, apparently including even Leo Baeck's father, voted to support the position of the executive. Only three rabbis voted against the resolution, one of them simply because, in his view, discussion had been shut off prematurely. Only two voted negatively out of principle: the Orthodox rabbi Saul Kaatz and the Liberal rabbi Leo Baeck. Here, so early in his life, was the first example of Baeck's willingness to act unhesitatingly on his beliefs, whatever the pressure on him not to do so. In this case, it was not that in 1898 he was an early supporter of Zionism; he was not. Rather, he consistently believed that there was room for multiple expressions of Jewish identity and that Jews of one opinion should not condemn those of another.

At the rabbinical group's session the following day, Baeck had the opportunity to give expression to this tolerant view when a different issue arose. In a short speech, he surprisingly suggested to the gathered rabbis that his own course of study in the seminaries of more than a single current of religious Judaism had been beneficial and should become the pattern for all rabbinical students. "It would be desirable, for a start," he said, "if young people from the Lehranstalt were to go to the [Orthodox] Hildesheimer Seminary. Why should a person have only a single denomination?"[21] According to the transcript, Baeck's comment provoked "great amusement," and he had to ask for patience so that he could explain that he was referring to a matter of educational method—not that a rabbi could be traditionalist and reformer at the same time. The purpose behind his suggestion was broader. Such study in a variety of institutions could lead to mutual tolerance among rabbis of differing views. Here, in this brief statement to a gathering of his colleagues, was Rabbi Baeck's first publicly expressed conception of a broad-based Judaism whose adherents had more in common than the differences that divided them. These unconventional views in later years would make him so extraordinarily acceptable in the German Jewish community that it tasked him with one leadership position after another. Eventually, he was chosen to be president of that very rabbinical association where initially he had been so decidedly in the minority.

Baeck's call for a broad rabbinical education was grounded in a theological position to which he had given expression while still a student in Berlin.[22] Like the eighteenth-century Jewish philosopher Moses Mendelssohn, Baeck held that Judaism did not possess dogmas; hence, one Jew could not rightfully call another a heretic. That lack of dogma not only differentiated Judaism from Christianity; it meant that—at least literally—there was no Jewish orthodoxy. The consequent freedom from intellectual constraint was a blessing, for it lent Judaism a flexibility that would have been restricted by any fixed creed. It allowed for a pluralism in interpreting the word of God, a diversity among generations, and the acceptability of different currents within contemporary Judaism. No party had the right to claim that its interpretation of the faith was *the* Judaism; the Jewish religion was sufficiently broad to include them all. The true point of differentiation among Jews lay not in the area of belief but rather in practice—in worship and ritual observance. The so-called Orthodox were best defined simply as those who were more loyal to the ceremonies.

Religious practices, according to Baeck, were not ends in themselves but merely means to a higher religious goal. They were not divine commandments, which, clearly revealing his Liberal perspective, Baeck limited to the moral sphere both here and in his later writings. The dietary laws served as an example. They were intended to "sanctify," a word taken from the Hebrew language root *kof dalet shin*, which, he noted, means both "holiness" and "separation." Jewish ritual both sanctified the Jewish people and set it apart for its moral tasks in the world. In Baeck's view, it served as a means to a higher end: the collective moral task of all Jews.

Baeck's instrumentalization of Jewish religious practice did not mean that ritual was of little value. Personally observant, he rejoiced when—at a later time, after the difficult years of the postwar inflation—he was able once more to purchase his own *lulav* (palm frond) for the appropriate blessing at the Sukkot holiday.[23] The Baecks had separate dishes for Passover, and much later, when he visited the United States and was taken to restaurants, he invariably ordered fish in place of meat. He noted that Jewish ceremonies differ from Christian ones in that they are not limited to the religious sanctuary but encompass the secular sphere as well. Thus they serve to transform all existence into religious service. "Ceremonies," he wrote, "are the language in which religious ideas achieve expression."[24] His liberalism emerges only when he adds: "But they must effectively speak to us—they must tell us something; that is the criterion for judging them. A worship exercise that no longer possesses meaning for us is not religious, but [in a negative sense] ceremonial." However, in a later article,[25] perhaps realizing the anarchic consequences of this unmitigated position, Baeck withdraws from it slightly: religious observance as such is also commanded but with a different source and purpose. Observances like keeping the Sabbath, for example, are commandments of the community whose intent is preservation of the Jewish people as the embodiment of religious values. In the language of the rabbinic sages but more broadly interpreted, they constitute a "fence around the Torah," protecting Jewish teaching from dissolving into the stream of history. They differ from the divine command to seek righteousness in that they are subject to the requirements of each age.

Decisions regarding worship in the synagogue become obligatory because they are made and carried out collectively in the community. But even certain rituals performed by individuals, such as circumcision, are a Jewish obligation. Even if the individual Jew finds no meaning in them, the act may possess immutable value in its being essential for the unity of the Jewish people. For Baeck, the relation to ceremony thus marks not only a distinction among the branches of Judaism; it also differentiates what he called the religion of the individual from the religion of the people. Individuals will always seek in the tradition whatever can provide release from the mundane and whatever can raise them to a higher level. What matters for them are the basic religious conceptions and moral laws. But that is not true for the community, whose concern must be for the external forms, since they provide continuity and protect collective Jewish life against the forces of dissolution. That was true in the ancient world when the challenge was presented by paganism, and it continued to be so for the Jewish minority in the Christian world. Individuals might suffer from the constraining effect that these concerns of the collectivity have upon them, and Baeck might at times have felt that effect himself. But as a community rabbi, he could not deny their necessity. This tension between the individual and the collectivity, expressed early in his career, remained one of the tensions that would become characteristic of Baeck's later religious thought.

Chapter 2

Restoring the Dignity of Judaism

Scholarship and Religion

Whatever the theoretical and practical differences among the currents in German Judaism, its religious leaders, with the exception of the most orthodox, were committed to harmonizing with, or at least relating to, the critical scientific study of Judaism known in Germany as *Wissenschaft des Judentums*. For Baeck, this common pursuit could serve as a point of unity, even if the results were sometimes divisive. In a book review that he published while still a student in Berlin, his discussion of how the Jews in medieval Muslim Spain had participated actively in its culture led him to the broader conclusion that "Judaism never sets itself in opposition to scientific progress, but rather regards it as a means for furthering religion."[1] This notion that unprejudiced critical inquiry would not damage Judaism but rather strengthen it remained Baeck's conviction throughout his life. Nonetheless, however much he was devoted to objective inquiry, Baeck's writings were almost always, directly or indirectly, historical inquiry for the sake of advancing Judaism.

From the very beginning of his career, Jewish scholarship played a central role in Leo Baeck's life. According to one of his students at the Liberal seminary where Baeck studied and would later teach for nearly thirty years, "of all his numerous interests and activities, scholarly research was really the main element in his life, which he pursued with particularly affectionate zeal and devotion."[2] Baeck's scholarly horizon was broad: he was able to write knowledgeably about philology, philosophy, history, and theology; his knowledge of Greek and Latin extended well beyond what was offered him in his formal humanistic education. Over the years, Baeck published seven articles in the principal Jewish scholarly journal of the time, the *Monatsschrift für Geschichte und Wissenschaft des Judentums*, as well as dozens of scholarly inquiries elsewhere.

As a scholar, Baeck was little interested in the external history of the Jews. He rarely wrote of Jewish economic achievement, nor did he dwell on the Jews' history of suffering, which, along with their history of learning, had made up an important element of the Jewish past for the Jewish historian Heinrich Graetz. Baeck's interest lay not in the Jews as objects of their history but only as its subjects, and he saw their historical creativity as dominantly religious. For him, it was the history of "the people of Judaism" before it was the history of the Jewish people.[3]

Among Baeck's articles in the *Monatsschrift* are some that lack any personal stamp of the author, especially the earliest articles. Here Baeck's religious commitment is not evident; the articles could easily have been written by another scholar, Jew or Gentile. His first published essay (1900) was on a Maimonidean epigone, Levi ben Abraham, and was severely critical.[4] After a careful reading of his subject's work, Baeck concluded that it contained nothing new of any value. Everything of consequence had already been proposed in the work of Moses Maimonides. Baeck's motivation, we may assume, was simply to fill a small blank space in historical knowledge—or perhaps, through a demonstration of critical capacity, to gain adoption into the circle of Jewish scholars. No present purpose or religious motivation is noticeable.

Baeck's full commitment to critical inquiry meant that he did not set limits to his research, unlike more traditional Jewish scholars. For Baeck, even radical biblical criticism was not destructive of faith. In a brief article published in 1902, during the middle years of his Oppeln rabbinate, Baeck argues that the Hebrew word *s'neh* in the Book of Exodus—usually assumed to mean "bush," the so-called Burning Bush that Moses discovers in the desert—is, in fact, a linguistic variant of the word *sinai*. He goes so far as to conclude that there never was a burning bush but only a burning mountain, the volcanic Mount Sinai. Baeck never retracted this unusual, though not entirely novel, hypothesis, repeating it even late in life.[5] An incongruous suggestion at the end of the article, proposing that it would nonetheless be more appropriate to remain with the traditional interpretation of Exod. 3:2, may well have been forced on Baeck by the conservative editor of the *Monatsschrift*, the journal in which his article appeared.

In succeeding years, Baeck would occasionally publish studies whose purpose was strictly limited to the advancement of scholarship. But the vast majority of his writing was devoted to the defense or propagation of the Jewish religion. This intent set Baeck apart from leading figures of Jewish historical scholarship in Germany. Although a religious Jew, Leopold Zunz, universally recognized as the father of modern Jewish studies, took a different position, expressed most emphatically: "Our Wissenschaft should first of all emancipate itself from the theologians."[6] Living most of his life in a Germany where Jews were not yet fully emancipated, Zunz directed his historical writing toward the political achievement of civic equality and the academic recognition of scholarship on Judaism in the German university more than to any religious purpose. His pupil Moritz Steinschneider held a similar view. Still, Zunz's scholarship, unlike that of Steinschneider, was largely devoted to the history of the Jewish religion rather than to the accomplishments of Jews in the sciences and the arts. In the twentieth century, some Jewish scholars, Fritz Bamberger among them, began to regard the critical study of Jewish sources as, by its very nature, a religious enterprise, thereby eliminating the need to use scholarship for an extrinsic religious purpose.

Baeck's approach in his scholarly work differed from all these. It was mediated by its location within religious Judaism, even as it reached out to the criteria of objective scholarship. In the preface to his first collection of essays, *Wege im Judentum* (Paths in Judaism, 1933), he wrote that the essays in that volume were "not so much written about Judaism but rather emerged from within Judaism."[7] He saw himself—and all Jews—as placed within (*hereingestellt*) the Jewish religious experience. It was the task of the Jewish scholar to begin from this position, not from an artificial one looking in from the outside. Although not consistent in the matter, Baeck frequently chose the expression *Wissenschaft vom Judentum* rather than *Wissenschaft des Judentums*. The preferred formulation could mean that Jewish scholarship by its very designation indicated that it flowed outward from within and was not externally applied. Certainly for Baeck, his own Wissenschaft was of that sort. He noted that the purely academic study of religion, on account of its method, was incapable of producing faith, whose sources lay elsewhere. Religion, he believed, could not be fully understood by cognitive research (*wissensmäßige Erforschung*) alone.[8] But the two could be combined in an academic investigation that was imbued with faith. In Baeck's eyes, the study of religion required that faith and scholarship be inseparable. A penetrating study of religion required writing it from a religious standpoint, shaping the material in one's own consciousness rather than allowing its history, separate from the investigating scholar, to shape the account. In his last major work, *This People Israel: The Meaning of Jewish Existence*, Baeck wrote: "One can understand history only if one has penetrated into faith, and one can understand faith only when one has grasped history."[9]

For Baeck, scholarship was likewise intimately related to personal virtue or to the lack thereof. It was more than a collection of techniques; it was the Wissenschaft of a particular person, a reflection of the scholar's character. When, in his later years, Nazi scholars twisted their studies to fit an internalized ideology, he wrote: "As is the person, so is his Wissenschaft."[10]

Attack and Defense

In his fourth year in Oppeln, Baeck chose once again to set himself in opposition to a majority-held view. This time, the issue was not one that divided Jews—not Zionism or rabbinical education—but rather a bitter issue between Jews and Christians; and this time, the field of combat was scholarship.

At the beginning of the twentieth century, Adolf von Harnack was the leading theologian among liberal Protestants in Germany. His influence radiated outward from his prestigious position at the University of Berlin. As a theologically progressive professor, he prided himself on rejecting what he regarded as historically and scientifically untenable Christian dogmas. Yet he had little regard for any faith but his own. In his famous inaugural address as rector of the university in 1901, he argued against the broad academic representation of religion, since, as he put it with regard to Christianity: "Whoever does not know this religion knows no religion, and whoever knows it, along with its history, knows them all."[11] That same year, Harnack published a series of sixteen popular lectures that he had given in Berlin during the previous winter semester, titled *The Essence of Christianity.* The lectures were decidedly not antisemitic, in the narrow sense of the word. As a critical scholar, Harnack did not rehearse old canards about the Jews' accusatory role against Jesus, as it is portrayed in the New Testament. His "liberal" arguments, he said, were based strictly upon historical Wissenschaft, though together with what he called his own "life experience, the product of witnessed history"—in other words, a basis that included the subjective along with the objective. By their author's own admission, Harnack's lectures eschewed a narrow conception of Wissenschaft, which he feared might constrain his message. Instead, he chose a scholarly approach that could be stretched to satisfy the needs of both heart and spirit. Thus when Harnack came to a discussion of the Judaism that was contemporary with Jesus, he avoided a strictly objective study of the Judaism of that age, choosing to proceed rapidly to a moral and comparative evaluation in relation to the Master's teachings. His conclusion was that while Jesus offered no radically new doctrine, his recorded statements rose to a level of purity and earnestness that stood in stark contrast to a Pharisaism polluted by excessive adherence to Jewish law.

Harnack's attack on rabbinic Judaism in its formative stage was a challenge that could not be left unanswered. Among the rabbis who replied, the youngest was Leo Baeck, whose lengthy critique, appearing in the *Monatsschrift*, first brought the Oppeln rabbi to broader attention. His response to Harnack's work comprised several elements, all resting on the prominent lecturer's having forsaken the canons of Wissenschaft as he proceeded to a biased, personally motivated, moral condemnation of Jesus' Jewish contemporaries. To Baeck's mind, despite the professor's protests to the contrary, Harnack had abandoned history for the sake of apologetics. Leaving out New Testament passages with which he could not identify, he had shaped Jesus in his own image; the essence of Christianity became the essence of Harnack's personal religious values. According to Baeck, the lectures should properly have been called "My Religion" or "My Christianity." He had "mixed himself up with Jesus," projecting his own ideals upon the past. In short, he had acted the role of defense lawyer rather than that of scholar.

It was only after attacking Harnack's general approach as unscholarly (*unwissenschaftlich*) that Baeck proceeded to undermine his portrayal of Pharisaism, which, according to Baeck, served Harnack as the dark background against which Christianity could shine the more brightly. Instead of acting as historian, by trying to understand the Judaism of that time and thus better understand the Gospels, Harnack had simply cast it aside as unworthy. Baeck concluded that there was nothing wrong with a Christian writing a glorification of Christianity but then he should have recognized that what he was writing was not history but rather apologetics.[12]

Apologetics

Ironically, apologetics is exactly what Baeck would write three years later, even borrowing the term "essence" in titling his own work *The Essence of*

Judaism and, like Harnack, composing what was ultimately a statement of Baeck's own faith rather than an objective study of Judaism. Like Harnack's lectures, Baeck's book was as much determined by religion as it was by scholarship. Writing from personal commitment, Baeck shaped the sources to fit that commitment rather than allowing the material—with all its inner contradictions—to shape the account.

Just as Adolf von Harnack's *The Essence of Christianity* mirrored his spiritual attachment to Christianity, so Baeck's first major work reflected his attachment to Judaism. In commenting on a later edition, the Jewish intellectual and philosopher Franz Rosenzweig stated bluntly that Baeck's theme was not the essence of Judaism but rather his own religious essence.[13] That prompted Baeck to respond to Rosenzweig that apologetics was virtually unavoidable. Were not the Platonic dialogues apologies in search of the "essence" of Socratic philosophy, and so, too, the works of Kant and Hegel apologies? There was simply no clear border between judging objectively and defending. Citing Wilhelm Dilthey, he maintains that the values and goals embedded in historical writing are interwoven with one another.[14] Already in the first edition of his work, Baeck had suggested that with regard to the Hebrew Prophets, one might perhaps see his treatment of them as apologetic. But it was simply not possible to speak of certain subjects other than apologetically. "For some matters, understanding them means *admiring* them."[15]

The Essence of Judaism is divided into three parts. The first of these, titled "The Character of Judaism," speaks in general terms, relating Jewish essence especially to the revelation vouchsafed to the biblical Prophets and its universal implications. The second, "The Ideas of Judaism," descends to specifics of belief: in God, in ourselves, in our fellow human beings, and in humanity as a whole. The brief final part, "The Preservation of Judaism," outlines the sustaining influence of religious practice as the Jews progressed through history.

As in the case of Harnack, and contrary to the criteria of impartial scholarship, Baeck's reading of history is selective rather than balanced and comprehensive. His intent is not to present Judaism in its full compass but to isolate its viable elements. He is attempting to provide Jewish readers with a usable past that they can claim completely and without ambivalence. Baeck admits that occasionally in the history of Judaism, base or inferior elements emerged. But he argues that, in due course, they were vanquished. He passes silently over any particulars that are discordant with his apologetics—or at least, places them outside the category of essence.[16] One example is Baeck's proud discussion of the humane manner in which ancient Judaism treated the slave, wherein he locates it morally above the cruel practices of Greeks and Romans. However, he fails to distinguish between the relatively well-treated Hebrew slave and the considerably less desirable position of his Canaanite counterpart. Like Harnack, with regard to early Christianity, Baeck minimizes outside influences on Judaism, limiting them mostly to externals that fail to touch the essence of the faith as it is expressed, especially in the originality of the Hebrew Prophets.

The Prophets, according to Baeck, were the religious geniuses of Judaism, occupying a role in religion equivalent to that of the greatest painters or sculptors in their respective fields. Seeing a world removed from the will of God, they condemned its manifestations and envisaged a different and morally superior society. "They possess the strength to set their psychological certainty against all the alleged facts and in opposition to the entire apparent reality. With the mighty paradox of a confidence grounded in faith, they speak their 'and nevertheless.' By their lives they have taught humanity to bear testimony to this 'and nevertheless.' The Prophets stand fast; they do not bargain or make deals. They will not allow anything to be stripped away or subtracted from their demand."[17] Thus the Prophets embody the essence of Judaism, which Baeck defines as the unmitigated moral imperative. It was the Prophets, not the priests, who distinguished Israel from other nations and made the religion of Israel unique. For Baeck, not surprisingly, it is the history of the prophetic message—not the history of judges, monarchs, and Second Temple priests—that constitutes the true history of Judaism in biblical times and up to the present day.

Baeck was aware that in *The Essence of Judaism*, he had crossed the boundary between unprejudiced Wissenschaft and an approach structured by his own religious commitment. In his preface to the English edition, first published in 1936, he wrote that "the writer must possess a personal, spiritual relation to the details and to the whole; he must be filled with the conviction that there is contained in them a permanent and decisive value."[18] Thus for Baeck, *Wesen* (essence) is intimately related to *wesentlich* (essential), meaning "to be of vital significance." The enduring essence of Judaism, his book suggests implicitly, is not determined by what is objectively and dominantly central in the Jewish tradition but by those doctrines (not dogmas) that possess a personal attraction for Baeck himself and that should possess no less attractive power for other Jews of his time. It was indeed to contemporary Jewry that *The Essence of Judaism* was directed and not, for all its scholarship, principally to a community of scholars. This is especially evident in the last pages of its first 1905 edition, whose language migrates from description to prescription, its author evolving gradually from scholar into rabbi. Here Baeck speaks of what his fellow Jews should do to embody their Judaism and spread its message. He writes not in the impersonal third person but in the first-person plural: "We should allow our way of life to announce the majesty of our faith."[19] His ultimate goal clearly does not lie in simply revealing the essence of Judaism but in inspiring Jews to express that essence in their lives.[20]

For Baeck, Zionism was not part of the Jewish essence. He did not believe that the future for all Jews lay in the ancient homeland. But, as we have seen, at the first rabbinical conference that he attended, he refused to be part of a protest against it. A few years later, shortly before Baeck's departure from Oppeln in 1907, Emil Bernhard Cohn, a rabbi employed by the Jewish community of Berlin, was suspended from his position because he had expressed Zionist views from the pulpit. When Cohn sent Baeck a copy of the booklet, which outlined what had happened and in which he defended his position, Baeck read it and was outraged by what had occurred. He sent a letter of sympathy to Cohn: "What has happened to you is so illiterate, so unreligious and so un-Jewish that one can scarcely grasp how it could have happened in a Jewish religious community that calls itself liberal. . . . Our situation is not so rich in men who possess their own steady views as to venture throwing [such] a man overboard!"[21]

By spring 1907, Baeck had completed a decade of rabbinical service in Oppeln. He had demonstrated his capability as a teacher and a scholar, even if his oratorical effectiveness still lagged behind that of his colleagues. He was now ready to move on to Düsseldorf, a larger, more challenging, Jewish community. Since Baeck did not keep the texts of his sermons, which he usually wrote out and then memorized, we know little of what he spoke from the Oppeln pulpit. However, the final sermon that he gave there, his farewell address, has been preserved. It was delivered, most appropriately, on the Jewish holiday of Simhat Torah, when the last portion of the Torah in the Book of Deuteronomy is read along with the first from Genesis. The sermon is remarkable in that Baeck's request is for the congregation to remember not himself but the messages he had sought to deliver. The sermon reveals a personal quality attested to repeatedly by those who knew Baeck: his genuine humility, almost to the point of self-effacement. He notes that in none of his sermons had he used the word "I"—until that moment when its use became necessary in order to render thanks to all who had supported him. He stresses that in Judaism, there is no distinction between clergy and laity. The rabbi, like everyone else, is only a member of the community. He must not fall victim to arrogance simply because he speaks from a raised pulpit, in a loud voice, and in a situation where no one is given the opportunity to refute him. He needs to remember that he is proclaiming not his own ideas but the word of God. Petty vanity and exaggerated self-affection, he insists, have no place in a rabbi's message.[22] Years later, as a senior rabbi in Berlin, Baeck would look askance at a younger generation of German rabbis who did exactly what he here eschews, speaking not as impersonal conveyers of the word of God but as personal commentators on the Jewish events of the day.

Düsseldorf

In moving from Oppeln to Düsseldorf in October 1907, Baeck was going from the east of Germany to its west, from a relatively small town and Jewish community to a sizable Rhineland city with a Jewish population of about three thousand. In the early eighteenth century, Düsseldorf was the home of the wealthy court Jew Joseph van Geldern and, at the end of that century, the birthplace of the poet Heinrich Heine. When Baeck arrived, its Jewish community had absorbed a large number of Eastern European Jews, attracted by the economic opportunities that the city offered. Baeck's task was to serve the settled middle-class Jews who had their roots in Germany. They were dominantly adherents of a lazy Liberal Judaism that was peripheral to most of their lives. Christianity had long tempted them, with its advantages of greater social acceptance. Judging by his publications during the years of his rabbinate in Düsseldorf, Baeck was determined to convince those Jews who had become distant from Judaism that they should not leave it for the dominant faith. Instead, they should recognize what Baeck himself believed: that Judaism was more in harmony with modern culture than was its religious rival.

During the nineteenth century, traditional Judaism in Germany gradually declined; by mid-century, it had become a diminishing minority. In the heady atmosphere of the 1840s, as political liberalism sought to unseat the tyranny of monarchs, religious liberalism—Catholic, Protestant, and Jewish—experienced a period of enthusiastic and hopeful activism. Liberal rabbis gathered in conferences to discuss changes in liturgy and ritual law.

But with the suppression of the revolutions of 1848, a new period of political reaction squelched the newfound enthusiasm. Although some religious reforms entered individual Jewish communities, public interest shifted away from thoughts of religious and social progress and toward the establishment of a firm German unity and a state that kept religion under its control. It became the age of Otto von Bismarck, the German chancellor who suppressed social movements and moved a newly united Germany toward the achievement of empire. Liberal Judaism, now led mostly by aging rabbis, was hard-pressed to combat the dominant religious indifference. However, shortly after the turn of the century, a renaissance began to emerge within the circles of an incipient Zionism as well as within Liberal Judaism. For the first time, Liberal rabbis and Liberal laity in Germany formed national organizations to advance their cause.

Liberal Judaism was a current (or denomination) in German Judaism that gradually gained a clear identity in the second half of the nineteenth century. Initially, any deviation from traditional Judaism was simply branded "Reform," but when a radical congregation in Berlin, which held its religious services on Sundays and virtually eliminated Hebrew from its prayer book, took the name *Reformgemeinde* (Reform community) in the 1840s, the relatively more traditional reformers chose to call their interpretation of the faith "Liberal Judaism." Leo Baeck considered himself a Liberal Jew.

The nature of Baeck's Liberal Judaism stands out more clearly when compared with two non-Orthodox contemporary Jewish thinkers who were close friends and respected associates: Martin Buber and Franz Rosenzweig. Both would develop distinctive philosophies that set them apart from the Liberal rabbi. Baeck differs from Buber in that, although, unlike the Orthodox, he speaks of commandment in the singular, not in the plural, he affirms God's moral imperative as divine revelation. Buber, in his best-known work, *I and Thou*, does not use the language of commandment.[23] His God relates to human beings as the Eternal Thou, a presence in whom out of the wordless mutuality of relationship the lines of all intrinsically valuable I-Thou meetings converge. Whereas Buber's God in relationship speaks "Thou," Baeck's God speaks an additional word: "Thou shalt." Thus morality becomes fundamental to the relationship between God and humanity, and I-Thou relationships among persons come into existence from a common response to the moral commandment. In addition, unlike Baeck, Buber finds no role for ritual or even for organized prayer, since he believes that all forms of organized religion militate against the spontaneity that, in Buber's eyes, is essential for true religiosity. Obviously, for Baeck that is not the case.

For Franz Rosenzweig, God does indeed command—not the traditional 613 commandments, to be sure, but potentially more than a single moral command. Ritual commandments, along with moral ones, he believes, are contained in divine revelation, even if they are heard differently by different individuals, and thus become binding in varying modes of practice. Moreover, Rosenzweig's God initially demands a personal response. God, the lover, requires human love in return. It is this love of God that Rosenzweig calls the "commandment of all commandments."[24] Baeck does not emphasize God's love; rather, his God turns those who hearken to God's voice immediately toward their fellow human beings, near and far. Unlike for Rosenzweig, therefore, for Baeck the Jews are not defined as a people that dwells eternally with God, remaining untouched by time. Such a notion runs counter to Baeck's prophetic model, wherein knowledge of the good requires redemptive action in the world and in history.

During his five years in Düsseldorf, Baeck became a regular contributor to a recently established magazine, *Liberales Judentum*, founded by the Liberal rabbi of Frankfurt am Main, Caesar Seligmann, in 1908, shortly after Baeck's arrival in Düsseldorf. Neither a strictly scholarly journal nor simply a Jewish newspaper, the publication was directed to a Jewish public with *Bildung* (cultural sophistication) but not necessarily Jewish learning. In his essays for *Liberales Judentum*, Baeck repeatedly sought to counter the notion that modern European culture was a form of Christian culture. Were that the case, Jews who regarded themselves as modern men and women would be—as many were—inclined to complete their Europeanization by converting to Christianity. Baeck sought to undermine that attraction by demonstrating that whereas a genuine Christian culture existed in the Middle Ages, that had ceased to be the case ever since the Enlightenment of the eighteenth century. In opposition to the current culture of the free individual, much of contemporary Christian leadership was dominated by a church that had set itself against civic equality for non-Christians and that remained suspect of scientific inquiry. By contrast, what Baeck calls "Jewish culture" had been open to secular knowledge all along, making it easier for Jews to adapt to modernity.

In recent decades, the contrast had diminished. Liberal Protestantism had begun to change course, manifesting a greater openness to critical modes of thought. That shift, Baeck argues, resulted in a turn toward Judaism.

Within its ranks, one now heard the call: "Away from Paul, back to Jesus." And, for Baeck, the significant teachings of Jesus were nothing other than Judaism. If, in his reply to Harnack, Baeck had defended Judaism by objecting to the Protestant theologian's denigration of its ancient manifestation, here he seeks to strengthen Jewish pride by showing that Judaism—even the Liberal Judaism that, in some respects, imitated Christianity—was not moving in the direction of its rival. Rather, its rival, Christianity, was moving toward Judaism. Christianity was leaving behind the dogmas that set it apart and was converging on the teachings of Jesus, the very teachings that Baeck believed were fundamentally Pharisaic and hence Jewish. "Modern Protestantism, in very un-Lutheran fashion is taking pains to be 'an ethical religion,'" he wrote.[25] Baeck's chosen example of the Protestantism closest to Judaism was to be found in Great Britain, where piety clearly entailed the struggle for social justice. The Protestant church in Germany had always regarded despotism and serfdom with mute indifference; its British counterpart had not done the same. There, religiosity had been linked to social concern.[26] But now, German Protestantism was learning from across the channel that social consciousness was integral to religion, and in learning from Great Britain, it was gradually adopting a form of religion that was precisely what Baeck believed Judaism to be: a religion in which salvation lay not in deliverance from Original Sin through God's grace but in obedience to God's moral law.

Baeck thus presented a twofold argument whose parts did not fit smoothly together. On the one hand, he pictured a Christianity inimical to modern culture that therefore should not be attractive to modern Jews. On the other hand, it was moving closer to Judaism. The first argument should have deterred Jews from apostasy. But the second raised a question that had first appeared at the beginning of Jewish modernity in Germany a hundred years earlier: if a trend in Liberal Christianity has now made it resemble Judaism so closely, why not obtain the social advantages that being a Christian offers? Did it really substantively matter whether one called oneself a Christian or a Jew?

Baeck was compelled to insist that, after all, Protestants had not moved fully in the direction of Judaism. Liberal Protestant theologians might doubt some Christian dogmas, but other dogmas, such as belief in the Trinity and the divinity of Jesus, remained binding for many sitting in the pew. Therefore, Baeck could conclude that in practical terms, "the firm, sharp boundary between Judaism and Protestantism persists before and after."[27] And there was, according to Baeck, yet another fundamental difference that remained between Judaism and Christianity. In contemporary Protestantism, Christian scholars were at odds regarding the historicity of Jesus. Were it to turn out that there never was a historical Jesus, Baeck maintains, Christianity would not be able to sustain itself. But such reliance upon a single individual was not true of Judaism. Even the historicity of Moses, the most important of the Prophets and Judaism's central figure, was not essential for the faith. Unlike Christianity, Judaism was not dependent upon the attestation of a single personage or historical event. Rather, wrote Baeck, "We regard the essence of religion to lie in the ideas, which carry their certainty within them. . . . Religious history is revealed to us in the living, endless development of the religious idea, not in testimony regarding a unique all-determining personality in whom the religious ideal has found its final fulfillment, its sole realization."[28] The notion of an incomplete, continually evolving, religion, Baeck believed, set Judaism apart not only from Christianity but from other faiths whose veracity centered for all time on a Gotama Buddha, a Zarathustra, or a Muhammad. To be sure, Baeck's argument would not have persuaded Orthodox Jews, or, as they preferred to call themselves, "Torah-true Jews." For them, the truth of Judaism depended upon the historicity and finality of the revelation vouchsafed to Moses at Sinai. But it was an argument that could appeal to Liberal Jews like Baeck himself.

In 1910, Leo Baeck presented a major address to the newly formed Association for Liberal Judaism in Germany, which was holding its meeting in Berlin. His subject, the ongoing discussions among Christians regarding their faith, was, on the surface, not a Jewish topic. But for Baeck, it was not possible to discern trends in Judaism without knowing what was on the Christian agenda. It would not do, as he put it, simply to stand outside and occasionally peek into a window, curious to see what Christian scholars and religious leaders were saying. Displaying evidence of the continuing influence of Dilthey on his thinking, Baeck sought to convince his listeners that "feeling your way" into the spiritual struggles and strivings of others was a fundamental step toward the love of humanity. For Jews to enter into a discussion by Christians on Christianity—for example, on the nature of Jesus—was not inappropriate. On the contrary, it was a mark of respect that, sadly, had not been paid by Christians to Jews. Unfortunately, what agitated Jewish theological discourse had been, and still was, of little interest to non-Jews. This was the more regrettable, as the fundamentals of Liberal Christianity, in Baeck's view, were so close to Judaism. In one of his most radical statements in this regard, he argued: "In Christian literature there is no noble and pious statement that does not since ancient times also clearly and nobly echo Jewish writings. With all of the respect that we owe to those of a different faith, but also with all the self-respect that we owe to ourselves, we say: We have received nothing new in the New Testament; for us the New Testament, insofar as it proclaims morality and piety, is something old."[29] Although in this address, Baeck urges respect for Christian deliberations, it is clearly Jewish self-respect that is his principal concern; for its sake, he is willing to make statements to this gathering of Liberal Jewish laity that culminate in self-congratulation. Too many Jews, he believes, seem in word and deed to be saying as Jews: "Please pardon me for existing." To them, Baeck wants to shout out derisively: "If in these times, you don't want to say or know who you are and what you are, then you should have remained in the nursery where you belong!" Instead, Jews should be willing to state with perhaps exaggerated pride: "We are Jews because we know of God above us and that truth is on our side; we are Jews because we are convinced that in our religion we possess the future."[30] Like the Zionists, who were also concerned with instilling Jewish pride but from a national perspective, Baeck sought to do the same in more ambitious, even grandiose, terms from the perspective of Jewish faith.

In his Düsseldorf writings, Baeck first presented an idea that he would repeat in later years: his notion that the Jews were inherently a people of nonconformists. Conformity, as he saw it, meant giving up one's own values and beliefs for the sake of avoiding conflict with a ruling power or a socially dominant element in society or culture. He criticized the Protestant churches in Germany for conforming to the desires of the state—for becoming state churches, dependent on political authorities and following their desires. At the same time, he criticized German Jews, especially his fellow Liberals, for their conformism to the mores of German society. For a Jew to be a conformist, in Baeck's view, was to betray the Jews' historical vocation. Borrowing a phrase from the prominent English preacher Charles Spurgeon, he calls the Jews the "great nonconformists," those who are consistently willing to think differently from others.[31] It was as a people of nonconformists, Baeck believed, that Jews were destined to play their unique role in striving for universal tolerance. Within a Liberal Judaism, most of whose adherents sought an expression of their religious identity that differed little from that of their Christian neighbors, Baeck's call for nonconformity was at least unconventional, if not a bit audacious.

Figure 2. Leo Baeck as a young rabbi (undated).
Courtesy of Leo Baeck Institute, New York.

Leo Baeck was more skilled as a writer than as an orator, a deficiency he needed to remedy—or, at least, diminish—if he was to be effective in the practical rabbinate. More than in Oppeln, that shortcoming became apparent in the large synagogue in Düsseldorf, with its more than 1,300 seats, but also when he was teaching children. One student recalled: "We couldn't understand the new rabbi, Dr. Baeck, not so much because of what he said, but rather because of how he said it. His pronunciation, his intonation, the melody of his speech were so grotesquely different from the usual manner of speech in the Rhineland that at first we couldn't help laughing."[32] To correct this deficiency, Baeck took private speech lessons from Louise Dumont, a well-known actress of the time who ran a theater in Düsseldorf located near his residence. He never did become as dynamic a speaker as some of his colleagues, but the help she gave him no doubt made him more acceptable for his final rabbinate in the demographically and culturally dominant Jewish community of Berlin.

Chapter 3

Rabbi in the World War

First Days in Berlin

With his arrival in Berlin, Baeck had climbed the professional ladder from the rabbinate of a small Jewish community, to a middle-size one, and finally to what was by far the largest in Germany. He had made a reputation for himself as a scholar, a defender of Judaism vis-à-vis Christianity, and a man willing to express his views even against the sentiments of the majority. In the German capital, he now faced a sophisticated, highly educated Jewish community, culturally deeply German but, for the most part, greatly estranged from Judaism. By and large, the Jews of Berlin were moderately wealthy, though there was also a socially separate community of Jews who had immigrated from Eastern Europe and whose members struggled to make a living. In the eighteenth century, Berlin was the home of Moses Mendelssohn, the Jewish philosopher who had done more than any other individual to bring Jews out of intellectual isolation and into participation in the culture of Germany and Europe. The career of Abraham Geiger, the leading religious reformer of the following century, culminated in Berlin, after he was drawn to the prospect of teaching at a modern center for Jewish learning, the Lehranstalt für die Wissenschaft des Judentums, where he became an instructor and where Leo Baeck would later study as a rabbinical student and teach as a member of its faculty. Baeck, too, was drawn to Berlin largely on account of the Lehranstalt, where he was now promised an academic position in addition to his work as a community rabbi.

On December 27, 1912, a few weeks after his arrival, Leo Baeck stood in the pulpit of Berlin's enormous and magnificent New Synagogue to be installed in office. The building had been constructed half a century earlier, in the popular Moorish style that set it sharply apart from church architecture and echoed the experience of Jews in medieval Muslim Spain, where they had participated actively in the scientific and literary culture of a highly productive age. For this occasion, every seat in the synagogue, which could hold three thousand, was occupied well before services began. At about four o'clock that Friday afternoon, Baeck festively entered the synagogue, along with a second new rabbi for the community, Julius Lewkowitz, and accompanied by rabbinical colleagues and lay leaders.

The chairman of the community spoke first, expressing the hope that the new rabbis would work to satisfy the religious needs that had recently been felt in the community. "The times when one prophesied the death of religion, and of the Jewish religion in particular, were over," he insisted. But in this widely spread-out community, there had regrettably been a lack of personal relationships between laity and clergy, which he hoped the newly elected rabbis would be able to remedy. When Baeck ascended the lofty pulpit to give his inaugural address, he spoke, as he had in the past, humbly and without the insertion of his own person: "In the evanescence of earthly existence," he said, "the human being must not make promises. Only the idea, to which he wants to devote his life's activity may he express. It is the idea of religious truth."[1] Despite this reticence, Baeck then spoke optimistically of the present. It was a time, he suggested hopefully, when a religious wave was sweeping across Europe and directing fresh new waters toward Judaism. It gave one a new lust for life. In this atmosphere, Judaism had regained present-day significance and a guarantee for its future. Recalling the American philosopher Ralph Waldo Emerson, whom he greatly admired, Baeck insisted that Judaism was not simply a religion that dwelled in the past; it was not just historical memories. Rather, the God of the ancestors was also their God and the God of their children and grandchildren.[2] Baeck was urging Jews, many of whom regarded Judaism as relevant only to previous generations, to make it their own for themselves and for future generations.

Most of Baeck's time during the less than two years he served in Berlin before entering the German chaplaincy was undoubtedly spent in becoming acquainted with the new community and his rabbinical responsibilities. But, as before, he did not neglect scholarship. A few months after his installation at the New Synagogue, he delivered his inaugural lecture as a faculty member of the Lehranstalt. He had been assigned the academic field of homiletics and midrash, the latter itself a traditional form of homiletics. It was therefore most appropriate that his first lecture should be titled "Greek and Jewish Sermons." Not only did the subject fit his designated academic task at the Lehranstalt; it was also a topic that played to Baeck's interest in historical comparison. In the past, his comparisons had been especially between Judaism and Christianity; here he chose to examine similarities and differences between ancient Greeks and Hebrews. Not surprisingly, the differences in sermons reflected variations in values between the two civilizations. For the Greeks, it was the artistic form of the sermon that mattered most; for the Jews, whether the style was elegant was of little consequence. For the authors of the midrashim, who had the advantage of a canonical book, the Bible, from which to interpret, it was the moral content that mattered. Baeck concluded with a critique of the sermon as preached in the contemporary synagogue. It tended to lack deep learning in classical sources, employed worn-out phrases, and sometimes resorted to cheap appeals to sentiment in a questionable desire to bring forth tears. Heavily footnoted, Baeck's lecture was included in the proceedings of the Lehranstalt and later in a volume of his essays.[3] The attachment to scholarship he displayed, as he had earlier—and, of course, typically culminating in a message for the present—remained a constant in his life, a pleasurable activity in optimistic times and a consolation in later more difficult ones.

Becoming a Chaplain

On the eve of World War I, Baeck published an essay that can be seen as an attempt to reach beyond the militant nationalism leading up to the war. It was neither a sermon nor a piece of scholarship but rather a contribution to a volume on social ethics published in 1914 by the Union of German Jews.[4] Its subject is the human being, the *Mensch*, and the fellow human being, the other person who shares my humanity, the *Mitmensch*. Baeck points out how the idea of the *Mensch*, a universal concept basic to human rights and human dignity, emerged only gradually, following earlier ideas of the people (*Volk*) and the state. It was in ancient Israel, argues Baeck, that the idea of the fellow human being first found expression in the Hebrew Bible. The notion of a single humanity was the natural consequence of the single God. "Beyond the borders that peoples and races, estates and castes, powers and talents want to mark out dwells the unity and the majesty of the human. Whoever is the other, may he be distant or foreign or even be my enemy, he belongs to me as essence of my essence, tied to me on account of God." To be a *Mitmensch* is God's command, which implies accepting the duty of common responsibility, one for the other. For Baeck, this meant more than goodwill; it meant undertaking the striving for social justice, the highest expression of religion. There was no true piety except in relation to the *Mitmensch*. But now came the war, a test of religious men and women, determining whether narrow national identification would, under these circumstances, fully drive out the universal one.[5]

A few months later, when he was already serving as a chaplain in the German army, Baeck composed a Hanukkah message to the Jewish troops that drew upon the same universal idea—but now in the context of war. "The principal love of fatherland is to be a *Mensch*," he declared, "who stands upright in his place and has the courage to be among the few when it is necessary, even against the many. Love, too, demands courage; it is love that provides strength and value."[6] To be among the few, as were the Maccabees in ancient times, meant in the present not to be swept away by the military fervor of the many, not to forsake love in favor of lesser values, but to gather the courage to set it before oneself as the highest ideal. As a chaplain, Baeck would seek to instill this view: his notion that love of the fatherland did not place fatherland above love.

Jews were first called upon to serve in national armies in the eighteenth century. Some responded negatively, fearful that it would be difficult to maintain Judaism in an army camp. However, some believed that only through military service alongside non-Jews could they prove their unqualified allegiance to the state. In Germany, Jewish soldiers participated eagerly in the War of Liberation against Napoleon and later in the Franco-German War of 1870–1871, even though fellow Jews were on the other side. With the outbreak of the World War, ten thousand German Jews speedily volunteered for service, certain that the kaiser's call for fraternal unity among all political and religious factions would include them as well. Once and for all, they would prove their loyalty to Germany. Ultimately, nearly a hundred thousand served, with about two thousand becoming officers, though almost exclusively of lower rank. Like the non-Jewish soldiers, they entered the war with an enthusiasm that bordered on euphoria. By its conclusion, many of them had been rewarded with medals, especially the Iron Cross.

Treatment of Jewish soldiers in the army varied. Some officers welcomed them, and some did not. One high-ranking officer thought it desirable that there be Jewish chaplains to guide Jewish soldiers, since, as he put it, "a God-fearing soldier, regardless of the religion to which he may belong, is also a good soldier."[7] However, antisemitic attitudes in the army were not uncommon. When Jewish chaplains complained that anti-Jewish literature was all too readily made available to soldiers, their complaints were turned down. At one point, General Ludendorff released a secret order in which he insinuated that Orthodox Alsatian Jews were carrying spy information in their phylacteries.[8] Most disturbing to Jewish soldiers and to German Jewry as a whole was the decision in 1916 to conduct a census that would determine how many Jews were serving on the front lines. The clear intent was to suggest that Jews were shirkers—that out of petty self-interest, they were neglecting their patriotic duty. Although results of the survey were never publicized, since the census apparently failed to show what was intended, this attempt to help account for German military failures was frightening. It was also the first example of a sentiment that, following the war, led to the popular accusation that Jews had stabbed courageous Germany in the back. Thus, Jewish chaplains in World War I were faced with the difficult task of maintaining morale among Jewish soldiers who, for all their enthusiasm, had to tolerate, at the very least, an incomplete acceptance in the ranks.[9]

Jewish chaplains first appeared in the German army in the Franco-Prussian War. Three rabbinical students from the seminary in Breslau served as best they could, with little support from the government. In World War I, eighty-one rabbis volunteered for service, of whom six were initially chosen as military chaplains. During the war, their numbers grew to thirty regular rabbinical chaplains and fifteen chaplain assistants. Unlike their Christian counterparts, they received no salary from the state but were supported instead by the Jewish communities, which continued to pay them as if they were still serving at home. Jewish chaplains were to be treated as officers but without specific rank. Their uniforms sported a Star of David fastened to their cap or sometimes dangling from the neck. Occasionally, they consulted with one another in rabbinical conferences held on both the Western and the Eastern Front.

In September 1914, Leo Baeck left his home in Berlin to become one of the first six rabbis to serve as a chaplain in the war. Like almost all German Jews, he felt that his country's cause was just. But unlike Hermann Cohen, Baeck did not fully conflate Germanism and Judaism. In two controversial wartime essays, each titled "Deutschtum und Judentum," Baeck's philosophical mentor argued that German humanism and Jewish universal messianism were fundamentally alike, each aiming at the same ultimate goal. Baeck

Figure 3. Leo Baeck as a chaplain in World War I.
Courtesy of Leo Baeck Institute, New York.

did not agree. With all of his respect for the humanistic tradition in German culture, he did not consider it the full equivalent of Judaism. And unlike some of his Christian counterparts, he avoided any resort to chauvinism. Judaism, he always maintained, needed to remain apart from the state in a separate realm, where it could exercise independent influence.

Though Baeck served without a government salary and was required to pay for his uniform, the army gave him a wagon and two horses and promised free accommodations.[10] The Berlin community agreed to pay for his uniform as well as his regular salary, even supplementing it with a war service bonus. He was initially sent to the Western Front, where he immediately undertook to visit the widely scattered army camps and field hospitals where

Jewish soldiers might be found. In the first of some sixty-five biweekly reports that he sent to the Berlin Jewish community, Baeck described how, sometimes riding a horse and sometimes driving a wagon, he traveled from place to place in order to make his presence known and to gain an overview of his duties. The logistics were difficult, since, unlike their Christian counterparts, Jewish soldiers were widely scattered with small numbers in many locations.

Baeck considered his principal task to be diverting wounded Jewish soldiers from their pain in seventy field hospitals placed in churches, schools, and even French châteaus. He brought the soldiers news from home and, in turn, dispatched news to their families. He wrote letters and postcards that they were unable to write themselves; occasionally, he had to announce a death. But mainly, he counseled and comforted the men, encouraged them to link up with fellow wounded soldiers for camaraderie as a way to overcome loneliness and to dispel thoughts that centered on their own affliction. Sometimes, he would bring them a small gift. Stressing the importance of this work, Baeck wrote in one of his reports: "The wounded receive a piece of home, and their self-confidence is raised. As I could often discern, they take heart from the fact that to them, too, just as to those of a different faith, a pastor has come."[11]

In one report, Baeck describes his field hospital experience: "The smaller the room, the sooner those who are gathered become like a family and the conversation that the rabbi begins with his wounded or sick soldiers soon becomes a general one; everyone wants to take part, ask questions, tell of their experiences, express wishes and hopes. But mostly what happens is that toward the end, only he [the rabbi] speaks, and the conversation becomes an amorphous sermon, and the edge of the bed or the table in the middle of the room becomes a pulpit."[12] Thus the rabbi would speak not only to the soldier he has come to visit but to all those gathered about him. Baeck believed that his presence was also important in what it did for the Jewish faith: Jewish soldiers could take pride that their religion, like that of their Christian brothers-in-arms, was officially represented among them. This recognition through Judaism's spiritual leaders made it easier for Jewish soldiers to feel that they, too, deserved the respect of their comrades.[13]

In view of the suffering caused by the war, Baeck early asked himself whether the conflict had any more profound justification than merely narrow national interest or, as he put it, "national egoism." War could be affirmed, he concluded, only if its goal was more than military. To justify the suffering, it had to be motivated by an ideal; for Baeck, that ideal was justice. War laid a burden not only on the shoulders of those who made the decisions but also on the consciences of those who carried them out. Only one consideration could liberate the soul from succumbing to the resulting stress: "the awareness that the war is of universal consequence . . . that it has value for the whole, that it is being conducted for culture and morality, for the future of the human race."[14] There must not be war for the sake of war, Baeck believed, not even for the sake of a peace that will relax tensions. War had significance only when it served a future, the great peace of culture. Baeck did not define what he meant by culture. But, as we shall see from his writing after the war, it did not mean the culture of Prussian militarism—not war as a value in and of itself but the culture that was a product of the tolerant tradition of the Enlightenment and that had been anticipated in Jewish monotheism.

In addition to visiting the wounded, Baeck was expected to conduct religious services on holidays and Sabbaths under conditions very different from those at home. On one occasion, a dimly lit cave at Saint Léger, north of the Aisne River, was the safest location available. Instead of standing on a raised pulpit speaking down to assembled congregants, as he did in Berlin, at army worship Baeck kept near the usually small group of Jewish soldiers who attended. He worshiped as one of them, in their midst. Here formal arrangements did not matter. Participation in prayer and familiar melodies became essential elements in making the worship meaningful to the soldiers and in raising their spirits. In a letter home, one Jewish sergeant described a service that Baeck led in northern France: in a room of the local church, twelve comrades gathered, along with a Christian petty officer who had asked to be present and who was totally carried away by the service. Baeck spoke of the need to hang on, to have patience, and to trust in God, who would direct everything for the good. "Only now," the sergeant concluded, "had many found God."[15]

In 1915, Baeck related that during the previous months, without his prompting, soldiers had repeatedly told him how powerfully they all felt their religion and the Jewishness that united them. By contrast, Jewish internal divisions, based on a narrow definition of Jewish identity, whether exclusively secular or exclusively religious, now seemed of little consequence.[16] That broader view, of course, had been Baeck's own opinion all along. Anticipating his later thought, he wrote in Martin Buber's periodical *Der Jude* (The Jew): "Jewishness is sui generis and therefore to be explained only through its existence; it has remained unique in the history of humankind, a word of the Creator of the world for all time. . . . It is a futile endeavor to attempt squeezing Jewish existence either into the bare concept of the nation or into that of a pure association of faith."[17] In other words, neither a secular Jewish nationalism nor a solely religious conception of Jewishness could encompass the fullness of Jewish identity. Baeck hoped that these expansive feelings, sensed by Jewish soldiers during the war, would persist in future peaceful times.

During the war, Baeck edited a pocket-size prayer book for the soldiers, designed to be broadly acceptable across the Jewish religious spectrum. Bound in plain black linen, it looked from the outside like its Christian equivalents. Inside were twenty-nine pages of German text and twenty-three of Hebrew. In the German section, opening from the left, were traditional prayers and selected psalms and also some patriotic songs, labeled "folk songs." The Hebrew section, opening from the right, used traditional, but much abbreviated, formulations.[18] Soldiers expressed gratitude for the prayers and songs in the prayer book, which could be used during formal worship. But Baeck maintained that the fixed prayers and even the sermon were, under these special circumstances, not nearly as important as the silently expressed prayer within the setting of a service or even in the trenches, when each soldier could reflect inside a group or alone upon his own place amid the ongoing strife and his personal relationship to God. The ambience of collective or individual worship could raise the soldier out of the anxious environment of the war and into a healing and comforting sphere. Baeck relates that toward midnight in April 1915, as together with his soldier-congregants he left the Passover service he had just conducted, they departed from "an island of peace" lodged amid an all-too-familiar turbulent sea.[19]

Later, on the Eastern Front, when Baeck conducted celebrations of the Passover seder in Novoalexandrovsk, no fewer than six hundred men attended during one of the two evenings. Unlike other German Jewish intellectuals, Baeck did not idealize the Polish and Russian Jews he encountered in Warsaw, Vilna, and other places in the East, although he appreciated the strength of their faith and was appalled by their poverty. He was focused on providing for their welfare. Thanks to his army connections, he succeeded in obtaining military passes for representatives of the local Jewish population, enabling them to purchase wheat from which he then had matzot baked for soldiers and civilians alike. So that their unleavened bread would be broadly affordable, he set a price for its sale that was not to exceed a given maximum.[20] Baeck was not alone in his efforts; it was not unusual for chaplains, especially in the East, to serve the indigenous Jewish population as well as the German Jewish soldiers.

Baeck's duties, of course, also included burials, often not of single individuals but rather mass burials of soldiers, some of whom were not Jewish. Occasionally, there were also exhumations, which likewise required appropriate prayers. For group burials of Jews and non-Jews, Baeck would at times co-officiate with Christian chaplains. On such occasions, Catholic, Protestant, and Jewish chaplains would take turns speaking and then follow the funeral cortege together. At other times, Baeck would speak as the sole clergy representative for Jews and Christians alike. For him, the war provided an opportunity for closer contact with Christian counterparts that had been largely lacking in peacetime.

Although Baeck was still in his early forties, his Jewish chaplain colleagues chose him to chair their rabbinical conferences whenever he could be present, during the time when he was serving in the West (September 1914 to October 1915), and in the East up until his return to Berlin (June 1918). Fellow rabbis congratulated him for being awarded, as were some other chaplains, the Iron Cross Second Class for his exemplary work as a chaplain. At the conferences, the army rabbis shared their experiences, discussed sermons and pastoral duties, and, on at least one occasion, considered how to deal with "the sexual question," which meant the temptation of Jewish soldiers, like their comrades, to seek out easy local sex when given a few days' furlough. The rabbis, no doubt Baeck among them, concluded that it was a rabbinical duty to discuss this issue with the soldiers following the religious services they conducted and make clear to them that self-control was also a form of courage, as well as a religious and patriotic duty.[21]

In the final months of the war, while he was serving on the Eastern Front, Baeck's reports became more reflective and began to consider what would happen after the war. He was now especially concerned to liberate himself and others from the narrow nation-centered morality of war that bore no understanding for the other side. In his last report to the Berlin Jewish community (March 1918), he denounced the abundance of hatred among nations that the war had managed to unleash. He mused on what it would mean if one could capture for oneself the view from the opposite side: "to see our world from the place of the other." All self-understanding, he insisted, depended on the extent to which one could view oneself through the eye of fellow human beings. Of course, he put it in religious terms: "All justice is conditioned by the degree to which one is able to think and feel oneself into the other, how far one is able, in the words of the Bible, 'to understand the soul of the other,' inwardly to pass over to the place of his feelings." Both sides had suffered immensely during the war; it was time to transcend patriotic phrases. Returning soldiers, Baeck believed—or, more likely, hoped—"will be able to tell how they experienced helpfulness and kindness even from people of other lands." Reiterating his theme at war's beginning, Baeck states it reflectively near the war's end: "The human [*das Menschliche*] always penetrated everything that serves to separate, and all particularity and difference only strengthened this sense of commonality. Though the nations stood distant from one another, the human beings soon came close to one another." It was this human quality, Baeck believed, that would have the capacity to strike a bridge from nation to nation after the war.[22]

It seems strange that, as far as is known, Baeck's reports and other writings during the war avoid reference to the antisemitism that the war unleashed, especially in its final months. Perhaps Baeck was concerned that such comment would increase the anxiety at home of soldiers' relatives who would read his reports. But that is not the complete answer. Baeck was consistently reluctant to dwell on recent or current animosities directed against the Jews and especially to cast aspersions on the Prussian monarchy. On the eve of the war, he wrote an essay recounting the history of Jews and Judaism in the Prussian province of the Rhine, in which Düsseldorf, where he had served, was located. It was intended for a volume that described various aspects of life in the province and therefore included its Jews and their religion.[23] Although Baeck does not omit Jewish suffering in this essay, he is unwilling to cast blame for discrimination against Jews on the Prussian monarchy. Thus, for example, he stresses what he regards as the extraordinary tolerance of the Great Elector in admitting a few Jews to his domains in 1671, but he fails to mention the severe restrictions accompanying his action. He dwells upon enlightened officials working for the Prussian regime, attributing anti-Judaism to a contrary "romantic spirit" that was able to garner adherents in the early nineteenth century. By ending his narrative with full Jewish emancipation at the beginning of the Second Reich in 1871, Baeck avoids having to deal with the antisemitism of the succeeding years. Contemporary hatred of Jews stood in conflict with the religiously based optimism that characterized Baeck just before the war. Possibly also this essay displayed early evidence of a psychology that moved him to suppress any emphasis on evil and that, after the Holocaust, which was incomparably more devastating for the Jews and for Baeck personally than anything that had occurred earlier, would make him almost invariably want to avoid bringing that subject into discussion.

Aftermath

In June 1918, a few months before the end of the war, Baeck returned to his duties in Berlin. But the war remained on his mind. As it drew to a close, he expressed the opinion that the war experience had diminished the rationalism that had been dominant in Judaism in previous decades. It was being replaced by personal religious experience and by an intuition of the depth and private nature of the world of religious devotion. That insight would soon manifest itself in his own thought. Upon reflection, he became even more confident of the importance of the Jewish message in the postwar world. Speaking to fellow rabbis, he expressed optimism about the future and, perhaps unrealistically, revealed a certainty that in the future, Judaism would play a central role: "It is for us to acknowledge that only through Judaism can the present wounded world be healed."[24]

It is a curious fact that in his biweekly reports, Baeck avoided naming the countries in the war. Even Germany is scarcely mentioned. One must conclude that for Baeck, the war was ultimately not about one nation against another but one system of values against another, and each could be found on either side. Shortly after the war, speaking at the Lehranstalt in memory of the students who had lost their lives in the war, Baeck suggested what the war, on a deeper level, was really about. Two powers were in conflict with one another, each represented in Prussia. On one side was the heritage of conservative Lutheranism, which allied itself with temporal power; on the other was an independent Calvinism and Kantian moral philosophy. The former abdicated its moral responsibility to the state; the latter did not. As represented by nineteenth-century theologian Friedrich Schleiermacher, the Lutheran attitude meant divinely ordained dependency upon the political status quo at the expense of progress; Calvinism meant the acceptance of individual responsibility. Baeck could not have been more explicit than when he said: "The war that we have had to endure is in a certain sense a war between Lutheranism and Calvinism."

Clearly, Baeck, who continued to identify as a Prussian, did not want to criticize Prussia directly, so he avoided mentioning the Prussian militarism or imperialism, with which he emphatically did not identify. Rather, he made his intention clear when he turned to a third force outside the bounds of both Lutheranism and Calvinism, which he hoped would be the final victor in the years ahead. That force was the Germany of Gotthold Ephraim Lessing, friend of Moses Mendelssohn and propagator of the *Aufklärung*, the German Enlightenment, who placed universal morality above the state. It was this spirit of the Enlightenment that had helped bring about the emancipation of the Jews. It was what Baeck called "Prussian idealism, with its optimistic belief in the future of the human," that was venerated in the Jewish communities of Germany. Looking backward and forward, he concluded the Lehranstalt address with characteristic optimism: "A new time wants to begin, a time that will connect again with the old Prussian idealism, in which ideas that are also largely born from the spirit of Judaism, are striving to prevail. The world wants to become different."[25] To consider how it might become different, Baeck wrote to Martin Buber, suggesting the establishment of a small circle to discuss the religious issues of the postwar world.[26] But as far as is known, such a group did not come to be.

Not all German Jews shared Baeck's forward-looking vision of a postwar world that transcended narrow nationalism in favor of concern for the individual human being. Jewish veterans remained intent upon proving that they had done their share in the war, and there were good reasons for them to feel the need to do so. Despite the Jews' full and faithful participation in the military, the German political Right still branded them as outsiders, unsuited for positions of authority in the new Weimar Republic. When Walther Rathenau, the Jewish foreign minister in the Weimar Republic, was assassinated in 1922, Baeck was given the sad task of delivering the funeral address. He had been close to Rathenau's family; upon Rathenau's death, his widow presented Baeck with her husband's library.[27] Many years later, in post-Holocaust Germany, Baeck lectured on four significant German Jews, and Walther Rathenau was among them—not only as a Jewish industrialist, intellectual, and statesman but also as a searcher who was ever more closely approaching a personal Judaism.[28] Following the war, Baeck dedicated a memorial to the Jewish soldiers who had given their lives for Germany. The inscription pointedly notes that they died not as Germans but as German Jews.[29]

As it did other rabbis in Germany and elsewhere, the war left Baeck an advocate of peaceful policies that would prevent its recurrence. A decade after its conclusion, he wrote an essay for a publication of the German Red Cross, titled "Neutrality." He praised the attitude of restraint and moderation, which was the gift of remaining neutral. That neutrality, which he had long advocated among the parties in Judaism, he now applied to nations. But neutrality was often passive and hence inadequate. As Baeck put it, *Zurückhaltung* (restraint) had to give way to *Haltung* (taking a stance), resulting in what he called a "positive neutrality" in place of a negative one. What was ultimately decisive was not holding back but stressing the factors that united and unified. That was the basis on which Baeck hoped that relations among nations would be structured, a new war would be avoided, and a "new Europe" would be brought into existence.[30]

Chapter 4

A Thinker Engaged

Weimar Ambivalence

The new, peaceful Europe for which Baeck hoped did not emerge. The League of Nations, formed after the war, proved a weaker instrument than competing national ambitions. In Germany, attempted revolutions of the Left and Right created disunity and chaos. Not long thereafter, heavy reparations exacted by the victorious powers precipitated an unprecedented inflation, reversing for many German Jews the upward mobility that they had enjoyed since the mid-nineteenth century. To be sure, in the new Weimar Republic, Jews enjoyed a greater ability to attain prestigious positions in government and society, but antisemitism, though not always perceptible in the larger cities, remained beneath the surface, occasionally breaking into view. The influx of Jews from Eastern Europe during the war divided the larger communities where the *Ostjuden* settled. By 1925, there were more than 85,000 Eastern European Jews in Germany.

Still, in the urban centers—especially Berlin, where about a third of German Jewry now resided—a new spirit was felt. In ever larger circles, Jews came into social contact with their Gentile neighbors. Despite varying degrees of continuing antagonism toward Jews, non-Jews increasingly were willing to marry Jews, thereby, without intent, aggravating a situation of low fertility that put the future of a demographically substantial German Jewry in doubt. There were also more Jews with little interest in their communal institutions and who were eager to avoid paying for their maintenance. They made their exit from organized Judaism without conversion, remaining Jews only by the racial definition that would, in little more than a decade, be imposed on them from the outside.

Especially the younger generation was drawn to the freer lifestyle of urban Weimar culture. Marriages, rarely any longer arranged affairs, were now determined by the wishes of the couple. Leisure hours were spent in cafés; sexual restraints were ever more frequently disregarded. In the general press, Jewish writers became paragons of biting satire and critique. With the exception of the Orthodox, attendance at religious services was limited to once or twice a year, at the High Holidays. The magnificent New Synagogue, dedicated in 1866 in the heart of Berlin, may have been a lasting source of Jewish pride, but Berlin Jews visited it only seldom. Baeck's preaching there on Sabbaths could scarcely fill the cavernous structure.

Although, in keeping with his reluctance to write about personal feelings, there are few explicit indications of them, one could sense that Leo Baeck was exceedingly uncomfortable in the anonymous and morally lax atmosphere of 1920s urban society. His own culture remained that of the earlier Wilhelmine era, with its stricter codes of bourgeois behavior. A product of tiny, traditional Lissa, he wrote critically of the metropolis to which he had been drawn. Urbanization, he believed, had come at a heavy Jewish price. With a tinge of nostalgia, he described how the communal piety of village and small-town Jews had given way to an individual religiosity—or, more often than not, to a lack of any religiosity at all. In the urban centers, Jewish philanthropy had become the replacement for religious obligation; the drive for constant change pushed aside the continuity of tradition. Unlike the small Jewish communities, many of which were ceded to Poland after the war, Weimar Jewry lived in a society that lacked reciprocated warmth and intimacy.[1] What emerged among Jews in the Weimar cities was no longer the closeness that resembled a family but a mass of individuals who voted for whatever party was vying against competitors in communal elections. Berlin Jewry in its interactions was more political than genuinely religious. Culturally, it lacked reverence; its sensibilities were distorted, its intellectualism focused upon what had already been accomplished and what could easily be accomplished with little effort. In the metropolitan environment, artificially induced enthusiasm replaced natural feelings, giving way to a thoughtless haste in quest of pleasure. "Joy retreated in favor of variety or of excitation with an ever changing program," Baeck complained. "In place of empathetic humor came a wit that derided everything."[2]

The urban Jew, Baeck believed, was in danger of losing the qualities that were primordial, immediate, and natural. Moreover, as a strict moralist, he could not agree with some of his younger rabbinical colleagues who had adapted their own way of life to the culture surrounding them. Bowing to the environment, some in the younger generation reveled in the new morality. Rabbi Joachim Prinz, for example, frequented cafés and adopted the laissez-faire of the youth culture.[3] The popular sermons that he and some of his colleagues delivered aimed at dramatic impact and at relevance to the contemporary Jewish situation. Unlike Baeck, they were not reluctant to speak about themselves. In response, Baeck and some in the older generation of rabbis remained critical of their younger colleagues' rabbinate and style of life. As Baeck saw it, the pulpit was a place for the rabbi to deliver a strictly religious and moral message, and the rabbi's life outside the synagogue required exemplification of his spoken word. Worst of all, in Baeck's eyes, was the rabbi whose goal it had become to entertain, for whom even religiosity was nothing more than playing a role. As an educator, Baeck believed that "all education consists, first of all, one might say, in awakening a feeling for what is clean, for the corporeal and spiritually pure. It therefore says to the child first of all: 'You may not, watch out!' . . . Fear of the Lord is wisdom, and avoiding evil is reason."[4]

With unfeigned admiration, Baeck cited the words of the late eighteenth-century German writer Jean Paul as appropriate to his own age, which was smitten with a "culture of personality." According to Baeck, Jean Paul had preached a decidedly Jewish view when he suggested that one should begin to develop the culture of the heart, not with the reinforcement of good drives but with exclusion of the bad ones. Only after evil was totally banished could the good emerge. Baeck's strict insistence on driving out the inclination to evil set him apart from many laypeople in the Jewish community as well as from some of his colleagues. Unlike some of them, he consistently maintained distance, always appearing publicly in a three-piece suit. Rabbi Prinz described Baeck as "a leader of the people without being of the people. He never danced or laughed with the people."[5] Baeck had little understanding of or respect for colleagues who did dance and laugh with the people, the less so for those who, like Prinz and numerous Jewish and non-Jewish intellectuals, adopted Weimar's urban morality. His own view of the rabbinate differed from theirs: it involved preserving dignity and maintaining a measure of separation from his flock even as he evinced concern for their welfare. His stance required self-deprivation, but he believed that to be necessary if the rabbi was to be a model of Jewish behavior. Years later, speaking to rabbinical students in America, he said: "The rabbi must be a man of the Jewish way of life, and perhaps the Jewish way of life means also a bit of puritanism, a bit of asceticism. The new rabbi does not mean the fashionable rabbi. His sermons must be a part of his own life."[6]

Yet there was also a religious culture in Weimar Jewry that, while it may not have seriously touched most Liberal Jews, did find its adherents and supporters, among them Leo Baeck.[7] In 1923, in the north of Berlin, a group of religiously serious Jewish men and women formed an independent synagogue. Unlike in the Liberal synagogues administered by the community, women sat together with men and all were expected to participate in the liturgy. The two hundred seats in a hall supplied by a Jewish orphanage were regularly filled at weekly services, largely by young people. "Community evenings" provided forums for discussing topics of contemporary concern.[8]

Wherever Jews lived in German-speaking Europe, they could access the products of a religious and cultural renaissance. Interested readers could peruse the philosophical writings of Martin Buber and enjoy his popular modernized Hasidic tales; Max Liebermann and Lesser Ury, Jewish painters of the Impressionist school, included Jewish subjects in their work. In Frankfurt, philosopher Franz Rosenzweig organized a Jewish *Lehrhaus*, an adult education institution directed to reintroducing assimilated Jews to the sources and ideas of classical Judaism. A small Zionist movement drew idealistic youth while, during the last Weimar years, the newly founded Schocken Publishing House in Berlin devoted itself to Jewish literature. At the Liberal seminary in the capital, recognized once again in 1920 as having the higher rank of a *Hochschule*, a faculty that included outstanding scholars, such as the historian Ismar Elbogen and the philosopher Max Wiener, published significant books and articles. Along with the older, more conservative, seminary in Breslau, and the Orthodox one in Berlin, the Hochschule was actively engaged in producing a new generation of rabbis for the Jewish communities. Throughout the Weimar period and beyond, Baeck continued to be a popular teacher at that seminary, specializing in midrash and homiletics. Baeck had long felt that midrash, especially, possessed ongoing significance because, grounded in the Bible, it had always allowed for a wide variety of interpretation, and it was able to do so even in the present. "The thread of the midrashic literature," Baeck held in a very early essay, "has, in fact, never been severed."[9]

It was in this latter Jewish culture, existing alongside its broader secular counterpart, that Baeck felt fully at home; it allowed him, for all his moral critique, to be optimistic about German Jewry. Reflecting later upon the World War and a decade of the Weimar Republic, he argued that the experiences during the military conflict and the consequent hatreds and political extremes thereafter had paradoxically deepened religious feelings. For all their negativity, even the outbreaks of antisemitism had produced a positive effect: they had awakened and strengthened Jewish pride in the possession of Jewish faith. "Even if everything that the age brought about has drawn some to extreme ways of thinking that led away from Judaism, in essence a certain piety was awakened and all of the currents in German Judaism have gained thereby."[10] Baeck could sense that newfound commitment to Judaism in his teaching at the Liberal seminary, which was a source of profound satisfaction both for him and for his appreciative students. But neither his teaching nor his scholarship—which reached only the small number seriously devoted to Jewish religion and its study—nor his regular preaching from the pulpit sufficed to fulfill the obligation that Baeck felt to sustain and strengthen Jewish life in a community, most of whose members, despite Baeck's occasional optimism about its future, were so strongly drawn away from it.

The Organization Rabbi

Berlin Jewry grew immensely in the last half of the nineteenth century; by the census of 1925, it numbered more than 170,000, about a third of the total Jewish population in Germany. Likewise, the great majority of the Eastern European Jews in Germany, then constituting more than 15 percent of German Jewry, lived in Berlin, especially in the so-called Scheunenviertel, the area of the stockyards. Although the Zionists preferred that the Jewish collectivity define itself as a *Volksgemeinde*, an ethnic community, the ruling majority saw itself as a *Kultusgemeinde*, a religious association. As such, it employed Liberal as well as Orthodox rabbis, each responsible to the community as a whole rather than to any one local synagogue. However, German Jewry was linked by far more extensive bonds than religious ones. And Baeck's role in the community extended well beyond purely religious functions. In Berlin, Baeck the rabbi became, as well, Baeck the communal leader, undertaking a variety of leadership roles. He held most of them simultaneously, and most were directed at those Jews who rarely visited the synagogue.

It seems remarkable not only that Baeck had the energy to perform so many leadership functions at the same time but also that so many organizations should turn to him for guidance. The explanation rests partly on his carefully nurtured refusal to engage in Jewish party politics, let alone internal polemics. Baeck continued to regard himself as a Jew first and the adherent of a particular religious stream or political ideology only second, just as he had in his youth. He deliberately refrained from divisive propaganda and thus could maintain his bona fides with most Orthodox Jews and not just with his own Liberal faction; with Zionists and anti-Zionists alike; with learned and unlearned Jews; with those whose Jewish identity was central in their lives and those for whom it was peripheral. But it was not only his public neutrality that made him so broadly accepted; it was also his character. The distance that differentiated his rabbinate from the camaraderie of younger colleagues had the advantage of lending him stature. Because he was not fully one of the crowd but nonetheless interacted with its members in a manner respectful of their individuality and compassionate regarding their concerns, people looked not across toward him, but up to him. He evinced a certain stateliness, which elicited confidence in his decisions and actions. And his personal morality was never in doubt. One might differ with him on this or that matter, but one did not doubt his integrity.

The first nationwide group to call on Baeck to lead it was the General Association of German Rabbis, to whose presidency he was elected in 1922. Its members included rabbis from across a wide spectrum, ranging from radical reformers to conservatives. Only the Orthodox chose to have their own separate organization. Aside from Baeck's personal qualities, his reputation as a productive Jewish scholar and thinker and the fact that he held a prestigious rabbinate in Berlin made him an obvious candidate for a position that required the ability to mediate and exercise influence over his colleagues.

Two years later, in 1924, Baeck was elected chairman of the Central Welfare Institution of the German Jews, the representative body established in 1917 to coordinate among the local welfare agencies. When Baeck became its chairman, welfare was gaining increased importance, as numerous Jewish families had become impoverished following the disastrous inflation of the preceding years. Welfare included not only providing for the growing number of poor Jews, especially among immigrants to Germany from Eastern Europe, but also dowering impecunious brides and providing for the homeless. Among artists, Baeck was especially moved by the work of Käthe Kollwitz, who depicted the hungry and impoverished. In his writings, Baeck frequently distinguished between the Christian attitude toward the poor, which was motivated by goodwill and by pity for the individual, and the Jewish attitude, which strove for a just society and aimed at preventing poverty from gaining a foothold. Employing a Hebrew word that derives from the root for both charity and justice, Baeck wrote that "the true human society is the community of *tsedakah*."[11]

In November 1924, Baeck was unanimously elected Grand President of all the B'nai B'rith lodges in Germany.[12] He had already joined the fraternal order, which came to Germany in 1882, during his stay in Düsseldorf, finding among its members, as did Sigmund Freud in Vienna, a group of Jewish men seriously committed to intellectual and social endeavor. B'nai B'rith was, for many in its ranks, a Jewish substitute for the religious life of the synagogue. It was attractive to its members in general, and certainly to Baeck, as a religiously and politically neutral organization that studiously avoided inner ideological conflict. The "brothers," as they called one another, devoted themselves to such social causes as fighting against the sex trafficking of Jewish girls and assisting Jewish orphans. In the cultural realm, they raised funds to support the comprehensive archives of German Jewry, established in 1905. When Baeck was elected president, a delegate arose and exclaimed: "A rabbi has become Grand President of the German District!" That apparently noteworthy fact was, to this delegate's mind, not just an honor for Baeck but a tribute to the status of the German rabbi. As president, Baeck admitted that, while he was not a nervous person, he was perhaps not altogether pliant, adding, "but, my dear brothers, it is necessary that there also be such persons."

In his first address to the group, Baeck consciously avoided all references to himself, calling to mind the words on a memorial to British statesman William Pitt: he lived without showing himself off. Instead, Baeck focused on what he regarded as the organization's most urgent current task: "a stronger emphasis upon consciously Jewish motifs within the order." He took issue with those members who regarded their bond of Jewish brotherhood as merely temporary, thinking that it would soon give way to a universal, purely human one. To them, Baeck responded: "Not in departing from our Judaism, but by way of our Judaism runs the path to our humanity." He was eager to prevent the further dissolution of Jewish identity, which would occur if B'nai B'rith were to open its doors to non-Jews. On this subject, he was not at all pliant, despite the wishes of certain members who wanted to make the order wholly nondenominational.

Baeck urged that B'nai B'rith should pay greater attention to the more independent and public position of women in Weimar society. Although he was not advocating that women become members of the various lodges, he believed that they should enjoy some participation in the order, perhaps as an auxiliary organization. And he warned his "brothers" of the decline of the Jewish family due to the growing number of interfaith marriages where the partners raised their children as Christians. Clearly expressing his objections to Weimar morality, he spoke of the current widespread "indifference and infidelity, of sexual impurity and promiscuity." Perhaps some listeners had difficulty accepting such words from Baeck, which they deemed analogous to pulpit preaching. We learn from the protocols that a few members were concerned about a "clericalization" of their district. But Baeck was determined to carry out his office as democratically and faithfully as any layman. In exercising his presidential duties, he traveled widely, not only visiting lodges in Germany—for which he occasionally traveled third-class on overnight trains, to save expenses—but also twice sailing to the United States in order to connect with the American movement in the country where B'nai B'rith had been founded back in 1843. He continued to serve as Grand President of the German branch until its dissolution in 1937.

In 1925, though not in a presidential capacity, Baeck was elected as a rabbinical delegate to the thirty-five-member council of the Prussian State Association of Jewish Communities. This organization, established in 1921, was intended to further the collective interests of its constituent communities internally and vis-à-vis governmental authorities. In retrospect, it was also an early effort to create a representative body for all of German Jewry, a process that would reach complete fruition only after the Nazi takeover, when Baeck would become president of the Reichsvertretung der deutschen Juden, the representative body for all German Jews in the Third Reich.

Whereas all these organizations were neutral regarding divisions within German Jewry, Baeck also played leading roles in two that were not. One was the international organization supporting Liberal Judaism, the World Union for Progressive Judaism, on whose governing board he served from the outset; the other was the Central Association of German Citizens of the Jewish Faith, the Jewish defense organization that, along with combating antisemitism, spent much of its energy fighting Zionism. Most German Jews who subscribed to Liberal Judaism were likewise opposed to the Zionist movement, believing that the universalism of their faith contradicted the particularism of the Zionist message and its program. Baeck, however, despite his activity in the Central Association, did not recognize that contradiction.

Liberal Judaism

Throughout the nineteenth century, the Reform movement in Judaism was bent on the modernization of Judaism, so that the gap between it and the surrounding culture would not extend beyond a few points of theology and liturgy. The commonly held belief in sustained moral and political progress made an ever closer approach to that aim seem realistic. However, when the German ambience became less friendly toward Jews in the 1880s and the Great War discredited the notion of ongoing progress, the goal began to seem questionable. By the 1920s, Liberal Judaism in Germany was facing a crisis that required a leader who could guide it to a more relevant and realistic outlook. In this realm, too, Leo Baeck played a central role.

Baeck inherited a Liberal Judaism that had become a party. By his time, the larger Jewish communities in Germany were religiously divided into three major sectors: the Orthodox, the Liberals, and the Zionists. Regularly, they fought against one another in community elections. Baeck distanced himself from these acrimonious debates. He saw Liberal Judaism as having a larger purpose. "A Liberal Judaism that finds its satisfaction in petty community concerns," he wrote in 1926, "denies itself; liberalism draws its sustenance from the large problems."[13] Baeck spoke scornfully of the "little Judaisms," or separate streams, which he regarded as less significant than the "great Judaism," which was Judaism in its totality. At its origins in the early nineteenth century, the advocates of Jewish religious reform had not sought to create a denomination but rather a movement within Judaism as a whole. Baeck wanted to restore that original vision. "We do not want to be a mere party, great or small," he wrote, "but a movement; not a sect but an energy in Judaism."[14]

Despite this breadth of vision, Baeck was not reluctant to involve himself in organized Liberal Judaism. When the World Union for Progressive Judaism held its first international conference in Berlin in 1928, following its founding in London two years earlier, Baeck was chosen to be the principal speaker. His eminence as a scholar and the broad respect he enjoyed within German Jewry lent stature to the gathering and to the World Union itself. When British scholar and philanthropist Claude Montefiore, who had founded the World Union along with the leading woman in the movement, Lily Montagu, died in 1938, Baeck was chosen to be its president. It was a position he could exercise only sporadically during his final years in Berlin, and not at all during his incarceration in Theresienstadt. But he took it up again following World War II and continued to hold it until 1953, when he became the World Union's honorary president for the last three years of his life.

In his writings, Baeck was more critical of his own Liberal stream than of other religious groupings in Judaism. In the nineteenth century, Liberal

Jews had devoted their efforts to the civil advancement of the Jews, to what was called their "emancipation." Baeck noted that, although it had been "a noble battle," it was waged for the Jews themselves, not for the Jewish religion. The time had come to shift the focus. In his view, Liberal Judaism's true objective was not to gain status by adapting the Jewish message to fit easily into the present age, inside the contemporary zeitgeist, but rather to be critical of the present state of culture and society for the sake of a better future. In its eagerness to be relevant, Liberal Judaism had tried too hard to be modern. For Baeck, in 1928, associating Judaism with being up-to-date meant to combine opposites, to make of Judaism an idolatry and provide divine justification for a society that was witnessing a rising racist madness. Subservience to regnant values in state and society, Baeck believed, was a negation of the Jewish message. The time had come to speak a great no to the present—to stand against it, as the Prophets had stood against their present, in order to speak a great messianic yes to a universal future.

Judaism had the moral advantage that, unlike Christianity, it was a nonpolitical religion—not a state religion but a world religion. It should therefore not regard the state as having greater authority than Jewish tradition, or follow the example of German churches by bowing to it; rather, when morally necessary, it should act in opposition to the laws of the state—for example, in matters of marriage law, when conscience or human kindness made that demand.[15] As he had before the war, Baeck stated again that Jews were ideally the world's great nonconformists. They were, at least ideally, always out of step with the times.[16]

Baeck did not perpetuate the Reform movement's focus on liturgical change. He did not write about the elimination of this or that passage from the prayer book. He argued instead that what mattered most was not the formulation of the prayers but the devotion of the person who prays. He told a 1930 meeting of the World Union that the topic most worthy of discussion was not how the prayer service should be constructed but rather, the meaning of prayer itself and why it was important that Liberal Jews pray. "What is decisive is that we pray," he said.[17] No less decisive for Baeck was observance of the Sabbath, the day of rest and devotion so much neglected by Liberal Jews. Nineteenth-century Liberal Judaism had the virtue of bringing personal choice to the fore in religious observance, but at the cost of widespread neglect of the Sabbath. Nonetheless, Baeck believed, choice could also become the principal consideration in the Sabbath's recapture. It was therefore not Jewish law (halakha) that Baeck emphasized with regard to keeping the Sabbath, but rather the subjective religious experience. Sabbath observance raised the Jew from the realm of prose to that of poetry. "The basic element in the battle between religion and indifferentism," he told the conference delegates, "is the battle of the poetry in our souls against the prose, the battle of the mystery within us against the superficiality that intends to penetrate and understand everything, to pass an immediate definitive judgment on everything."[18] Much of that mystery had been lost. For Liberal Judaism to be vibrant, it needed to rediscover the Sabbath as the chief path to regaining religious transcendence. Baeck's own observance of the Sabbath required his walking, whenever possible, to the synagogue where he was preaching that week, even when it was quite far away.

The Zionist Challenge

By the years of the Weimar Republic, the heated religious antagonisms that split German Jewry in the nineteenth century had mostly cooled. The burning conflict now was over Zionism. On one side were those Jews intent on being fully German, to the exclusion of any other national identity; on the other side were the Jewish nationalists. The latter were likewise very much embedded in German culture but sought a homeland in Palestine for persecuted Jews in the East and, in some cases, also for themselves. Baeck did not withdraw fully from this conflict. Instead, he associated himself, if not completely, with each side, and each proved appreciative of his sympathy. It was a feat that few others sought to accomplish.

The anti-Zionists were mostly to be found in the Centralverein deutscher Staatsbürger jüdischen Glaubens (CV), the aforementioned Central Association of German Citizens of the Jewish Faith, established in 1893 as an organization whose principal purpose was to combat antisemitism. It was, by far, the largest Jewish membership organization in Germany. As Baeck noted in a letter to a fellow rabbi, most of its members were not religious. "It is the spiritual barrenness of many Association members," he wrote, "that they want to make their Germanism into a sort of substitute religion."[19] In that regard, the association was like B'nai B'rith, except that, unlike the fraternal lodges, it was not neutral on the Zionist issue.

Leo Baeck not only joined the CV but served as a member of its governing board. Of his active participation, a contemporary wrote: "The fact that he considered the struggle for the civic rights of German Jewry important brought him close to the leaders of the Centralverein, and this organization regarded him as one of their own, one who commanded great authority within their ranks."[20] He was welcomed into their circle, although its leaders were certainly aware that, regarding anti-Zionism, he did not share their views. Fortunately for Baeck, even within the CV, a minority among its members held attitudes toward Zionism that were not at all extreme. He was part of that minority.[21]

In contrast to his active role on the inside of the Centralverein, Baeck did not officially join its antagonist, the Zionistische Vereinigung für Deutschland (Zionist Association for Germany), a much smaller and less influential group than the Central Association. Nor was he a regular delegate to Zionist Congresses. Given the outsider status of Zionism within German Jewry of the 1920s, if he had been a clear protagonist of the Zionist ideology, it is doubtful whether Baeck could have maintained his broad acceptance by German Jewry. But his motivation in remaining officially an outsider to Zionism was not purely political. There was a narrowness in Zionism that he could not affirm. Early in his career, Baeck had, albeit obliquely, expressed his belief—and that of Liberal Judaism—that the destruction of the ancient Temple and the Jewish dispersion had been a positive phenomenon. Unlike Christianity, Judaism was not the official religion of any state nor should it become that, even of a state composed of Jews. Fundamentally, it was a world religion. The ultimate goal of Jewish history, for Baeck, always remained universal.

Yet he was never hostile toward Zionism; he generously gave it its due as a positive force in German Judaism, especially for the young and for Jewish immigrants from Eastern Europe—and not only for them. In a remarkable speech to fellow Liberal rabbis, Baeck said of the German Jews: "We are bourgeois. And along with this admission there arises the summons to remove ourselves spiritually from the bourgeoisie. There can be no such thing as a religion of the bourgeoisie. Bourgeois religion is degeneration. Zionism is an expression of the desire to get out from under it."[22] Zionism, he believed, was a justified response to a religion that endorsed the values of the self-satisfied. He told rabbis that their sermons were in trouble because they were preaching only to the bourgeois members of the community, not to those inspired by the Zionist cause. Here Baeck's views associated him with some of the younger German rabbis who, in a countercultural protest to the German Jewish bourgeoisie, were preaching Zionism as a means for renewing religious life and making it more challenging.

Baeck was intensely interested in the Jewish settlement in Palestine. Following the Balfour Declaration of 1917 and the first steps toward the establishment of the British Mandate in the Land of Israel, he preached in 1920 of the "Hanukkah miracle of our days, the possibility of rebuilding the Jewish land."[23] His nostalgia for his own childhood, close to the soil, mingled with an admiration for the idealistic Jewish immigrants who were establishing agricultural settlements in the land. When some were massacred by Arabs in 1929, Baeck spoke of them in religious terms as Jewish martyrs who had died for the sanctification of God's name. Using characteristically Zionist language, and to hearty applause, he told a broad audience: "As much as we are aware of what it means that Jews have been led back to the soil, to agriculture, it is not simply a question of farming. What is arising there before our hopeful eyes is *the new man, the new Jew*."[24] Baeck hoped that this new Jew would also be a Liberal Jew. In a letter to Lily Montagu, executive secretary of the World Union for Progressive Judaism, he expressed his belief regarding Palestine that in scarcely any land was the religious work of Progressive Judaism as important as it was there.[25]

Whereas the German Zionist movement had initially regarded everyone outside its ranks, especially Liberal Jews, as the enemy, by the mid-1920s, it had changed course. The Zionists realized that they could exploit the growing division in Liberal Judaism between those who opposed Zionism and those who sympathized with it, even if they did not join the movement. Now they regarded the sympathizers outside their ranks, although they were not political Zionists, as potential recruits. They were especially interested in wooing Baeck—and their chances for doing so with a measure of success looked very favorable. Following the war, he had embarked upon a trajectory that would bring him ever closer to Zionism. Although he still did not join the Zionist party, he did join a number of organizations associated with the cause. When Keren Ha-Yesod, the organization created to purchase land for Jews in Palestine, was created, Baeck became an ardent supporter and a member of its executive board. In 1922—along with Albert Einstein, among others—Baeck signed a major appeal on its behalf. Four years later, again along with Einstein, he joined a German Pro-Palestine Committee. Composed of Jews as well as non-Jews, the committee dedicated its efforts to informing the broader public of the settlement work in Palestine, characterizing it as an outstanding means for the cultural and economic development of the Orient.

The final step came in 1929. The Jewish Agency, the body that directed the Jewish Palestine project, had until then been strictly under Zionist organizational control. But now its leadership determined that it could be more effective if the Agency expanded its international body to include nonmembers of the Zionist Association from various countries who were sympathetic to the cause of settlement. Governance would be split: half Zionists and half non-Zionists. When the founding assembly of the expanded Jewish Agency's council took place in Zurich in August 1929, Baeck was among the German delegates. Although he was not asked to be one of the speakers, he was chosen as a permanent member of the non-Zionist section of the administrative committee.[26] As early as 1921, the head of the Zionist Association, Kurt Blumenfeld, had believed that working with Baeck was "for us a lasting benefit," since Baeck was "a man of spiritual and human qualities of which his writings provide only a wholly inadequate idea."[27] Though he remained officially a non-Zionist, Baeck unquestionably contributed to the Zionist cause.

But was Baeck's support of Zionism limited—as it had been for an earlier generation of committed Zionists—simply to providing an avenue of philanthropy for persecuted Jews in Eastern Europe? Or was Zion, in Baeck's view, also a potential place of refuge for German Jews who, during Weimar, felt quite secure in the land of their birth? One piece of evidence suggests that as early as the 1920s, Baeck was not wholly certain regarding that security. In a speech that he gave in Königsberg in 1925, he declared that theologically, "Palestine . . . is a fact that God has set before us." He went on to say: "We cannot know what will be in Palestine and we cannot know what will be here in Germany. We cannot know it, but who will therefore say whether one day the grandchildren of those who today feel secure will have to emigrate to the land of their ancestors?"[28] He then drew a parallel to the Jews of medieval Spain, who likewise felt safe for many generations, only to be expelled in 1492 and forced to wander about desperately seeking a new haven. Hence, building a homeland in the Land of Israel was more than charity; it was a deed on behalf of the self. In 1925, his audience was startled and incredulous; Baeck could not have imagined how right he would be.

"Romantic Religion"

If Baeck, even in passing and not consistently, doubted just how secure Jews were in Germany, that doubt may well have been linked to his judgment of contemporary Christianity. In 1922, he wrote the first version of an essay that severely criticized the regnant German Protestantism. Although it contained themes he had outlined earlier, in this piece he drove his views to an extreme.[29] He gave it the general title "Romantic Religion," but it was aimed directly at Paul and Luther. A major theme in Baeck's writing, beginning with his response to Harnack in 1905 and continuing thereafter, was his wish to differentiate Judaism from Christianity, not only out of scholarly intent but also to justify the continued existence of a separate and, he believed, morally superior Jewish faith. In "Romantic Religion," he differentiated the two religions most sharply.[30]

Christianity appears in this essay as the close approximation of a specific type of religion that Baeck calls "romantic," in contrast to its opposite, "classical religion," which he thought was best represented by Judaism. The former, Baeck argued, was characterized by sentimentality, inwardness, and the desire for personal salvation; the latter strove for social morality. Playing upon two German words, he characterized Christianity as concerned with experiencing (*erleben*), while Judaism was concerned with living (*leben*). He termed the former "a religious egoism" because it was focused on the self, not on "the claims human beings have on each other." The desire for religious experience, for a sort of spiritual enjoyment, pushed social conscience aside. As Baeck saw it, Paul was the founder of romantic Christianity, and Martin Luther its most influential modern exponent. Like Saul of Tarsus, who became Paul, the great German religious reformer despised the Gospel of works and dwelled on the doctrine of salvation by faith alone. In the nineteenth century, such Christian romanticism found renewed expression in the Protestant theology of Friedrich Schleiermacher, for whom Christian faith meant the acceptance of complete dependence on God. As a striking contrast in Christianity, Baeck held up Calvinism, declaring it a form of Protestantism much closer to Judaism—despite its insistence on predestination—since it recognized "the free moral power of worldly activity." But the most direct Christian countertrend to Lutheranism was Kantianism, with its strong emphasis on the ethical element in religion, on the "ought." In Baeck's eyes, Kant and Luther were simply cut from different cloth; Kantianism and religious romanticism were antithetical. Although he did not explicitly say so, it is evident that Baeck regarded Kant, despite his critique of Jewish "legalism," as standing more within the Jewish tradition than the Christian one with which he was associated.

Critics of Baeck have rightly pointed out that his essay was both unfair to Christianity and highly selective in its reading of Judaism. As balanced history, the essay is indeed questionable. But it is significant in understanding why Germany chose Nazism, a point that clearly emerges from it, though Baeck does not make it explicitly. Christianity, or at least some strands within it, was conducive to the abandonment of political conscience. Paul had taught belief not in the teachings of Jesus (which Baeck regarded as within the Jewish tradition), but in the person—in Jesus himself. It was only with Paul that Christianity distinguished itself clearly from Judaism, setting itself apart, as well, from what Baeck calls the "original Christianity," which had been in harmony with Judaism. "The direction and intent of the Pauline teaching," writes Baeck, "led deliberately away from Judaism and from the original Christianity and toward an antagonism to them."[31] As Baeck noted a few years later, when explaining the basic teachings of Judaism, Paul did not oppose the ritual laws of Judaism alone, but "every demand in the Bible, every 'Thou shalt' that is in it."[32] Thereby Baeck made Paul into the negator of what was essential in Judaism, not only to Orthodox Jews but to Liberal ones as well.

In keeping with the Pauline faith, Christians raised a human being to the status of divinity and placed their trust entirely in his saving power. Romantic religion, Baeck noted, was the faith in such a salvation, one that removed the individual from the burdens of autonomous decision making. It was a salvation that "fulfills the longing for passivity, the desire to be rid of the commanding will, the craving to be captivated and to experience pure dependence."[33] The romantic ignores the call to conscience, choosing to locate his trust completely outside the moral self. Baeck recounts the history of personality cults, noting that "the romantic always requires a person to worship."[34] Writing of Luther, he does not mention the virulently antisemitic writings that the reformer published in his old age, apparently because these could be attributed to personal factors. It was not Luther but Lutheranism that Baeck saw as a danger. Since Baeck wrote explicitly of the bond between romanticism and the reliance upon external authority that was tucked into it, it is not surprising that the Nazis confiscated the volume in which "Romantic Religion," in its final form, appeared in 1938. In his critique of Christianity, launched initially in the essay's original version of 1922—whether or not he was fully conscious of it at the time—Baeck was revealing some of Nazism's deep roots within the country's dominant religion. In 1922, it had barely come into existence, so Baeck could hardly draw an explicit comparison; but in its essence, Nazism was a demonic form of romantic religion.

Baeck admitted that there were romantic elements in all religions; indeed, his reevaluation of mysticism in Judaism, to which we will soon turn, could be regarded as a newfound appreciation of the emotional element in the Jewish faith. But, unlike in Judaism, romantic elements were at the heart of Christianity, especially in its Pauline/Lutheran form. Baeck does not deal at length with Catholicism, within which good works historically balanced faith. He also does not hold Islam up to the romanticism test; it scarcely plays a role in his writings. When he does sporadically write about Buddhism, he distinguishes it even more sharply from Judaism than he does Christianity. Writing historically, he notes: "There are only *two determinative fundamental forms* of religion, the *Israelite* and the *Buddhist*."[35] The former affirms a moral relationship to the world; the latter sets itself the goal of negating the world and focuses only on the self. Moreover, Baeck has little regard for the separation that Buddhism makes between the monks, who are designated as the true community, and the larger circle of believers, which is little more than a sort of appendix to it. The Catholic monk, Baeck notes in contrast, is devoted to the service of others; not so his Buddhist counterpart.

Jew Among Gentiles

For all his critique of the dominant faith in Germany of the 1920s, Baeck found that there were German Christians eager to read and hear what he had to say about Judaism. They turned to him as its most authentic representative. When, for example, the influential German Evangelical theologian Carl Clemen, who had written two volumes on Paul, published an exceedingly popular work on the nature and history of the religions of the world, he chose Baeck to write the essay on Judaism. When Hugo Gressmann, an Old Testament scholar at the University of Berlin, decided that Jews could best represent their own faith to a Gentile audience, Baeck was among those asked to lecture.[36]

Most extraordinary during these interwar years was the intellectual and personal relationship that Baeck established with at least three members of the German-speaking nobility: Count Paul Thun-Hohenstein, Count Hermann Keyserling, and Baron Hans-Hasso von Veltheim-Ostrau.[37] All three sought to carry the old "imperial mentality" into the postwar period. They valued character, dignity, and restraint, attributes of aristocracy that appealed to Baeck. In 1924, he wrote to Thun-Hohenstein: "With what you write about the task of the nobility in Germany and in the Europe of our days I am in total agreement. Its time may now again have come."[38] Not that Baeck wished a return to the political order of imperial Germany, but as he wrote to this Austrian noble and diplomat, Germany was currently lacking the powerful culture and elegant style that characterized the intellectual nobility and that he believed necessary for the restoration of a Europe torn apart by the war.

These men were devoted to intellectual enterprise, to global travel, and to understanding religion beyond the boundaries of Christianity—both Judaism and the religions of the Orient. They were cosmopolitans in an increasingly nationalist time. Keyserling was of the old Baltic nobility that had lost its relevance after the Great War; Veltheim was a Saxon nobleman with an attractive family estate at Ostrau, near Halle, that could even boast an old-fashioned surrounding moat. Both men were well connected; Keyserling's wife, for example, was a granddaughter of the longtime German chancellor Otto von Bismarck. Their prestige came from their lineage and their extensive writings, which often told of their travels to distant lands. Keyserling published *Travel Diary of a Philosopher*, which became one of the most popular books of its time. Neither Veltheim nor Keyserling had a university position, but both held their place in the German intelligentsia. From the world before the war, these men drew the vision of a new supranational Europe that was united in its spirit, a vision that stretched beyond narrow nationality and one that Baeck shared. During the following years, neither of these two men showed any sympathy for Nazism. Both held Leo Baeck in high regard and, as we shall see, did not abandon him after 1933.

In 1920 in Darmstadt, Keyserling founded what he called a "School of Wisdom." Its conferences, held annually until 1927, were sometimes attended by as many as five hundred listeners. "Wisdom" was understood to be an attainment that went beyond the academic. It rested as much on spirit as it did on knowledge. Spirit, drawn especially from the Orient, was to combat the all-too-prevalent materialism of the age and to prepare for a new European humanism. Invited speakers came from a broad range of disciplines and backgrounds. Some were exceedingly prominent individuals, including the Christian theologian Martin Dibelius, the theologian and historian Ernst Troeltsch, the Swiss psychiatrist Carl Gustav Jung, and the philosopher Max Scheler. Lecturers were expected not simply to transmit knowledge but to convey something of themselves. Keyserling's own thought included certain characteristics that he shared with Baeck. Both men wanted to stretch their minds beyond knowing to empathetic understanding; each man dwelled on the tensions and polarities inherent in religious thought; and both were engaged thinkers, critical of the present that had displaced the old order and seeking a better, transnational future. Keyserling believed that the Jews had the potential to become the international nation and thus play a beneficent political role—provided that they did not abandon their Judaism.[39]

Keyserling was a controversial figure. Prominent individuals, including Nobel Prize winner Thomas Mann, held him in high regard. Some even came to the conferences at Darmstadt as if on a pilgrimage, while newspapers in the United States lavishly praised Keyserling's originality when his works were translated into English. But his frequently bombastic style and exaggerated self-regard could be off-putting, as it clearly was for the Jewish satirist Kurt Tucholsky, who declared: "Most amusing is his mixture of instructive wisdom with ill-mannered audacity, which must be his very nature. . . . In all seriousness, after everything that we have heard about him, Hermann Keyserling represents nothing but a certain wretched and trivial, worthless and ephemeral layer of Germany."[40] But then Tucholsky was very much a Weimar personality and social critic who could have no love for contrary personalities of a bygone imperial age. Not so Leo Baeck, who was drawn to Keyserling just as Keyserling was drawn to him. Three times the count invited Baeck to speak at meetings of the School of Wisdom, each time asking him to present the Jewish view of a subject dear to Keyserling's heart. Like Keyserling's, Baeck's introductory lectures phrased his topics in sets of dualities (*Doppelbegriffe*). In 1922, he spoke on "The Tension Within a Person and the Completed Person"; in 1924, "Death and Rebirth"; and at a special jubilee conference in 1930, "Spirit and Blood." On one occasion, the Baltic aristocrat chose to relate how he had learned of the rabbi: "I was referred to Leo Baeck by an envoy of Orthodox Judaism who asked me whether I didn't want for once to allow a genuine Jew to speak. For sure, I replied, provided that there is one who has the internal right to represent the Old Testament, that ethically most powerful [book] that humanity has brought forth. I received the answer that there was in any case *one* such Jew."[41]

Following Baeck's first lecture, Keyserling wrote to him that it had been the "highlight of the conference."[42] With regard to his second lecture, "Death and Rebirth," Keyserling claimed that Baeck had taken what was factually age-old and, with great depth of spirit, had provided it with new life. And thereby he had plainly given it rebirth. With his characteristic tendency to hyperbole, he added: "I believe I would not be guilty of arrogance if I maintain that this lecture, in my opinion, marks one of the most important hours in the history of Judaism since the death of Christ, given that probably for the first time, outside his own circle, from a platform visible from far away,

[Baeck was able] to place the accent on what was completely positive [in Judaism] and on that alone."[43]

Like Baeck, Keyserling deplored Jewish conversions to Christianity, since Judaism thereby lost its significance for the future, and Keyserling strongly believed in the value of religious pluralism. In sharp contrast to Harnack, he asserted that, from an ethical point of view, Judaism was superior to Christianity. But ethics was not his sole criterion of judgment. Judaism possessed a lofty ethics, yet it lacked pathos; it lacked the Christian concept of grace. In Keyserling's view, Judaism's religious goal was reconciliation with God—a less exalted idea than salvation. For Keyserling, spirit stood above ethics, as it never did for Baeck. But by the 1920s, Baeck was gaining a greater appreciation of the role of spirit in Judaism. When, in 1932, Keyserling published a book of meditations on his trip to South America, Baeck wrote to him: "The book accompanies me inwardly ever since I began to read it and when I speak with people I'm always compelled to speak of it."[44] In this volume, Keyserling wrote of the unprecedented dehumanization of the present age and of the potentiality of creative spirit, reborn ever and again, to transform the world.[45] The rebirth of persistent creative spirit was an idea that Baeck would ever more frequently apply to the history of Judaism and of the Jews. Impressed by Keyserling's book, he made efforts to publicize it in America and Palestine.

All three of Baeck's lectures at the School of Wisdom appeared in the 1933 collection of his shorter works, *Wege im Judentum* (Paths in Judaism). The first, whose title in print was shortened to "Perfection and Tension," was a comparison between the Greek view of the world and the Jewish, the former holding up a consummated ideal of finality as represented in art, the latter characterized by an ethics immersed in tension between past and future, between creation and commandment, and driven forward toward a redemption that lay always in the future. It was a contrast perhaps drawn too starkly, but it was a theme that fit well into Keyserling's own view of ongoing spiritual rebirth. It was also perhaps the first time that an audience of non-Jews in Germany, who were so distant from Judaism, had heard the faith of which they knew so little explained to them in considerable depth, historically and philosophically.

In 1924, Baeck addressed a topic even closer to Keyserling's thought, "Death and Rebirth." The lecture did not concern itself with physical death and resurrection but dealt instead with death as loss of the ability to overcome fate and to create one's life ever anew. According to Baeck, the ability to renew one's life was the true religiosity. As an example, he referred to the Sabbath, which weekly renews the spirit and thereby deprives death of its meaning. Like an individual, he argued, a people, too, can find renewal. This was a theme that would gain urgency and become more prominent in Baeck's writing after the Holocaust.

In his final lecture in 1930, Baeck spoke of "Spirit and Blood." Not surprisingly, he associates race with romanticism, a connection that was becoming ever more apparent during the last Weimar years. To speak of blood was to speak biologically of the past, this in direct contrast to spirit, which looked infinitely forward to the future. Spirit, Baeck insisted, is the image of God in the human being, manifesting itself in every moral commandment that a person obeys.

Baeck's lectures spread his fame beyond the Jewish community, not so much among Christian academics who, for the most part, remained hostile to Judaism, but within a less likely circle whose interests lay beyond the academic realm. Like Baeck, they were relatively less interested in a critically analyzed history of Judaism than in its significance within the larger family of religions and cultures.

Mysticism

As a disciple of Kant and of the Jewish neo-Kantian philosopher Hermann Cohen, Baeck was initially hostile to mysticism. In the 1905 version of *The Essence of Judaism*, he noted favorably, regarding the Hebrew Prophets, that they understood genuine religion to be free of any tinge of metaphysics or mysticism. Although he could scarcely deny that the Kabbala had played a role in the history of the Jewish religion, Baeck regarded it as a foreign intrusion to which Jews resorted in times of distress.[46] Judaism was inherently ethical, not mystical, he believed. Yet mysticism attracted Baeck's scholarly attention. He lectured to rabbinical students on the Zohar.[47] He wrote penetrating essays on two early Jewish mystical compositions, *Sefer yetsirah* and *Sefer bahir.* He was familiar with Rudolf Otto's influential *Idea of the Holy*, published in 1917, and cited Otto's revival of interest in the irrational. He even got to know Otto personally during the late 1920s, when Baeck, as a visiting lecturer in Marburg, was a guest in his home. For Otto, he wrote to a friend, "I, as well as my wife, felt sincere affection."[48] Otto, in turn, praised a lecture he had heard Baeck deliver on the 1929 riots in Palestine.[49]

Following the shock of the war and within the circle of other Jewish thinkers like Martin Buber, who were drawn to a more embracing approach to Judaism than the ethical alone, Baeck began to reevaluate his own religious thinking, which hitherto had been circumscribed by the ethical imperative. He told his B'nai B'rith brothers that in the present age, a sense of the hidden, of the irrational in life, had emerged anew. "We know today that in every person there is a secret remainder, which lies beyond calculation and analysis. What is decisive in a person's life is not mere rational consideration, not only the clear direction of ideas but rather what is mysterious—that anonymous remainder in every person. Innermost in every person dwells something that is hidden."[50]

This more profound awareness of the unanalyzable in human beings opened them to a view of the world that embraced a mystical component. But Baeck's admission did not make him into a mystic in the usual sense. He rejected every form of gnosis, which he characterized as inherently non-Jewish; for him, as for the medieval Maimonides, the nature of God remained impenetrable. Nowhere in Baeck's thought does he affirm the existence of knowable intermediary spheres between God and humanity in the manner of the Kabbala. He continues to attribute the entry of mysticism into Judaism to "times of distress," calls the heated imagination of some mystics "artificial" and "idle amusement," and terms engagement with the occult "trivial curiosity."[51] In the quest for complete religious truth, it was all too easy to forget the divine commandment. Mysticism could be "a flight from moral responsibility."[52] But now, Baeck also discerns a positive result: mysticism lifted the Jews "above the arid channels of their existence, above their constraints and fears; it was able to deliver the wondrous stillness of the faraway, the descending world of the Sabbath."[53] Mysticism revived Judaism when excessive ritual requirements had dulled the religious spirit.

Baeck came to recognize that a religious ethics alone lacked the depth and vitality that religion required. Commandment remained of the essence, but it now became for Baeck only one element in a duality. To *Gebot* (commandment) he now added *Geheimnis* (mystery). But the latter was emphatically not in the plural; he did not believe in Jewish mysteries. He denied that Jewish prayers revealed any secret teachings. In the revised edition of *The Essence of Judaism*, Baeck distinguished Jewish mysticism from its Christian counterpart, which had absorbed mysteries from the ancient world and given them substance in the mystery of its ritual: "Whereas in the Church [the mystery] is something concrete, something that becomes tangible in the sacrament, in Judaism it is something ideal. [In the Jewish faith] it designates that which lies beyond inquiry, that which belongs to God and not to human beings, that of which one can have no more than a notion."[54] Even this Jewish mysticism, as Baeck understood it, could not be the totality of Judaism. It was the counter-pole to the moral imperative to which it was necessarily attached. Together they were what Baeck called a "mysticism of life" and a *Gebotsmystik*, "a mysticism of the commandment."[55]

Not only had Baeck now set mystery into a duality with commandment, he was ready to argue its value for the contemporary modern Jew. In Judaism—unlike in Buddhism, for example—mysticism was not a negation of the self but its elevation; not a loss of the self in God but its communion with God. The mystery was the source of the commandment and that which embedded it in the cosmos. Without mysticism, Judaism remained shallow and incomplete. Ethics alone left out a vital element in religion, an awareness of the creative source behind the ethical imperative. If Liberal Judaism were to be vibrant, it could not ignore the transcendent mystery—it could not rest on moral action alone. Mysticism would supply "the certainty of the unmediated connection to God." Finally, mysticism supplied a messianic message. The piety of the contemporary Jew too often lacked the impulse to gain the future. Mysticism could turn that Jew toward "the days to come."[56]

What mattered to Baeck was that the moral and the mystical be understood as existing in a creative tension, which would be broken if one were to drive out the other. "The commandment is true commandment only because it arises from the mystery, and the mystery is true mystery because the commandment always speaks from its midst."[57] To Franz Rosenzweig, he wrote: "Most essentially Jewish is the inner unity—unity therefore with all of its tension—the ethical and the mystical, the earthly and the cosmic, the unity of mitzvah [commandment] and *kavanah* [piety] or, what has the same meaning, of Torah and Sabbath."[58] And in the new edition of *The Essence of Judaism*, Baeck wrote: "Mystery and commandment connect with each other; only the two together give full meaning to our lives. The unity of the two is religion in the manner that Judaism possesses it."[59]

Revelation Versus Relativism

If, as Baeck believed, God's essence was mysterious, fully beyond human ken, how could one be certain that the divine moral commandment "Thou shalt" was not entirely of human origin? Unlike Orthodox Jews, Baeck did not believe in a literal divine revelation at Mount Sinai of both the written Torah and its oral interpretation. Yet unless there were some manner of communication from God, Judaism would become subject to relativism: If God's will were simply a human construction, it would be open to multiple and contradictory versions. Like other Liberal Jews before him, Baeck needed to posit a revelation that was not confined to a Sinai experience, with its miraculous character—and that was also not a human invention but rather an ongoing breakthrough of the mysterious God into human consciousness. In the nineteenth century, the leading reformer, Rabbi Abraham Geiger, called the Jews "the people of revelation," explaining revelation in its essence as "the contact of human reason with the First Cause of all things" and also as "an illumination emanating from the higher spirit, which cannot be explained and which, though subject to later evolution, was not evolutionary in its origin."[60] Put differently, the Jewish faith for Geiger could not rest on secular history and could not be seen as a wholly self-contained phenomenon explicable by historical research. Likewise for Martin Buber, Judaism could not do without some contact with God. Buber saw it as arising from intrinsically valuable personal relationships that pointed to a divine source. Later, Abraham Joshua Heschel, Baeck's former student at the Liberal Seminary, would understand God to be in search of human beings; God created an awareness of the divine through a sense of wonder at nature's magnificence. Baeck stands out from these other religious thinkers by his insistence that revelation manifested itself predominantly by an awareness of moral obligation.[61] But for such a faith, historicism posed a severe challenge. The sense of moral obligation could all too easily be reduced to an awareness of conscience that was the product of historical and personal human experience, without reference to a divine source.

Baeck clearly recognized the problem: for a Liberal theology to be credible, it was necessary to fulfill "the unmistakable longing to overcome the historicism that dominated the nineteenth century and to escape the relativism it brought in its wake."[62] In its emphasis on historical evolution, Liberal Judaism had undermined a theologically rooted norm, not fully realizing that "evolution always means relativity." Protestant thinkers across a wide spectrum were dealing with the same issue, from the neo-orthodox Karl Barth's dialectic theology to the liberal theologian Paul Tillich's doctrine of the epoch-making moment, whereby he sought to give absolute significance to a particular point in history. In response, Baeck sought language that would raise the transmission of the Jewish "ought" above the level of a self-imposed imperative and set it apart from the oughts of other peoples. That was a complex task. To be religiously persuasive, he had to argue that the source of moral obligation and responsibility was not self-given. He did that in a powerful essay titled "Theology and History," initially published in 1932, the last year of the Weimar Republic.

In the nineteenth century, Baeck noted, *Wissenschaft des Judentums*, the scientific study of Judaism, brought about a revolution: some of its practitioners began regarding Judaism as a fully historical phenomenon. At the price of historicism, they examined it from the outside; they did not attest to it from within. As the study of Jewish history became an end in itself, its inner religious meaning was lost. As a result, the continuity of Jewish existence was lost, as well. History pushed theology aside. The time had come, Baeck believed, not to abandon the historical approach to Judaism but to regain a doctrine of faith, and such a doctrine required a new conception of revelation. Baeck stated: "This problem, through and on account of which Judaism in all of its particularity has become universal—this specifically Jewish problem of world history—is that of the incursion of the Infinite, Eternal, the One and Unconditional into the finite, temporal, manifold and limited, and of the spiritual and moral tension of the human fiber which is its result."[63]

Here was a conception of revelation both Jewish in its character and universal in its potential. It was not static like the *eidos*, the Platonic idea in Greek thought, but dynamic and imperative. The tension it produced resulted in "a never-ending battle with the task, the way, and the future." The subsequent battle, fought anew in each generation, Baeck believed, created the continuity that critical historical study emanating from the outside had severed. It was a theology of the teachers who stand within the tradition and pass it on from age to age, who wrestle with the tension, personify it, and provide it with a personal nuance. Systematic reflection upon the problem created by the gap between divine demand and human response was, in Baeck's eyes, the function of Jewish theology. It was also the way in which historicism could be overcome.

Awareness of that gap, which revelation created between the actual, the limited, and the imperfect, on the one hand, and the infinite ideal, on the other, brought about the impetus for Jewish messianism, a central element in Baeck's thought, as it was in the philosophy of Hermann Cohen. Although Baeck relegated creation of the world to the realm of mystery, and revelation proceeded from a God whose essence was beyond human knowledge, the goal that revelation set before humanity was clear: the establishment of God's reign on earth. This was the true response to the revelation of God's "Thou shalt," which was not an imperative transmitted only at Sinai but a commandment heard down through the ages. Its goal was infinite, but that did not render it less powerful. What one generation did not accomplish was left to the next, until the final redemption at the End of Days. Meanwhile, Jews strove to bring it even a bit closer, living its peace in their observance of the Sabbath, struggling to set society on the path toward it. Moreover, it was a task in which both Christians and Muslims could play their own role. But it was not a self-imposed secular task. God sets the process in motion and continues, through command and through loving encouragement, to drive it forward. Human beings, in turn, respond with either acceptance or rejection.

Baeck does not give up the idea of Providence: "However much human beings may suppose that they fashion the course of history, its outcome is determined by God."[64] Nonetheless, it is human beings who take God's presence into their lives, who accept the moral task, and who nurture the hope of realizing the universal messianic goal. Baeck was, of course, well aware that the initial Jewish conception was of a personal messiah who would miraculously bring salvation to Israel, reestablishing its ancient glory. But he suggests that in time, and well before the Reform movement, that conception was at least partially displaced by "Days of the Messiah" and, more tellingly, by "The Sovereignty of God."[65] For Baeck, the promised deliverance was linked to no single individual but was the task of all—each person's burden. He cites the Jewish prayer book, which stresses the human role "to order the world under the rule of the Almighty."[66] Revelation imposes both the task and a vision of universal justice, which Baeck believes is the future-oriented goal of all human life. He writes: "Where the new principle, revelation, has entered, there history on that account is no mere series of events, no mere motion forward. It is not simply individuals coming and going or the mere recurrence of attacks and resistance to them. Rather, history here is the encounter of the principle [of revelation] with ever new personalities. It is revelation and human beings meeting and grappling with one another. It is always the same and yet always unique: God reveals Himself to the person and the person reveals himself to God."[67]

Thus seen, human history rises to a level above the secular. As Albert Friedlander noted: "In contrast to historicism, which had made revelation a predicate of history, history here became a predicate of revelation."[68] In religious terms, Baeck's understanding of history, viewed theologically, approaches what is called in German a *Heilsgeschichte*—in this case, a Jewishly understood partnership of God and humanity aimed at a collective salvation.

Baeck believed that only the Jew who accepted the messianic burden was a religious Jew and only the religious Jew was "truly" a Jew. But what did it mean to act messianically in the world? Baeck's own aforementioned activities in the 1920s in the area of social welfare and B'nai B'rith social causes provide examples. But there are also others, which point to reflection on his politics.

A Rabbi's Worldview

Before the war, Baeck quoted Ralph Waldo Emerson: "Let your faith be seen in your deeds,"[69] a saying that Baeck had taken to heart. Given his admiration for the German nobility and his own preference for the genteel ways of the imperial upper class, one might have expected that Baeck would have been a conservative in German politics or at least a right-wing liberal, as were many German Jews. Instead, Baeck chose to associate himself, as well as the Jewish people, with the socialist enterprise. He was not officially a socialist; he explicitly rejected an equal distribution of all goods.[70] But his championship of the claims of the poor suggests that it would be most accurate to describe him, at least informally, as a social democrat.[71] Of particular interest is what he said about socialism at the 1928 conference of Liberal Jews in Berlin: "It is no coincidence that leaders of socialism have been Jewish. This is not simply so because, as one has often said, from ancient times, a social sensibility has been alive in the Jew. . . . The workers and we Jews are . . . comrades in fate in that we, each in his own way, have acted similarly, perhaps had to, in that they and we put on the discarded clothes of others."[72] Oppression of the workers, Baeck believed, had its counterpart in oppression of the Jews, inducing a sense of common fate and common purpose in the pursuit of justice. To be sure, organized socialism, especially in its Marxist version, had been secular and even militantly antireligious. As such, Baeck could not support it. But he detected a change: "May I say something personal? I have occasionally been asked by German workers to speak in socialistic circles. . . . The workers came to me and said: We thank you, you are right, that is the way it is and has been! A leader of the socialist youth, to whom two years ago in a smaller circle I said the same thing, pressed my hand and said I was right. Things have gotten better in socialism today; we Jews feel it even more gratefully than anyone else. Today one has insight; today religious life . . . is beginning to stir. There too something is new. Rebirth!"[73]

Baeck's ideal was a religious socialism or, put differently, a welfare society. He rejected what he called the *Machtstaat*, the authoritarian state. That state could take two forms: the Fascist variety, as it had developed in Italy; or the Communist state, as it existed in Russia. Both were forms of dictatorship; in each, power considerations displaced ethical ones. The authoritarian state, Baeck believed, was ultimately self-destructive. It was also based on a false conception of what was just. The true conception of social justice, "even as prophetic religion proclaims, is determined by the days of the messianic age."[74] In that prophetic conception, social concern is not an added element dragged in from elsewhere. It is "the essential element of religion without which this religion is unable to exist."[75]

Baeck castigated those who disregarded the misery and misfortune all around them. Satisfied with the status quo, they made themselves oblivious to the admonishing, pressing divine commandment. What they called their "good conscience" was nothing more than a "soft pillow" on which their lack of spirit and their godlessness found rest. "Whoever possesses spirit," wrote Baeck, "that person's conscience is never satisfied, never stilled." To act justly was to be willing to act against one's own interest and to eschew every moral compromise.

Although Baeck, as we have seen, played a leadership role in the central Jewish welfare organization in Germany, he warned of the danger in assuming that charity for the poor was the sole obligation. It was all too easy to soothe one's conscience by charitable acts, ignore injustice and social inequities, and so turn attention from the righteous society that still needed to be built. To fellow Liberal Jews, he argued that the divine imperative was not to fix the world in the image of the present but in the image of God's kingdom. The social task, Baeck held, was at the same time the religious task. In Judaism, there was no piety without concern for the other, and, obversely, all social action was service of God.[76]

Beyond concern for the poor lay concern for the future of Europe after the Great War. As a military chaplain, Baeck had favored the German cause, but he had witnessed firsthand the war's devastation. Following its conclusion, he turned his concern to preventing recurrence. By the late 1920s, he

had declared for pacifism. When the Jüdischer Friedensbund (Jewish Peace League) was founded in Berlin in 1929, Baeck became a member, joining Albert Einstein and other prominent Jewish personalities, Zionist and non-Zionist, rabbis and laypersons. Within this circle, it was left to Baeck to stress the Jewish character of the peace idea by citing relevant Jewish sources.[77] He now condemned all war as merely an exercise of force leading to no positive goal. *Shalom* (peace) in the Bible, he pointed out, was not the absence of war; rather, it had a positive content. Its true opposite was sin, and its true meaning was truth and the fulfillment of God's commandment.[78]

Linking social concern with the struggle to move history morally forward, Baeck distinguished two forms of peace, which shared only the same verbal designation: one was established by force of arms—the peace that gave dominance to the stronger military power. In Baeck's eyes, a peace of that sort failed the moral test. The other, more noble, peace, he maintained, was "the peace of the hungry and hopeful," the peace of righteousness. It was only that peace that was worth struggling for, and it alone represented progress toward the messianic goal.[79] Not surprisingly, the Jewish Peace League was forced to disband in 1933.

At the same time that Baeck was outlining his universal vision of peace, he sought to reconcile it with the particularist vision of a Zionism that he was coming to favor. In a special issue of *Der Jude*, the journal of the Zionist intelligentsia, cofounded by Martin Buber and the publisher Salman Schocken, Baeck traced the historical interaction between two Hebrew terms: *eretz* (land) and *olam* (world). In the agricultural society of ancient Israel, *eretz* meant both "land" and "soil"; it also meant "world." It was only with the Israelite population gradually distancing itself from the soil that the new term, *olam*, unrelated to land, came into use; with it, Jewish messianism moved from the particular to the universal, even as Jewish particularity reasserted itself through the Jewish community, the synagogue, and the house of study. But in the medieval and modern Jewish diaspora, *eretz*, as a possession of land, was lost—and along with it, according to Baeck, the beneficent tension between the two concepts. Fortunately, it was within the power of Zionism to restore the connection and create a new balance between the opposing, equivalent forces. That balance could occur in Zionism, with its "strong desire for the old *eretz*, the old this-worldliness, with its immediacy and its presentness of the land, its mystery, its power, and its poetic magic." It would be complemented by "the strong desire for the eternal *olam*, the

powerful attraction to the transcendent with its own presentness, its mystery, its power and its poetic magic."[80] Baeck concluded that such was the positive tension of the age in which Jews were then living.

Marriage, Family, and Feminism

Leo Baeck lived in an apparently happy marriage with his wife, Natalie, and their daughter, Ruth. They spent most of the year in the western part of Berlin; in the summers, he and Natalie enjoyed vacationing in nature, especially hiking in the hills of Switzerland. We know little of Leo Baeck's family life, since he was a very private person who scrupulously avoided writing about himself. A personal letter indicates that he had difficulty expressing his emotions. When on a trip to America for B'nai B'rith in 1925, he wrote the following to Natalie, on the occasion of her upcoming birthday: "You know that I am least able and lack the desire to speak of my life in great depth. And so I will not set into words the wishes that I carry within me and that are always with you. The best that is in them speaks to you without them; their best is the attachment of our lives. May what is given you, what is given us, always remain ours."[81]

Leo and Natalie's marriage seems to have been a very traditional one, in which the husband was active in the world while the wife managed the home, raised their daughter, and made visitors feel at ease. Natalie was the prime example of a rabbinical wife, the *rebbitzin* (German: *Rabbinerfrau*). Her duties included instructing other rabbinical wives in the proper performance of their tasks.[82] She was a helpmate to her very busy husband but without a career of her own outside the home. There is no indication that she desired anything more. However, unlike her mother, their daughter, Ruth, became a university student, meeting her future husband at the University of Freiburg.[83]

In his writings, Baeck gave marriage and the family—though not his own marriage and family—considerable attention. In 1925, his friend Count Keyserling published a popular book on marriage that was quickly translated into English. Its twenty-four contributors, referred to as "leaders of contemporary thought," included such well-known figures as Thomas Mann; the multitalented Indian intellectual Rabindranath Tagore; and the British expert on human sexuality Havelock Ellis. Baeck was the only Jewish religious figure asked to contribute. His essay was titled, perhaps not surprisingly, "Marriage as Mystery and Command."[84] As the title clearly indicates,

Baeck attempts to fit marriage into his own theology. The piece is highly abstract and unsentimental. The central ideal of marriage, as Baeck sees it, is trust. Surprisingly, the word "love" does not occur even once.

For Baeck, marriage is a religious act. "Its ethics are rooted in the divine mystery that two human beings experience in each other."[85] The result of this experience is a lifelong bond. Marriage possesses permanency, not simply on account of the nature of the couple's feelings toward each other but because marriage draws husband and wife to the Eternal. The adulterous partner is the one who lacks the mystery of connection with God and spouse. He or she has chosen to exit the mystery that surrounds them both. Baeck distinguishes the grammatically singular mystery, which seals a marriage, from the grammatically plural secrets, which destroy the mystery. For Baeck, a traditionalist in all matters of personal morality, "marriage is the home of mystery, and for that reason it can be so only in the marriage of one with one." No less important in marriage than the mystery is the divine commandment that the couple be bound together for their lifetime. "They must realize and fashion their entire lives through each other."[86] Together they maintain the *Poesie* (the magical poetic quality) that keeps out the destructive force of the prosaic and protects the mystery and the command.

Baeck noted that for many in his time, the family as reality and as ideal had fallen into a state of uncertainty. He attributed that regrettable situation to two causes: the rights and opportunities that had recently been given to women; and the broader spatial and emotional freedom given to young people outside their home.[87] Baeck was genuinely fearful of what this new situation in the Weimar Republic would mean for the Jewish family. Yet for all his own and his wife's traditionalism, he was an advocate of women's rights. On the occasion of the convention's celebrating the twenty-five-year anniversary of the Jüdische Frauenbund (Jewish Women's League), Leo Baeck was invited to give a major address. In keeping with contemporary understanding, he expressed his understanding of women and men as psychologically different from each other. Although the woman obviously shared human qualities with the opposite sex, she was from birth more given to receiving and to bearing than was the man. But that did not mean that she was, citing Goethe, merely "the silver bowl into which the man lays the golden fruits." She did indeed carry the destiny of receptivity, but Baeck believed that bearing that burden was a sort of heroism. Regrettably, up until the present, it had become a sort of dogma that the woman was dependent for her identity upon the man and that she was simply his object. The result was that women had begun to believe that their lives gained meaning only from men. For Baeck, that was an intolerable situation demanding attention by both men and women.

Fortunately, change was coming about. What Baeck calls a revolution perhaps more significant than any other was under way, and he believed that Judaism should fully recognize it. He later recalled that his wife had often reminded him that when, at the turn of the century, she had read to him from the newspaper that the Prussian high school and university were being opened to young women, he had said to her: "Now the revolution has begun."[88] He continued to believe that this revolution should be fully recognized even when it became necessary that it proceed to a second stage. The revolution had rightly sought to provide women with equal education, equal professional opportunities, and equal rights. To achieve that goal, it had for a time been necessary to stress the similarity of women to men. But now, it was possible to proceed to the next stage: "the woman reaching back upon herself, upon herself as a woman." Baeck went on in his address to compare the emancipation of women with the emancipation of the Jews. The Jews, too, had striven to be what they were not—to resemble non-Jews—in order to gain their rights. But now, they, too, should be turning inward, recognizing that they were different as Jews and, as such, possessed a particular task. Similarly, Jewish women, while seeking equality in the broader feminist movement, had lost their particularity as Jews. They believed that in order to become the "new woman," they needed to pay the price of their Jewishness. The rejection of that need, according to Baeck, was the great contribution of the Jüdische Frauenbund. He then went on to praise five of its most prominent members, beginning with Bertha Pappenheim, the Frauenbund's founder, for whom being Jewish was essential both to her personal existence and to her feminism.

Discourse, Baeck noted, was now moving toward the recognition of psychological difference within equality, toward a sort of complementarity. Men and women were each creative, Baeck suggested, but in different ways: in men, that creativity pressed from the mind to the heart; in women, it took the opposite course, from the heart to the mind. Baeck concludes his address on an ecstatic religious note, attributing the new equality, along with recognition of difference, to God: "God has created something new. That is the way the woman of our time has experienced it, the Jewish woman before most. History has been made, a new song may be sung. The Jewish woman may sing it for she has discovered herself. She has found what is most her own; she has become aware of her religious power. In that way, she has been renewed. 'Sing to the Eternal a new song!'"[89] But was the Jewish woman's religious sphere the same as the Jewish man's? For example, should men and women, in contrast to the practice even in Liberal synagogues in Germany, be allowed to sit together?

In 1929, the Berlin Jewish community was in the process of constructing a new synagogue on Prinzregentenstraße. It would be the last before the rise of Nazism put an end to such projects. At that time, only in the small independent synagogue, mentioned earlier, did the sexes sit together. To be sure, in Liberal synagogues women were not confined to an area behind a separating barrier in the balcony. But there were no "family pews," as had existed for some time in American Reform temples. Men and women sat in separate sections on either side of a dividing aisle. Before making its decision with regard to seating in the new synagogue, the lay leadership of the Berlin community requested expert guidance from the Berlin rabbinate. The results were indecisive. The more liberal rabbis came out in favor of mixed seating; the traditionalists were against it. In keeping with his long-standing desire to maintain communal unity and to respect all sincere feelings, Baeck offered a unique intermediate position.

After reviewing the history of the subject, he noted, as he had in his lecture to the Jewish Women's League, that a new Jewish woman was emerging who was seeking equality in German society; it was understandable that she should seek it in the synagogue, as well. This demand was not simply a matter of being in accord with the times—a notion for which, as we have seen, Baeck had little regard—but rather, a new idea that did not do violence to historical Judaism. But what form should that innovation take? Baeck had to recognize that there were male synagogue-goers whose religious feelings would be disturbed by the presence of women in their immediate vicinity. A unified community had to consider those feelings, as well. He therefore suggested a third way: the new synagogue should provide family pews for those who desire them; and separate seating for those who would feel that they could pray more comfortably among members solely of their own sex.[90]

We do not know what Baeck's own preference in this regard was during the years that he was leading services from the pulpit. Much later, in a rare personal recollection, he confided to a former student what had, at least for a time, been his practice during the Nazi period, when he no longer conducted services and had himself become a congregant. Baeck relates: "In the synagogue on Prinzregentenstraße in Berlin—which as to its religious services was scarcely different from the other synagogues—men and women sat next to each other, and if I may mention something personal: In the last year of my wife's life, we went there—I was no longer exercising liturgical functions—and I was deeply moved to be able to sit next to my wife in the days of her illness."[91]

Without specific reference to his own daughter, Ruth, who in the Weimar years was already an adult, Baeck devoted reflections to the Jewish education of children in the family and school and, not surprisingly, placed parenting and formal education into a religious context. Here, as elsewhere, Baeck emphasized *Poesie*, the poetic orientation that he saw as the opposite of the prosaic and the philistine. The poetic sense, which Baeck believed to be characteristic of children, was too easily lost in the process of maturation. Yet that sense was essential for "religiosity"—a term that Baeck, like Buber, preferred to the word "religion." It was the responsibility of the teacher of Judaism to guard the poetic consciousness as the child grew older and to implant it into thoughtful religious practice. The conscientious parent and teacher were to guide the child from the poetic magic characteristic of childhood through the idealism of youth, on to the responsibility of adulthood, whereby the earlier states of being were not lost in their successors and where rootedness in the family and community led gradually to identification with all humanity. All genuine education, almost regardless of subject, was, in Baeck's view, religious. It was only religion that repeatedly and from both major stages of life, from youth and from age, allowed for the capture of life's meaning. "In the Eternal, in the depths of life and its heights, teacher and student, age and youth, can come together." Only when they came together in mutuality could they communicate and not merely converse. "It is religion that creates the connection."[92]

During the "good" Weimar years between the disastrous inflation and the Great Depression, Baeck could scarcely imagine the political revolution that would occur in January 1933. However, after Jewish cemeteries in Germany repeatedly suffered desecration and the Central Association in 1932 issued a volume documenting them, Baeck wrote a foreword that included these words: "Guilty are those who do evil, but guilty in particular before the bar of history are those, as well, who witness the crime or who know about it and remain silent. They are the ones who, without intending it, allow it to occur. Violence gets its way only when freedom is lacking, and no one is less free than the person who remains silent when he should be speaking, who should be admonishing and warning."[93] That same year, although

Hitler had not yet gained power, Baeck wrote in a similar vein: "Injustice and sin exist in every nation; they come and they go and the people lives on. But if the nation as such, as a whole, joins in the guilt through silence, through indulgence, through looking on, then that misdeed destroys the foundation upon which a nation exists; it collapses under it. Nations have perished only when they first remained silent, when people ceased to resist sin and to speak out for justice."[94]

In the wake of the acts by a few, Baeck was saying that the complacent majority comes to share in their guilt, and eventually the silence of the people leads to its destruction. Ahead lay a supremely agonizing time for Leo Baeck, but, in the end, he would witness the accuracy of his words in the collapse of Nazi Germany.

Chapter 5

The Burden of Leadership

Reversal

As early as the French Revolution, the Jews of France had gained civil equality. But for German Jewry, achieving emancipation from the political exclusion of medieval times was a lengthy and arduous struggle. For the first two-thirds of the nineteenth century, that Jewish ambition was repeatedly frustrated, moving ahead only sporadically and differentially in the various independent states that then made up Germany. Only with German unification in 1871 did the constitution of the Second Reich finally, and uniformly for all of Germany, end official discrimination against all Jews. Yet even then, many Germans in high as well as low positions were unaccepting of Jewish equality. Not long thereafter, a wave of antisemitism swept across the country, and the slogan "the Jews are our misfortune" first made its appearance. Most Jews regarded this recrudescence of Jew-hatred, now often in racist garb, as a passing phenomenon, the last gasp of a prejudice that would have no place in the twentieth century. They felt themselves to be Germans and believed that their fellow citizens would soon accept them as such. Moreover, by the Weimar years, informal exclusion seemed to be declining. Public opinion, especially in the large cities—most of all, in Berlin, where a third of German Jews lived—was becoming more accepting of Jews in positions of prominence, whether in the arts, the academy, or the economy. Jewish opinion leaders may have admitted that the path had been rocky and that there were still some stumbling blocks on the road, but with the assistance of their defense organization and fair-minded non-Jews supporting them, the future looked bright. In 1931, Jewish self-confidence was higher than ever. That year, the anonymous editor of the Jewish address book for Berlin could declare in his preface: "However much enemies of the Jews may deny our Germanness, it exists, we live it every day and no power in the world will be able to tear apart our inner connection with the German people, to dispute our belonging to this German people."[1]

Few German Jews, whose numbers now stood at about half a million, were prepared for January 30, 1933, when Adolf Hitler became chancellor of Germany. Like many Gentiles, they regarded him as little more than a joke, a funny-looking Austrian corporal and demagogue. He was not a real German—not a man Germans would exalt as their leader and whom they would let whittle away the status that German Jewry had so long yearned for and finally gained.

Although National Socialism had numerous objectives, both economic and military, the transformation of German Jews from fellow citizens into nefarious enemies of the nation was clearly a central goal, especially for the new Führer. It did not take long for the process to begin. After scarcely two months, on April 1, members of the Nazi SA, the armed and uniformed branch of the Nazi party, placed themselves in front of Jewish stores, daring anyone to enter. That same month, the now no longer democratic government passed a law removing Jews from positions of influence, such as in education and public performance. Within a few weeks of coming to power, the Nazis had begun the reversal of Jewish emancipation. It would find its most explicit expression in the Nuremberg Laws of September 1935, which declared the Jews no longer *Staatsbürger* (citizens of the state) but only *Staatsangehörige* (state's subjects). Major steps taken against the Jews came at intervals—in 1933, 1935, and 1938—with the result that most Jews, at least initially, decided to wait it out, hoping and perhaps believing that the most recent setback would be the last and that, sooner or later, the German people would come to its senses.

The immediate and sustained Nazi objective was to force Jewish emigration by making life in Germany increasingly difficult. This intent was clearly indicated in a memorandum that stated the goal regarding the Jews: "The possibilities for life [in Germany] are to be diminished, not only economically. Germany must be for them a land without a future, in which, to be sure, the older generation will be allowed to die in place, but in which the younger generation cannot live, so that the incentive for emigration remains alive."[2] To further this objective, the authorities were determined to play off one Jewish faction against another, lest a sense of Jewish unity lead to the desire for minority rights in German society.[3] Given the deep-seated divisions within German Jewry, such a strategy held great promise.

German Jews, by this time, were deeply acculturated in Germany and, especially after their service in World War I, felt themselves entitled to being regarded as fully German. But given their internal differences, they reacted to the profound reversal of their status in various and contradictory ways. As fervent nationalists, the Zionists possessed their own appreciation of the power of nationalism. One of their leaders wrote: "When a people dedicates itself anew to nationhood and to a powerful state that embraces all aspects of existence, then we, as Zionists, . . . have an obligation to display a profound understanding for the genuine source from which all of this flows."[4] An editorial in the newspaper of German Zionism even used language similar to that employed by the Nazis when it defined Zionists as "national Jews who affirm the constitutive value of *Volkstum* [folk identity] and of the blood for the person and the people." They did, however, differentiate their movement sharply from Nazism by stressing, as well, the "higher unity of the human race."[5] On June 21, 1933, the Zionist Association for Germany issued a lengthy statement indicating its relationship to the new German state, in which it pointed to parallels between the Jewish and the Nazi understandings of ethnic identity. It, too, believed in a differentiation between the Jewish and the German race and in propagating the emigration of Jews—in the Zionist case, to Palestine. It was thus in accord with the Nazi policy of separation,[6] and it is not surprising that, of all the Jewish factions, Zionists were the ones whom the Nazi authorities tended to favor, initially granting them privileges denied to other groups.[7]

Yet Zionists, too, had seen themselves as patriots during the war and had difficulty in accepting the turnabout. To be sure, some Zionists wasted no time in leaving Germany for Palestine, but most remained in the Nazi state for the immediate future. And at least for the present, they recognized the need for a leader who could command broad support within German Jewry. So it was that they were among those who turned to Leo Baeck to be their leader for the days that lay ahead. Although most Zionists were not actively religious, they wanted to be led by someone with spiritual qualities as well as practical skills. German Jewry needed to be "strengthened in spirit," they felt, not only "physically maintained."[8] In Leo Baeck, the rabbi and scholar, they recognized "a man who cannot be categorized according to party because his singular personality and his powerful Jewish ethos, his immense Jewish knowledge and experience as well as his judgment and worldview elevate him above the usual divisions."[9] As we have seen, Baeck was not a card-carrying Zionist, but as a member of the expanded Jewish Agency and a supporter of Jewish settlement in the Land of Israel, he could be seen by Zionists, if not as one of their own, certainly as someone sympathetic to their cause.

If the Zionists, with some emotional pangs, were willing to give up their claim to full Germanness, at the other end of the spectrum were those German Jews who persisted in claiming that, in every respect, they were as German as the non-Jews. They virulently rejected Zionism and continued to attack it after January 1933. The followers of one of the factions in this category, led by the uncompromising Max Naumann, declared themselves *Deutschjuden*, meaning that their Judaism was of a specifically and uniquely German sort. When their opponents pejoratively branded them "Juden-Nazis," they joyously adopted the term, noting that it was not the first time a designation intended to be derogatory was, in reality, a title of honor.[10] Unlike the Zionists, and to their profound chagrin, these super-patriots, who tried so hard to prove that they were loyal to the state, did not find favor in Nazi eyes. Nothing that a Jew could affirm would make him or her fully German in Nazi eyes. The authorities condemned Naumann and others like him as "assimilationists"; in 1935, the Gestapo went so far as to forbid Jews from claiming that they were fully German. Unlike the Zionists, these 100-percent Germans among the Jews had little regard for Leo Baeck. In their eyes, he was part of the Zionist camp, leading the German Jews into a "Zionist ghetto," and hence he was among their opponents. When Baeck became head of the incipient Jewish representative body, they refused to join.

Navigating between these extremes were the Liberal Jews, the group to which Leo Baeck, as a Liberal rabbi, belonged. Like the Zionists, whose views on Germany were not wholly uniform, the Liberals were split on how to deal with the reversal. For them, it was particularly painful, since liberalism had posited a notion of progress that would lead to a more humane world, and Germany, with its rich culture, was expected to be the driving force. But Nazi authorities branded their political arm, the Central Association of German Citizens of the Jewish Faith (CV), no less than the Naumann faction, with the negative epithet "assimilationists," making them enemies of the intended separation between German Aryans and German Jews.[11]

Internally, the Liberal Jews, more than the other groups, were divided on the issue of Germanism versus Judaism. Factions that leaned toward one side or the other emerged both in their religious organizations and in their political defense organization, the CV. But all felt the dissonance between "their" Germany and what Germany had become. The most loudly German among the Liberal Jews—those who belonged to the Reform Congregation in Berlin—took the longest to recognize the new situation. The sharp reversal was a devastating blow to virtually everything they believed in—an erasure of their ideology. They had no intention of leaving Germany. As late as 1935, one of the congregation's rabbis counseled outright against emigration.[12] The deeply unsettling effect of the changed environment on some in the congregation was poignantly evident in a member's lament that she could no longer feel that she was German and that now she could feel only Jewish.[13] Although mainstream Liberal Judaism was less persistent in its Germanism than the Reform Congregation, it was divided, with some of its leadership close to the Reform position of holding fast to German allegiance. From that faction came the suggestion of a Jewish concordat with the government of the sort that Hitler had been willing to make with the Catholic Church.[14] In 1934, its members were of the opinion that Jewish rights in Germany could only be effectively maintained by those Jews who "feel themselves to be children of Germany and limbs of the German people. Whoever accounts himself part of the Jewish nation, whose national home is Palestine," their periodical stressed, "he remains a guest in Germany and a stranger, and he can and must necessarily become disruptive when he appears together with those who see their home as being here and want to assert their rights as among the home-born."[15] The anti-Zionist group among the Liberals held fast to its position until it became simply too absurd to do so, while the other faction, to which Baeck belonged, rejected hostility to Zionism and was gradually moving ever closer to the Zionist position with regard to emigration.[16]

In the weeks after the Nazi ascent to power, in his capacity as chair of the German Rabbinical Association, Leo Baeck gave an interview to the Berlin correspondent of a French newspaper, which was publicized in the Jewish press. The contents indicate that even for Baeck, the depth of the reversal had not yet penetrated his soul. In the interview, he stressed two points. The first of these, though fully in line with Nazi thinking, was to be expected from a religious Jew: the complete rejection of Bolshevism as a godless movement. A few months later, in the German Zionist periodical, Baeck expressed a similar thought, more broadly encompassing opposing notions of government and indirectly casting aspersions on Nazism: "There can be no true aristocracy and also no true democracy without religiosity, without the relationship to God, or, what is saying the same thing, without an awareness of the [moral] task. Every aristocracy and likewise every democracy, when it ceased to be pious, became a mere showpiece that then fell apart when a blast of wind forced its collapse."[17] Although Baeck was thinking especially of secularized Jewish leadership, he may also have been hinting at the Hitler regime, brought to power by a godless Weimar democracy and engaged in creating its own false aristocracy.

The second point made in the interview was Baeck's insistence (perhaps misquoted by the reporter) that the renewal of Germany was "an ideal and a longing among the German Jews." Supposedly, he added: "We Jews here cherish the honest wish and the honest hope that we too will be able calmly and candidly to fashion our relationship to the new rulers in Germany."[18] If the reporting is indeed accurate, then Baeck, like so many others, initially harbored the illusion that what had happened was not a reversal but only an unfortunate but manageable change of regime.[19]

As late as June 1933, Baeck could still speak of Germany as a Jewish *Heimat*, a home. That autumn, he would praise the "love and loyalty" that German Jews shared with their non-Jewish fellow citizens; and a few months after that, he still mentioned the "German home soil."[20] He, too, had difficulty in believing that the German people could have made so sharp a turnaround. As he told the prominent Zionist Arthur Ruppin, as late as the summer of 1937 he still continued to believe that 80 percent of the German people were opposed to persecution of the Jews but were simply afraid to express their opinion.[21] Yet Baeck also recognized the historical necessity of providing young people with an exit to a new land. Already in 1933, he wrote: "It has become a major task to look for locations and find ways as to how on the holy soil of Palestine, which Providence has provided with a new era, . . . the German Jews will be able to prove themselves." There, with character, sweat, and efficient labor, he believed, they would be able to take charity from none while providing bread for all.[22] That ability was the direct opposite of the situation in Germany, where, increasingly, there was not sufficient bread for all, and Jews who had been donors to charitable causes were soon forced to become charity recipients. When, in 1935, the Saarland returned to German sovereignty, Baeck did not welcome its Jewish population to a fatherland but only to a common Jewish fate—to common concerns and common tasks.[23]

Like many Jews and many non-Jewish critics of the Nazi regime, Baeck hoped that the German president, Paul von Hindenburg, would be able to hold Hitler in check. After the Nazi takeover, the ex-general insisted on privileges for Jews who had fought on the front lines of the war. In a letter to Claude Montefiore in England, Baeck wrote: "We are joyful that Hindenburg remains president."[24] When Hindenburg died in the summer of 1934, Baeck spoke at a memorial service held in a Liberal synagogue in Berlin. Here he compared Hindenburg to a rock, thereby implicitly implying that he had been a formidable rock blocking—though, in the end, ineffectively—Hitler's path to dictatorship. Baeck also stressed the dead president's aristocratic demeanor, in unspoken contrast to the demagoguery of the new chancellor. He must have speedily realized that with this last obstacle removed from his path, Hitler could move further ahead, entirely unhindered.[25] Nonetheless, Baeck continued to dream of a military coup against Hitler. He told one of his associates: "No one can prophesy, but it is still my view that one day I will wake up and find a posted notice that announces: 'I have assumed full authority,' General von. . . ."[26]

Initially, some of the Jewish factions tried to approach the new rulers on their own. Early on, representatives of the CV did get a meeting with Reichsminister Göring, during which they stressed that their organization had nothing to do with Communists and other enemies of the state. Supposedly, the minister replied that security of life and property was assured to loyal, law-abiding Jewish citizens.[27] However, such assurances—if ever seriously intended—proved to be increasingly worthless in the course of time. Moreover, other attempts to contact the authorities by individual Jewish groups—for example, by Naumann's faction and by Orthodox Jewry—were simply rejected or ignored. An Orthodox memorandum, sent to Hitler in October 1933, stressed the observant Jews' attachment to Germany and inquired whether it was the chancellor's intention merely to restrict the Jews' lives or to annihilate them. Their memorandum received no response.[28] A face-to-face meeting with Hitler was out of the question. When a delegation from the CV sought to obtain such an audience, the chancellor rebuffed them, stating explicitly: "I cannot find any interest in seeing Jews."[29] It soon became apparent that both the Nazi desire to maintain easier control over the Jewish population and the Jews' own desire for a single united representation to the regime required as broad and as encompassing an organization as possible, and that such an organization needed to be created as soon as possible. Given the dissent within the community, that was no easy task.

Creating Unity

On account of the ideological and religious differences, as well as local loyalties, German Jewry had hitherto been unable to establish an effective national organization. In 1869, it created the Association of German-Israelite Communities, but its activities were limited principally to education and social welfare. Moreover, being community-based, it did not include the later-created but increasingly significant CV or the Zionists. Finally, an all-Germany representation, comprising the individual German state associations, came into existence in 1932, and on February 12, 1933, a few days after the Nazi ascent to power, Leo Baeck was chosen to chair it. In this capacity, he and a colleague sent a letter on June 6, 1933, to the government, asking for an interview to discuss issues regarding the Jews that arose from the new political situation. It was followed three days later by a declaration that the German Jews were tired of reiterating their long connection with German soil, German culture, and German spirit. They now insisted on a relationship that would rest on law and mutual respect. Not surprisingly, their efforts did not result in a positive reply. Like the requests of the individual groups, this plea was rejected.[30] Such refusals only aggravated the need for a genuinely representative organization, if for no other task than to coordinate internal Jewish policy. The existing association, being dominated by the Prussian Jews and especially by the Berlin community—to the dissatisfaction of the rest of German Jewry—could not effectively fulfill that task. Baeck called it nothing more than "an enlarged Prussian association or an enlarged executive of the Berlin community," not an effective instrument for German Jewry at a time of severe endangerment.[31] Frustrated, he withdrew from the chairmanship on June 25, after less than half a year.[32] His departure unleashed a new initiative, one in which Baeck would be able to play a stronger leadership role.

It became clear that a genuine representative association would have to give significant influence to the major Jewish political organizations, the CV, the Zionists, and also the National Association of Jewish Front-Line Soldiers, whose members had all fought in World War I. Although they differed from one another in political orientation, these organizations collectively represented a new order in German Jewry. Unlike the leadership of the individual communities, they were led by elites who were generally younger and economically not as well established as the men who governed the local Jewish communities and the regional communal associations. The question was how to bring together this nationally based leadership and the older order of community leaders in an encompassing unity. To be effective, a membership was required that would include almost all German Jews, along with broad financial support and a universally accepted summit leadership.

There was another reason for action, although the Jewish leadership was possibly not aware of it at the time: according to the draft of a Jewry law drawn up in April 1933, the government was planning to set up a compulsory organization for all Jews, to be called a *Judenrat* (Jewish council), the very designation the Nazis later used for the councils, tightly controlled by the SS, that were set up in the ghettos of the East. Its function would simply be to implement orders from the Nazi regime.[33] This possibility may have added to the need for establishing a voluntary, democratic organization lest the new regime force German Jewry into a compulsory one—as would indeed eventually happen in Germany, though not until six years later, in early 1939. Meanwhile, the head of the Gestapo, Reinhard Heydrich, insisted that all Jewish organizations announce their meetings to the local police. Nazi officials would then appear at Jewish gatherings to ensure that nothing suspicious was said, even at religious services.[34]

The initiative for a new encompassing Reichsvertretung der deutschen Juden (RV, National Representation of German Jews), as it was first called, came from the Jewish community of Essen, in northwestern Germany. Three men—the Liberal rabbi Hugo Hahn, together with a banker and an attorney—set the process in motion. All three were members of the faction in the CV that supported the Jewish Agency for Palestine. Their strategy was to win over the major national organizations, isolating and then eventually gaining support from the powerful Jewish community of Berlin, which, it was anticipated, would initially oppose this diminution of its national influence.

Winning over the CV was relatively easy. In an article in the CV newspaper, titled "Unified into the New Age," its president, Julius Brodnitz, stressed the need for German Jews to put aside ideological differences at so difficult a time and to work together for their common interests.[35] The Zionists were harder to convince. Within their camp, one faction was in favor of unity, and the other opposed cooperation with non-Zionists.[36] Moreover, even those Zionists who favored cooperation complained that, although they were much smaller in numbers than the CV, they had the right to larger representation than they were initially offered: given their ability to aid in matters of emigration and their foreign connections, they deserved special consideration.[37] But they, too, soon became supporters, especially after one of their own, Siegfried Moses, was given the position of deputy chairman. As for the National Association of Jewish Front-Line Soldiers, they were suffering under the illusion that, as soldiers, they would be more respected by the Nazis and hence deserving of a position of central leadership in the new organization. They had, in fact, played a role in persuading Hindenburg to grant certain concessions to their members on account of their previous service to the state.[38] Their spokesman initially warned that deep-seated differences within the German Jewish spirit should not be ignored and that a forced unity would suffocate the richness of diversity.[39] But before too long, they also joined, declaring that the situation of the German Jews required an internal Jewish *Burgfrieden*, a truce analogous to that proposed by Emperor Wilhelm II at the outbreak of World War I when he declared that, in the face of military threat, he would no longer recognize parties but only Germans.[40] Baeck had their respect; as a chaplain, he, too, had been a soldier in the war. The religious Liberals likewise came aboard, as did the Jewish community leaders—though most reluctantly, in the case of Berlin.

But the smaller, most fervently Germanocentric, groups and the Orthodox did not wish to join. Naumann's *Deutschjuden* would have nothing to do with an organization that included Zionists; neither would the Reform Congregation in Berlin. The Independent Orthodox Jews, for their part, were also unhappy with the large role to be played by the Zionists as well as the effect that the new organization might have on the direction of Jewish education. In 1934, they publicly rejected the work of the RV since, being "spiritually determined by Buber and Baeck," it stood in opposition to Torah-true Judaism.[41] In addition, they felt left out of the leadership—snubbed—and therefore, they argued, they were forced to pursue their interests independently of what they regarded as an illegitimate leadership.[42] Not until the summer of 1938 did they finally join, much to the distress of one Orthodox rabbi, who branded their affiliation an act of apostasy.[43]

Fortunately for the founders of the new Reichsvertretung, they were able to gain support from certain influential sources within and outside of Germany. A central role was played by Max Warburg, the wealthy Jewish banker, then still living in Hamburg, who vigorously pushed for the project. Given the increasing impoverishment of the German Jews, large sums would be required to sustain the work of the RV. And unlike the Jewish communities, the RV had no standing in public law and therefore did not have the right to levy taxes on German Jewry. A large portion of the funding would have to come from abroad, from organizations such as the American Jewish Joint Distribution Committee and the Central British Fund.[44] Warburg could help in assuring the arrival of the necessary donations. In addition to a broadly representative membership and adequate funding, a third requirement was perhaps most important: there had to be a leader at the top who was respected by virtually all the factions as well as by donors abroad.

From the beginning of the formation of the new Reichsvertretung, only one individual was considered for the position of president as well as head of its associated social assistance agency: Rabbi Leo Baeck.[45] Members of the Essen group had Baeck in mind from the first, remarking on his broad worldview and diplomatic skill. They noted that he was concurrently a member of the CV Executive and a member of the governing body of Keren Ha-Yesod, the fund-raising body for Jewish settlement in Palestine. Both sides could claim Baeck as one of their own. So could the German B'nai B'rith, for which he continued to serve as president, and the General Rabbinical Association, over which he likewise presided.[46] However, having resigned from the earlier ineffective representative body, Baeck was initially reluctant to assume the top leadership position again. It was only due to the pressure exercised on him by Max Warburg that he agreed to take the presidency, although Warburg was later of the opinion, according to his biographer Ron Chernow, that Baeck was "too peaceful a man to enforce harmony among headstrong personalities."[47] Others, too, wondered whether his personality was right for a position of such responsibility. Robert Weltsch, editor of the German Zionist newspaper, noted that Baeck surely possessed spiritual authority, but wondered whether he could display the "toughness" that the job required "in a world full of antagonism and enmity."[48] However, a few months later, the same newspaper greeted the new president with enthusiasm. It noted that Baeck could not be relegated to a particular party, since "his extraordinary personality and his powerful Jewish ethos, his extensive Jewish knowledge and experience, as well as his judgment and his international perspective, rise above the usual divisions."[49]

More difficult was persuading the chairman of the Berlin community, Heinrich Stahl, to accept Baeck as president of the new organization. In Germany, community leadership had been exercised almost exclusively by

Figure 4. Leo Baeck at a synagogue during the Nazi period, with Heinrich Stahl on his left. Courtesy of American Jewish Archives, Cincinnati.

laymen, to whom rabbis were responsible, if not subservient. Baeck had been chosen as the leading Liberal rabbi of Berlin; but Stahl, the most powerful community leader in Germany, was not easily persuaded to accept his leadership in an office of secular responsibility. A wealthy insurance executive, Stahl had taken charge of the Berlin community in May 1933. Called to participate in the discussions concerning the founding of the RV, Stahl commented that "Baeck, whom we esteem and honor as a man of great learning, does not have our confidence in political matters."[50] Although he finally agreed to Baeck's leadership, Stahl would later repeatedly attempt to unseat him.

Baeck was fortunate that Otto Hirsch was elected by the constituent organizations to be at his side. As a former government official, Hirsch possessed administrative skills and political experience—just the sort of practical experience that Baeck lacked. During the Weimar years, Hirsch rose to a high position in the government of the state of Württemberg, in the south of Germany, but lost his position in 1933. Moreover, he had shown himself to be a seriously committed Jew, deeply in accord with Baeck's own convictions. In 1926, Hirsch helped found a center for Jewish learning in his native Stuttgart; he was familiar with the work of the contemporary Jewish philosophers Martin Buber and Franz Rosenzweig, whom he regarded as his religious mentors. Annually at Passover, the Hirsch family would join the Baecks for the festive seder meal. As executive chairman of the RV, Hirsch could provide a perfect complement to the spiritual and diplomatic qualifications of its president, Leo Baeck.[51] A memoirist recalled that "respect for Leo Baeck together with recognition of the integrity and unselfishness of Otto Hirsch created a harmony among the leading members of the [RV's] executive body."[52] Without Hirsch and a second close associate, Julius Seligsohn, Baeck testified after the war, "the Reichsvertretung could never have survived the difficulties that it encountered from time to time and the dangers that threatened its work." After both were murdered by the Nazis, it "left a vacuum that could not be filled."[53]

Baeck was installed as president of the newly constituted representative body of German Jewry on September 17, 1933, seven and a half months after Hitler came to power. That very day, its leadership issued a proclamation, which seems to have been written by Baeck. It spoke of days that were "hard and heavy, as ever were the days of Jewish history," and said that things had fundamentally changed for the Jews of Germany, who should realize that fact "without self-delusion." Since Jewish children were abandoning the general schools in ever larger numbers, the RV would have to do more for Jewish education, as well as train young people for new occupations that they could exercise "on the holy soil of Palestine." The declaration ended on a note typical for Baeck: "We build upon the living sense of community and conscious acceptance of responsibility by the German Jews as well as the sacrificial assistance of our brothers everywhere. We want to stand together and with trust in our God work for the *honor of the Jewish name.* From out of the sufferings of these days may the essence of the German Jews arise anew!"[54]

The Reichsvertretung was an anomaly in Nazi Germany: a democratically functioning organization, containing a variety of views, operating within a dictatorship. The freedom it enjoyed, according to historian Otto Dov Kulka, was "a freedom of the excluded, continuing to exist for years only finally to be revealed as a freedom of the condemned."[55] According to a sympathetic eyewitness, when Baeck conducted its meetings he "set the tone for unity of purpose. To watch him doing this was a lesson in leadership." He would introduce a subject with a few words and then allow an occasionally lengthy and sometimes divisive discussion to take place, with little intervention on his part. When it seemed concluded, he would sum it up in a few sentences and produce general agreement. Only after you left the room did you realize that "what Dr. Baeck had said at the end of the discussion was exactly what he had already outlined at the beginning."[56] Although there is no contemporary written source attesting to it, various individuals who were present have claimed that at the very first session of the RV, Baeck uttered words that have been cited in his name for many decades: "The thousand-year history of German Jewry is at an end."[57] Some believe that he made this assertion only after the Holocaust. However, it seems plausible that he could have spoken these words already in 1933, meaning that German Jewish life, as it had existed for two millennia, was seemingly at an end. At the very least, a new situation that offered little potential for the old existence had taken the place of what had gone before.[58] But, being Baeck, he could not let it go at that; his conviction that deeds could avert fate made him issue a challenge: "If we German Jews lose our internal morale, then the day could come when the foundations of Jewish communities abroad are likewise shattered."[59] German Jewry, in Baeck's eyes, was not only endangered; it had an obligation by presenting an example of holding together under pressure, to subvert that danger to Jews elsewhere, as well.

Physical and Spiritual Sustenance

The new situation of German Jewry placed unprecedented burdens on the Reichsvertretung even as increasing poverty reduced its internal donor base. By 1935, one German Jew in five required assistance.[60] Three years later, it was one in four.[61] In addition to providing for the poor, there were other tasks. A listing of RV responsibilities enumerated social welfare, economic assistance, education, occupational retraining, and preparation for emigration to any land.[62] As the younger people, who could more easily find employment abroad, left in increasing numbers, the remaining community grew older in average age, a population largely requiring old-age homes and social welfare assistance.[63] In addition to his tasks as president of the RV, Baeck chaired the Central Welfare Office, creating an effective personal union between the two. Just as he was ably assisted by Otto Hirsch in the work of the RV, he was blessed in the area of welfare with a deeply committed staff that included dedicated women with professional training in the field. Although Baeck may have been more of a figurehead than an active participant in the ongoing work of social welfare, his position at the apex inspired confidence from Jewish organizations abroad, whose contributions were an absolute necessity. His prestige enabled him to explain to Anglo-Jewish leaders that, with all appreciation that was owed them for financial support, their assistance should not imply the right to control matters in Germany. The German Jews had to be allowed to conduct their own affairs without interference by external donors.[64] But that necessitated German Jews undertaking a major effort to help their own.

Thus, when in 1935 the government withdrew all state assistance, leaving the Jewish community entirely dependent on resources that remained within its jurisdiction, the RV created a Jewish *Winterhilfe*, a fund-raising effort to enable impoverished Jews to get through the winter with all necessary food, coal, and clothing. The campaign opened with a formal ceremony in a large hall, where Baeck addressed the gathering. Frequently in the past, he had distinguished between the Christian conception of benevolence and the Jewish imperative for social justice. Now he again gave voice to the Jewish ideal of concern for the poor as a response to divine command, a duty incumbent upon every human creature of God and the source of his own action. Baeck's address included these words: "All around us fate has lifted its head. Often it threatens to crush us. But worst of all would be if life with its pressures were to become meaningless for us. All true faith is a faith that raises itself above fate: it is the will that springs up within this faith, the will to fashion and to create, to fulfill the [moral] law. Through our Winter Assistance we can become stronger than fate."[65]

For Baeck, helping the Jewish poor was not only to aid the needy. Charitable activity had the power to give meaning to a life that otherwise lacked it. By joining in the effort for others, Jewish contributors could transform themselves from objects into subjects, from victims of a cruel regime that had forsaken justice into propagators of the just society within their own ranks, as that society was envisioned by Israel's ancient Prophets. Reflecting upon Baeck's words, the editor of the Zionist newspaper claimed that Baeck had given the campaign a higher meaning. His address was followed by a selection from Mozart, after which a large number of women carrying collection boxes gathered the campaign's first fruits as the audience left the overcrowded hall.[66]

In succeeding years, Baeck was continually called upon to inspire those Jews who still possessed financially sufficient means to spend from their remaining resources for the benefit of less fortunate coreligionists. Liberal Jews, in particular, had taken pride in their individual capacity as capitalists to ascend the economic ladder. But now that Jews were dependent upon themselves, Baeck believed, individual strivings had to give way to sacrifice for the sake of the entire community. Once, native German Jews had needed only a sense of noblesse oblige vis-à-vis the impoverished Eastern European Jews in their midst; now, it was their own faction within German Jewry, the home-born, that required assistance, as well. It was necessary, Baeck wrote in an article on Jewish social work, to abandon the old attitudes of heart and mind that no longer sufficed and to think instead in a new way and, what is more difficult, to feel in a new way. Social work "is now work for ourselves," he concluded.[67]

Even as a greater number of German Jews, unable to manage fully on their own, now required physical sustenance, so too more Jews than ever in recent generations sought spiritual support. As noted earlier, during the Weimar years, most synagogues remained nearly empty, with the exception of the High Holidays. But now, they filled to an extent unprecedented in recent years.[68] They became places where Jews could feel secure among their own. Although this revival may not have touched the majority, it did mean that Baeck and other rabbis had an opportunity to speak to the heart of a spiritually devastated community. They could use traditional texts referring to villains of the past in order to cast oblique aspersions upon the tormentors of the present. We know that Rabbi Joachim Prinz did so frequently, and others, including Baeck, doubtless did so as well. The synagogue was also a place where one could look away from the idols of Nazi ideology to a higher source of strength.

Not only did the new situation unleash a modest spiritual revival but, as doors were closing on the German Jews in employment, education, and culture, there arose, at least for a time, a remarkable renewal of Jewish knowledge and appreciation for the Jewish heritage. Jewish parents in Germany had taken great pride in the accomplishments of their children in non-Jewish schools, especially on the level of the academic high school, the *Gymnasium*. Teachers had prized their Jewish pupils, often rewarding them for their accomplishments. But with the Nazi ascent to power, the atmosphere in the schools shifted sharply. Jewish children were no longer praised by teachers who had freshly joined the party, and fellow students, members of the Nazi Youth, harassed them on their way to and from school. Although, in general, parents tried to keep their children in the public schools as long as possible, they now increasingly withdrew them for their own safety and well-being. Quotas reduced numbers further. Parents who had neglected their own Jewish identity were now sending their offspring to Jewish schools, which, as a result, blossomed as they had not for many generations. Outstanding Jewish teachers, dismissed from their former positions, became their teachers. That growth in the educational realm was, of course, a further drain on the finances of organized German Jewry. And it was another element in the inward focus that the Nazi regime was forcing on the Jews; the Nazi Security Service insisted that those teachers in the Jewish schools who were still propagating a German Jewish identity be replaced by Zionists, who were more ready to abandon it.[69] In retrospect, that demand had the positive effect for German Jewry of strengthening Jewish consciousness among the young and inclining them more strongly to emigrate as soon as that was a personal possibility.

The turn inward was not limited to the growth of Jewish schools for the children. Adults who had received only the most minimal Jewish education, usually delivered by a rabbi for an hour or so per week in the general schools, now found themselves branded from the outside with a Jewish identity that was mostly hollow. A large number of German Jews in the years immediately following the rise of the Hitler regime sought to fill that void with classes on all manner of Jewish subjects. Under the auspices of the RV, Leo Baeck placed Martin Buber, a man he admired, in charge of Jewish adult education. When that appointment encountered opposition from the Berlin leadership and the Orthodox, Baeck persisted, giving Buber free rein to shape the program as he wished.[70] Adult education institutions, on the model of the *Lehrhaus* that had been established in Frankfurt during the Weimar years, now sprang up in various cities, and the classes drew astonishing numbers. Rabbi Prinz recalled that when he spoke on Jewish history, he had to deliver his lecture twice to hundreds, in the same large hall.

When the adult education center in Berlin opened its doors to an overflow crowd in 1934, it was, not surprisingly, Leo Baeck who was called upon to give the opening lecture. He spoke on "History and the Present," devoting a portion of his remarks to African Americans, whom he drew into relation with the Jews. "Perhaps the worst crime that the white race has perpetrated against the Negroes," Baeck stressed, "was tearing them from their homeland and thereby suddenly separating them from their tradition."[71] The German Jews had long been committing that same crime against themselves when, in the nineteenth century, they had cut themselves off from their own tradition. He then differentiated between the Greek view of history, which culminates in the present, and its Jewish counterpart, which leads into the future. Baeck wanted to banish the thought of a Jewish history that led only to an assimilated—or a persecuted—existence. He wanted instead to inspire with a history that led to a secure and revitalized Jewish life in Palestine or in some other land. In the Nazi years, that urgent message of hope was frequent in his writings and on his lips.

A few months later, Baeck returned to the same theme, but this time with a measure of sarcasm that is unusual in his work. He made fun of those German Jews who had hungrily chased after every opportunity to display their *Bildung*, that typically German value representing a broad higher secular education and culture. They had run to every exhibition and every motion picture, they had read every new book—lest, alas, they lag behind their peers. Such was the Jewish cultural haste of which one could justifiably make fun. True *Bildung*, by contrast, was not erased by the exclusion from general culture, nor was its concentration in the Jewish domain a cultural narrowness: "We are able to turn toward the genuine, the lasting, toward that which has its place in the millennia, and from which no one can separate us." A profound *Bildung*, Baeck was saying, is possible within Judaism and therefore even in the present. The way there "is the way to ourselves."[72]

Most German Jews, with the marked exception of the Zionists, had defined their Jewish identity almost exclusively as a matter of religion, analogous to Christianity. They thought of high culture as German, European, or universal. It existed in the theater, the opera house and symphony hall, art museums, and German and world literature. There were, to be sure, Jews who participated in that non-Jewish realm—one was proud of the philosopher Moses Mendelssohn, the poet Henrich Heine, the painter Max Liebermann—but it was not a Jewish sphere of creativity; rather, it was one in which Jews were simply participants and were mostly pushed to the periphery. Now, however, Jews were being driven out of the general culture and forced to create their own separate cultural milieu. In response, in Berlin and elsewhere, Jewish cultural associations sprang up that undertook to present both dramatic and musical events. Jewish culture would fill the vacuum for those Jews who were willing to support and attend performances held within a closed Jewish circle. Not all Jews welcomed this separate Jewish culture, and the *Kulturbünde* did try to maintain the connection with the European stream by presenting compositions by non-Jews as well as by Jews. Despite such efforts, those Jews furthest from Jewish cultural tradition resented what they regarded as constriction. They resented what was clearly an objective of the regime, as one Nazi document put it: to "slowly lead the Jews into a spiritual ghetto."[73] Regardless of this hesitancy on the part of some Jews, Baeck still needed, on behalf of the RV, to call on all Jews, whether they attended the performances or not, to support the Jewish cultural associations financially if for no other reason than that they offered a living to innumerable forcibly unemployed Jewish performers. Joining a local *Kulturbund* was therefore not just an opportunity for enjoyment in troubled times; it was also "an obligation of honor incumbent on all Jews."[74] Furthermore, beyond the fulfillment of obligation, participation in a Jewish cultural enterprise possessed survival value: "We German Jews," Baeck wrote in 1934, "will get through difficult, critical times if we grasp and comprehend what is intrinsically ours, our own culture."[75] Along with leading cultural figures such as Martin Buber and Max Liebermann, Baeck served as a member of the Honorary Committee for the Berlin Kulturbund.

In Leo Baeck's eyes, authentic culture was not an end in itself. It was intimately related to religion and, for the Jew, to religious Judaism. In an article that appeared in the Jewish intellectual periodical *Der Morgen* in 1937, he wrote: "Every genuine artist—it is often evident—is on the path to piety; all true art, consciously or not, aims at becoming religious art, for what is experienced as invisible, impenetrable, lying behind the visible, leads to the First and the Last, to the Eternal. . . . Only in the meaningfulness that derives from the Eternal, from the one God, does the Jew experience himself and all else as truthful. Only on that account does his life and his being acquire artistry."[76]

In addition to culture, the Reichsvertretung was a supporter of sports, which, like the cultural activities, needed to be organized separately for Jews. We know that Leo Baeck was an avid hiker, especially when he could get away to the hills of Switzerland, but little more is known of his attitude toward sports activities—with the exception of a brief note from 1936. Here he did not speak of sport as enjoyment but rather as providing the necessary strength and solidarity that young Jews required under the new circumstances. He conceived of sport as a kind of asceticism, a self-denying preparation for the difficult conditions that emigrants would face in adjusting to a very different and, in many cases, more physical life in their lands of immigration. For Baeck, sport could not be only about hardening the body; it had to be, as well, a strengthening of character. Even here, he could find a connection to Judaism and to God. Sport among Jews was to lead its participants to the point where they could let their "little egos step back behind the great ideas, becoming fully Jews, in awareness and in earnestness holding fast to the Jewish commandment and to Jewish life."[77] For

Baeck during the Nazi years, every area of activity—charity, education, culture, and even sport—could be raised to higher level, to the realm of a uniquely Jewish spirit.

Contestations

Baeck's ability to hold his position as head of the Reichsvertretung and later of its successor organization, the Reichsvereinigung, was not due only to the broad support he enjoyed within German Jewry. It was also because the government authorities, despite all their distaste for Jews, displayed grudging respect for this Jew whose behavior ran so sharply against the stereotype enshrined in Nazi ideology. Baeck refused to grovel. His tall slim figure stood erect before the authorities—dignified, restrained, and fully in control. According to Max Grünewald, a surviving member of the RV, Baeck displayed a politeness that bordered on contempt.[78] Arrested five times, Baeck withstood every attempt to reduce him to the Nazi caricature of the plaintive, pleading Jew. In 1936, Baeck wrote that the person who believes in the transcendent God of mystery and commandment does not bow down, does not submit; he does not fear to speak out either for or against.[79] On one occasion, Baeck and associates were summoned to the offices of the Gestapo, told that the Reichsvertretung was unqualified to represent German Jewry, and heard a proposal for different leadership, apparently composed of Baeck's critics. Yet according to a postwar report from an RV employee, the Nazi official, a man named Flesch, showed Baeck great respect even as the Jewish leader refused to submit. That treatment surprised Baeck and even frightened him. Flesch, however, must surely have been aware of the widespread recognition that Baeck enjoyed among the Jews in Germany.[80] Removing him against their will would have created a chaos that was not in the Nazi interest.

Despite the respect that some Nazi officials accorded Baeck and the high regard he enjoyed among the great majority of German Jews, there were those in the community who continued to object to his leadership and sought to empower themselves instead. Even among his supportive associates within the RV, some, with mild resentment, referred to their president disparagingly as "the cardinal," the Jewish equivalent of a prince of the Catholic Church. Others were bitterly opposed to his exercise of authority. The Reichsvertretung that, according to one recollection, had been established in Essen "with tightly closed fists and clenched teeth" suffered persistent attempts to unravel the hard-fought unity that it had to struggle to maintain all the way to the end of its independent existence following the pogrom of 1938.[81] A mediation center established in 1934 seems to have had little influence, so the task of reconciling the factions fell largely to Leo Baeck.[82] Initially, confronting the claims of those Jews who believed that they alone were proper Germans was the major concern. In response, Baeck insisted that loyalty to the fatherland was not limited to one or another faction but was the possession of all German Jewry.[83] That divisive issue necessarily declined in severity as ever harsher Nazi policy made claims of loyalty to the fatherland appear absurd. Other points of conflict, relating more to power than to ideology, took its place.

The two major lines of tension ran between Zionists and the CV and between the Berlin community leadership and the RV. Within a few months after the formation of the Reichsvertretung, Baeck found it necessary to issue a public statement calling upon all groups "in these serious times to cease the factional polemics"[84]—but to no avail. Again and again, he had to spend much of his time and effort as head of the RV to preserve its fragile unity. In 1936, a council comprising twenty-four members was added to the administration of the RV, but this broadening of authority, which benefited both the Zionists and the Liberal community leaders, did not relieve the pressure on Baeck and Hirsch for very long.

Two powerful men were a persistent thorn in Baeck's side. Their low regard for his leadership and their desire to replace him spawned a deep mutual antipathy between them and Leo Baeck. One, Heinrich Stahl, possessed both wealth and the principal position of leadership in the Berlin Jewish community, by far the largest and most powerful community in Germany. Stahl was deeply devoted to Jewish welfare, donating generously from his time and resources for the Jewish poor. In return, he expected the perquisites of leadership. To his mind, the Essen initiative that resulted in the formation of the Reichsvertretung was a coup that undermined the proper locus of national leadership. Stahl was also among those German Jews who, for a time, believed it best to await the demise of the regime. Rabbi Prinz claimed that Stahl told him: "My people will not be so cowardly as to leave."[85] Like Baeck, Stahl was not a Zionist, but, also like Baeck, he supported the establishment of Jewish settlements in Palestine.[86] Given Stahl's backing in Berlin, Baeck had little choice but to co-opt him by allowing Stahl to obtain various positions in the national leadership.

The other opponent, Georg Kareski, was a dubious financier of high political ambition and a militant antisocialist. He headed the State Zionist Organization in Germany, a form of Revisionist Zionism that favored massive emigration to Palestine. But he differed from the mainstream Revisionist Zionists, led by Vladimir Jabotinsky, in rejecting their support for the international boycott of German goods. Although the State Zionists had not joined the RV, in 1937 Kareski made a deliberate effort to take over its authority, both in concert with Heinrich Stahl, whose views on Zionism scarcely coincided with his own, and independently by requesting the Gestapo and the Propaganda Ministry to impose his leadership. Kareski, who, in an interview published in 1935 in Goebbels's paper *Der Angriff*, had embarrassingly expressed acceptance of the situation created by the discriminatory Nuremberg Laws, now sought the title "Commissar in Charge of Emigration." In that position, he would have been the German Jewish equivalent of the Norwegian collaborator Vidkun Quisling.[87] In place of the Reichsvertretung, the head of the State Zionists called for a fully centralized authoritarian leadership, with himself as Führer, that would drive forward the process of total emigration. Since speedy emigration—with no concern for how Jews might fare after their departure—was Nazi policy at the time, the Gestapo gave its support to Kareski in his endeavor, in conjunction with Stahl, to take over the RV in 1937.[88] This was not surprising, since the RV was, according to the Nazis, most regrettably, "an ever larger reservoir of assimilationist Judaism."

The main task of the authorities was self-understood to be "complete elimination of assimilationists from Jewish political life in order to bring the Jewish question closer to its conclusive solution." Having earlier favored a policy that split the Jewish leadership, the Gestapo now desired unity under an authoritarian leadership fully within its control and dedicated to freeing Germany of its Jews with utmost speed.[89] For that purpose, Kareski was a fitting tool. At the same time, the Berliners, led by Stahl, again threatened secession from the RV and the establishment of a counter-organization. Once more, the claim was heard that the Reichsvertretung should be led by a man of action and not by a rabbi—in other words, by Heinrich Stahl and not by Leo Baeck.[90] In response to a letter, signed by Stahl and Kareski on behalf of the Berlin community, that was clearly intended to unseat them, Baeck and Hirsch vowed that they would never submit to such threats.[91] Clearly on the side of Stahl and Kareski, the Gestapo entered the fray, summoning Baeck, along with other Jewish leaders, to its headquarters and urging them to give Kareski a position as a member of the RV's Executive Committee or even to give him Otto Hirsch's position.[92] At this point, the RV still had sufficient independence for Baeck to refuse the order. Supposedly, he responded: "You can force me to appoint Kareski as a member of the Executive Committee. But you cannot force me to continue as president of the Reichsvertretung."[93]

If Baeck was able to foil the Stahl/Kareski offensive, it was largely because of the backing that he received from Jewish leaders abroad, who were appalled at Kareski's cooperation with the Gestapo. On June 11, 1937, Baeck received from Sir Herbert Samuel, on behalf of the British Jews, a letter that expressed confidence in "the present personnel and management"[94] of the Reichsvertretung. At a meeting of the RV Executive Committee and Council a few days later, Kareski, with clear reference to the Nazi regime, loudly complained that the RV "had not understood how to gain the trust of certain circles on whom we are dependent."[95] But it was now certain that removal of Baeck would endanger a vital source of funds, and, as a result, he was able to withstand the Nazi pressure while strengthening the organizational structure of the RV. Stahl traveled to Paris and London to obtain funds from Jewish organizations there but failed in his effort. That left him little choice but to accept a subordinate position in the RV.[96] It was now formally agreed that the Reichsvertretung was the sole representative of the Jews in Germany both to the German authorities and to the Jewish assistance organizations abroad. A vote of "unlimited confidence" in Baeck and Hirsch and expression of "the desire that the Reichsvertretung carry on the work it has undertaken," proposed by Max Warburg, was adopted without objection.[97] The following year, the government not only withdrew its support from the State Zionists but dissolved the group, allegedly on account of its ongoing relations with the "very strongly anti-German Jabotinsky group" and the suspicion that young emigrants from the movement to Palestine were working for the Haganah, the illicit Jewish army whose very existence ran counter to the Nazi conception of "the effeminate Jew." Kareski emigrated to Palestine, where he was formally accused of collaboration with the Nazi regime.

Undergirding Endurance

Leo Baeck's tasks as president of the Reichsvertretung, though of undeniable importance, and as energy-sapping as they were from day to day, did not constitute his only crucial role in these difficult years. No less significant, and perhaps more so, was his fulfillment of the rabbinical role as a voice of consolation and encouragement, a voice that, when it still seemed possible, sought to offer a hidden critique of the Nazi regime and some hope for the future.

As we have seen, Baeck had already criticized romantic Christianity for its submission to the state a decade before Hitler's rise to power. Now he believed that it had played a role in the political upheaval. In 1934, choosing his words carefully and distinguishing Christianity from Judaism, he wrote, with a not so veiled reference to the contemporary situation, that religion in Germany had ceased to be independent; it had become a mere "tool of politics, a tool of the state." Under such circumstances, religion could not deliver an independent message criticizing decisions of the regime: "It loses its own word, the word of God, this power of assertion and persuasion."[98] Though lacking in political strength, Jews, because they were not tied to the state, could at least remain uncompromising in their own religious principles. At Hanukkah that same year, Baeck again stressed the advantage of Judaism over Christianity: not being bound to support political power, German Jewry alone enjoyed true freedom. To be sure, German Jews were ever more squeezed into a corner of society, but that did not need to produce narrowness but rather a breadth uncharacteristic of the rest of society. On Hanukkah, the Jewish holiday celebrating freedom from the constraints imposed on ancient Judaism by Antiochus the Syrian, Baeck noted that Jews in his time, too, though their external freedom had been diminished, still possessed the inner freedom to hold fast to what was theirs.[99]

In addition to urging appreciation for the unique Jewish identity that the Nazis could not demolish, Baeck's writings in the early Nazi period argued for a particular posture that he called *Haltung* or *Zurückhaltung*. By the former, he meant a composed stance, a self-determination that did not allow the oppressor to undermine self-image or self-esteem. It was an antidote to fate. If you possessed *Haltung*, you were in control of yourself—you upheld your dignity. *Zurückhaltung* was holding back, not allowing emotions to dominate your behavior, not getting swept away; it was the precondition for *Haltung*. Of *Haltung*, Baeck wrote in 1934, using unspecific language but clearly readable in reference to the present: "When a person is struck by fate, he retains one thing that enables him to confront fate: *Haltung*. . . . True *Haltung* is always the revelation of a spiritual possession; it is the expression of an inner solidity and dignity." Jews who had for so long judged themselves by how they were judged by others, who had been persons subject to public opinion and fashion, in this new, otherwise unfavorable, situation had the possibility of becoming self-motivated, of being "persons of *Haltung*."[100]

Baeck's messages point not to what was lost but to what remained. German Jews had been thrust into a situation not of their own making, a situation for which he repeatedly uses the term *hineingestellt*—indicating that they had been cast into a certain spot in history. Asking why and wherefore this was the case yielded no answers but only despair. The only helpful response was to look inward. German Jews were losing their place in German society, and their links to fellow Germans and to German heritage were being severed more completely every day. But their Judaism remained and could give them strength if only they would cease the vain struggle to change public opinion, the vain hope of restoring what had been lost. The old connections with the non-Jewish world had indeed snapped, but a togetherness with fellow Jews was being discovered anew.

Of course, Baeck could not refer directly to Adolf Hitler. But in a speech that he delivered to the Lessing Lodge of B'nai B'rith on its fiftieth anniversary in 1935, he made a reference that came as close to an attack on the Führer as any censor would allow. Referring back to the time when the lodge was founded, Baeck cited Jakob Burckhardt, the great Swiss scholar of art, who had written to a friend: "In the incipient twentieth century, authoritarianism will again lift its head, and [it will be] a terrible head." Baeck comments: "It seems to us today, when we read [the letter] again, to be a prophetic word."[101]

In 1935, the situation of the German Jews continued to deteriorate. That summer witnessed a wave of violence against the Jews. And that autumn, the Nuremberg Laws officially deprived them of the status of citizens, legally reversing the long struggle for civic equality that in 1871 had finally culminated for Jews in all of Germany. The Reichsvertretung der deutschen Juden was now no longer called the National Representation "of the German Jews" but rather—designating foreignness—"of the Jews in Germany." Officially, Jews were no longer Germans. The Nuremberg Laws clearly defined Jewishness according to racial criteria, and a pernicious antisemitic stereotype gained legal status when Jews were prohibited from employing maids under the age of thirty-five, lest their lascivious employers sexually assault them. Ever more German Jews were in need of inner strength to resist the persecution. It was in 1935 that Leo Baeck composed two messages intended to supply courage to a Jewry that was ever more disheartened. The two statements are well-known but are nonetheless worthy of recollection and of comment. The first is a message of comfort; the second, a religiously garbed act of protest.

Baeck composed the first of the two statements shortly before the Nuremberg Laws, on the occasion of Shabbat Nahamu, the Sabbath in August 1935 on which the portion read from the Prophets begins with a verse from Isaiah (40:1):

> "Comfort, oh comfort, My people." That is what today's Sabbath calls to us. From whence in these days when we are forced to traverse a flood of insults shall comfort arise? It arises from the answer that our faith, that our honor, that our youth give us.
>
> Against all insults we set the majestic dignity of our religion, [against] all offenses our steady persistence in pursuing the paths of our Judaism, in following its commandments.
>
> True honor is what each person grants to himself; he gives it to himself through a life that is unimpeachable and pure, modest and honest, as well as through a life of that self-control which is the mark of inner strength. Our honor is our honor before God; it alone will endure.
>
> Our youth—does it not give us a model of unpretentiousness and courage, of mastering this difficult life in new ways? Let us, parents and teachers, raise up a generation strong and hard against itself, ready to be of assistance to everyone else, with a strong body and a fresh spirit, faithful and firm, rooted in Judaism.
>
> Let yourselves not be cast down and let yourselves not be embittered. Trust in the One to whom the ages belong.[102]

In this brief message, Baeck laid stress on three possessions that the Nazi regime could not take away: the faith in God and the will to obey God's commandments; the honor that was self-achieved; and a Jewish youth that, unlike earlier generations, strengthened by its ordeal, was committed to the common welfare. Baeck's message was sent out to Jewish communities and regional organizations throughout Germany, to be read publicly before the religious service on the Sabbath of Comfort. It was not intercepted by the regime. Comfort had become a necessity, which religion alone could offer. Baeck spread that message orally, as well. In Hamburg that same year, he participated with Martin Buber and his friend Bruno Italiener, rabbi of the

Hamburg Reform Temple, in a series of lectures. They were appropriately titled "Comfort in Judaism."[103]

A few weeks later, in anticipation of Yom Kippur, the Jewish Day of Atonement, on October 6, 1935, Baeck formulated a second, yet more eloquent and powerful, message, this time containing words that the Nazi authorities could not ignore. He composed it shortly after the promulgation of the Nuremberg Laws and gave it the form of a prayer to be read publicly on the eve of the holiday:

> At this hour, all Israel stands before its judging and forgiving God. In His presence, all of us seek to examine our ways, what we have done and what we have failed to do, examine where we have gone and from where we have remained distant. Wherever we have failed, we desire openly to confess: "We have sinned," and with a strong will to repentance we desire to pray before God: "Forgive us!"
>
> We stand before our God. With the same strength with which we have acknowledged our sins, the sins of the individual and those of the collectivity, we say with a feeling of abhorrence that we see deep beneath our feet the lie that is turned against us, the libel that is cast upon our religion and its testimonies. We commit ourselves to our faith and to our future. Who announced to the world the mystery of the Eternal One, of the one God? Who revealed to the world a sense for the purity of human conduct, for the purity of the family? Who gave the world respect for the human being, the image of God? Who directed the world to the commandment of justice, to the social idea? The spirit of the Prophets of Israel, the revelation of God to the Jewish people, played a role in all of this. In our Judaism it matured and it still grows. These facts refute every slander.
>
> We stand before our God; we build upon Him. In Him our history, our survival despite all vicissitudes, our steadfastness in every torment, have their truth and their honor. Our history is a history of spiritual greatness, of spiritual dignity. We turn to it when attack and insult are leveled against us, when distress and suffering afflict us. From generation to generation God led our ancestors. He will likewise lead us and our children through our days.

> We stand before our God. His commandment, which we fulfill, gives us strength. To Him we bow down, and we stand upright before humans. Him do we serve and remain steadfast in every turn of events. Humbly we trust in Him and our path lies clearly before us; we see the future.
>
> All Israel in this hour stands before its God. Our prayer, our trust, our confession is that of all Jews upon the earth. We look at one another and we know ourselves. And we look up to our God and know what is everlasting.
>
> "See, the Shepherd of Israel neither slumbers nor sleeps." "He who makes peace in His high places will grant peace to us and to all Israel."
>
> We are filled with sorrow and pain. Silently, through moments of silence before our God, let us give expression to what fills our souls. This silent devotion shall speak more urgently than any words are able.[104]

A powerful refrain runs through Baeck's message. Five times, he repeats that on the Day of Atonement, Jews express their conviction that they are not accountable to cruel human authorities; they stand before God alone. God alone is their judge. Only the Creator can judge their worth as human beings: "To Him we bow down, and we stand upright before humans"; we will not let the Nazi authorities define who we are. In language similar to what Martin Luther King would say when forced to remain silent during his march into Arlington Cemetery at the time of the Vietnam War, Baeck alludes to a "silent devotion" that "shall speak more urgently than any words are able." Referring to this message after the war, Baeck recalled that one specific line in the prayer especially offended the Nazi authorities, since they could not help but see it as an attack upon them: "We say with a feeling of abhorrence that we see deep beneath our feet the lie that is turned against us, the libel that is cast upon our religion and its testimonies."[105]

Eight hundred copies of Baeck's prayer were sent out to synagogues throughout Germany, with the intention that when they would be read aloud, they would serve as a collective protest. Among those planning to read it was Max Warburg in Hamburg, who later wrote: "And since I would have thought myself cowardly had I caused it to be read by others while I took no share, I decided to deliver it in the synagogue of the Jewish Orphan

Asylum."[106] However, Baeck's prayer was not read all over Germany, as he had intended. The Nazi authorities got wind of it and insisted that it not be read. Baeck had no choice but to order its destruction wherever it had been sent, as in the telegram he wrote to the congregation in Potsdam: "By order of the Office of the Secret State Police I call upon you under no circumstances at no time and in no place to read the proclamation. Destroy it."[107] According to Baeck, his prayer had come to the attention of the Gestapo because one of the German rabbis had foolishly asked the minister of the interior of his German state whether there was any governmental reservation regarding its presentation. As punishment for the statement, Baeck was arrested, charged with failing to secure advance permission from the Gestapo, and briefly imprisoned. His release seems to have resulted because, at a time when the Nazi government was still sensitive to foreign opinion, a correspondent for the London *Times* learned of his arrest and reported it in his paper. Moreover, Otto Hirsch had assumed responsibility for sending out the prayer, whereupon he was then arrested, forcing Baeck to go to Gestapo headquarters to seek his colleague's release. He told the imprisoners that he could not carry on the work of the RV without Otto Hirsch. At first, Baeck failed to gain his colleague's release, but he succeeded on a second attempt. At that point, it was apparently still of some importance to the authorities that there be a representative body of the Jewish community with which they could communicate, even if its leaders did not act fully in accordance with their wishes.[108]

The following year, Baeck again wrote to the Jewish communities on the occasion of the High Holidays, in autumn 1936, but this time his message contained nothing that could offend the government. He did not again allude to the difference between standing before God and standing before a human regime. This time, he stressed standing within the Jewish community and accepting the welfare tasks that a common commitment entailed. In view of the tensions within the RV mentioned earlier, internal unity had become the dominant concern.

Nonetheless, Baeck could not avoid referring to the vicious anti-Jewish propaganda spewing from Hitler and his minions, to which Jews were unable to respond directly without provoking disastrous response. Hans Reichmann recalls Baeck's 1937 Yom Kippur sermon in the Lützowstraße synagogue in Berlin, where he said from the pulpit: "We hear insulting, tormenting, painful words. But within us loudly sounds the voice of silence." Reichmann adds that even children understood Baeck's meaning.

"Fifteen hundred people left the synagogue greatly stirred up but nonetheless encouraged. With unbowed posture they responded silently, yet loud and clear, to the madly insane reproaches that the menacing fanatic had once again bellowed out to his chorus."[109]

In 1938, Baeck's New Year message turned once more to the comfort theme of the summer of 1935: Let not the oppression on the outside destroy your inner life. Forsaken by the world about us, we turn to God. "As we are with God, God will be with us."[110]

Chapter 6

Enmeshed

Independence Lost

For more than five years, from January 1933 until November 1938, German Jewry suffered one discriminatory or exclusionary law after another, along with a persistent onslaught of verbal abuse and sporadic local acts of violence. Yet during this time, the Reichsvertretung was able to preserve a measure of independence from the regime as long as it did not try to confront it directly. That situation changed, beginning with the pogrom of November 9–10, 1938, and continued to deteriorate with the substitution of a differently structured central organization, a union under the direct control of the Gestapo.

The pogrom, later known as Kristallnacht—night of crystal, on account of the shattered windows of Jewish stores, their shards of glass strewn upon the sidewalk—was a planned and coordinated action instigated by the propaganda minister Joseph Goebbels, who had successfully solicited Hitler's tacit approval. It was publicized as an act of justified public anger in response to a young Jew's assassination of a German consular official in Paris. In reality, it was intended to frighten the Jews into a more speedy flight from Germany, leaving behind whatever wealth they still possessed. Ninety-one Jews were brutally murdered that night, and many more lost their lives in the aftermath; an indeterminate number were beaten up or raped; and as many as 2000 synagogues in Germany were destroyed, often set afire. The windows of approximately 10,000 stores owned or rented by Jews were shattered, their contents mostly plundered; as many as 30,000 Jewish men were sent to concentration camps in Germany; and a fine of a billion marks was levied upon a depleted and impoverished Jewish population. Some neighbors of the Jews, even women and young people, joined the Nazi *Sturmabteilung*, the SA, in carrying out the pogrom, while most remained passive. Few condemned the action, and even fewer intervened. In retrospect, this large-scale, carefully planned act of violence marked a watershed on the road to the Holocaust.

Baeck realized that there was nothing he, or any other Jewish leader, could do to stop the pogrom. A colleague from the Lehranstalt went to see him "seeking some words of advice and wisdom and wanting to hear Baeck's thoughts about God's justice. But the only solace Baeck had to offer was his view that the Nazi regime was bound to collapse any day and that would be our salvation."[1] Nonetheless, early on the morning of November 10, Baeck and Hirsch tried to reach the state secretary at the Reich chancellery, without success. There was no stopping the violence, until Goebbels finally called the action complete that afternoon. Baeck was deeply frustrated and despondent. He had been unable to avert the catastrophe. For him, and for others who had witnessed it, memories of the pogrom continued to haunt their dreams. Fifteen years later, Baeck wrote: "How often have the images of that night in which the great crime occurred, when the Jewish houses of God were destroyed, whether we wished to recall them or not, emerged once again before us? Once again, even if we turned our ears away, we thought to hear the voices which during that night called out to us: 'The synagogues are burning!'"[2]

Although two of his associates, Otto Hirsch and Arthur Lilienthal, were among the men sent to the nearby Oranienburg concentration camp following the pogrom, Baeck was not sent, perhaps because he was too well known outside Germany. This enabled him to approach the Gestapo in order to seek their release. Since the Nazi authorities needed Baeck to carry out the speedy emigration they so desired, he had grounds for the argument that he could not do so without the assistance of his arrested associates. When he was asked whether Hirsch was his right hand, he famously replied: "No, I am Hirsch's left hand."[3] In the wake of the pogrom, Baeck also sought to gain the release of rabbinical colleagues and rabbinical students. For a number of the arrested rabbis, he was able to obtain certificates for immigration to Palestine or entry permits for England, which he visited for that purpose. He wrote an article for the new weekly Jewish news magazine, the only press offering that was still allowed. It included these words: "At a fateful time, let a word go out to all the Jews in Germany—hold together, walk on the path of righteousness, believe in your future, trust in the Eternal our God." Baeck's words were not allowed to appear, presumably because of the reference to a Jewish future.[4] That future, it was now crystal-clear, could lie only outside Nazi Germany. To Ismar Elbogen, his colleague at the rabbinical seminary who had managed to flee to New York, he wrote: "The work here is vast; we try to help and to support and, above all, to prepare ways [for emigration]. The effort is great but it must be borne."[5]

Even before the pogrom, in March 1938, the Jewish communities had lost their legal status and therewith the right to tax their members. That led the national Jewish leadership to conclude that a tighter, more fully inclusive and effective, centralized organization was now required. At a meeting of the RV in July 1938, it was resolved to create a Reichsverband, a national association that would firmly unite the Jews in place of a Reichsvertretung, a mere representation to an unresponsive government. It would be based on all the communities, including those of the Independent Orthodox, and every Jew would be required to be a taxpaying member. The governing body would, for the first time, include a woman as representative of the Jewish Women's League, while the composition of the Executive would remain unchanged.[6]

The Reichsverband enjoyed only the briefest existence. As early as December 1, 1938, only a few weeks after the November pogrom, Reinhard Heydrich, head of the Gestapo, had laid the framework for a new compulsory national Jewish organization.[7] It would be known as the Reichsvereinigung der Juden in Deutschland (RVe), the National Union of the Jews in Germany.[8] By July 1939, it had officially come into existence. The Nazi newspaper, the *Völkischer Beobachter*, rejoiced that the law establishing it left no doubt that now the "Jewish Question" would finally be solved by totally getting rid of the Jews. "The main thing is that we get rid of them soon, soon and completely."[9] Although the leadership still remained largely the same and, like the Reichsverband, was strictly centralized, its leadership had now lost most of its independence. The RVe operated under the watchful eye of the authorities. All Jews by Nazi racial definition, even non-Aryan Christians and Jewish religious dissidents, were required to be members. One could exit only by death or emigration. Jews had been clearly identified as such since August 1938. All, even small children, were required to add a specifically Jewish name to their given name, if they did not already possess one. Women added Sarah, men Israel; Leo Baeck became Leo Israel Baeck.

Like its predecessors, the RVe, with the assistance of subsidiary organizations and using tax funds from its members, donations, and subsidies from Jews abroad, conducted social welfare, education, and activities to prepare for emigration. But it did so more exclusively and centrally than before. Only religious matters were left to the communities, which were now deemed to be private associations. The two Jewish organizations directly in charge of emigration, the Palestine Office for the Land of Israel and the Hilfsverein (Assistance Association) for emigration elsewhere, became departments of the Reichsvereinigung. Under pressure, Jewish leadership became more authoritarian and less democratic. RVe officials were appointed by the Nazi authorities and were responsible to them, not to German Jewry. The real power lay with the Nazi supervisors, under the direction of Adolf Eichmann, not with the Jewish leadership. As chairman of the new organization, Baeck had little room for maneuver; that ability had been limited from the start. His position was analogous to that of the heads of the *Judenräte*, the Jewish councils that, under supervision of the SS, later governed the Jewish ghettos of Eastern Europe. He did what he could, but he was enmeshed in a structure over which he had little control. It could not yet be foreseen at its official beginnings in 1939 that only two years thereafter, the Reichsvereinigung would be drawn into the anguished work of deportation.[10]

Baeck's final years in Berlin were—if anything—even more difficult than those that preceded them. Until March 1937, his wife, Natalie, had been his support. Their home had always been open to friends and students at the seminary. With her death from a stroke, arguably brought on by the extreme anxieties of the times, Baeck lost his life's companion, and only a housekeeper remained to serve his domestic needs. He called it "the hardest blow of these hard years." Two days after Natalie's death, he committed his thoughts to paper: "We shall now be without you, our life without the blessing of your life, without you, who were so pure, so true, so bright, so genuine, so pious. . . . You have returned home and left us behind without you. May God give strength to get through these days."[11] A friend who had often been in their home and had witnessed their matrimonial harmony wrote of their marriage that it had been "earnest, sacred, and deeply happy."[12] For months after Natalie's death, Baeck daily visited her grave in the Weissensee Cemetery of the Jewish community. On her gravestone, he asked that words from the last chapter of the Book of Proverbs be written in Hebrew: "But you surpass them all" (Prov. 31:29). According to an interview he gave after the war, each year on the anniversary of her death he suggested to his students at the seminary that they preach a sermon on women.[13]

Trusted colleagues and friends were now leaving, among them Ismar Elbogen, to whom he wrote almost despairingly but with acceptance: "It is getting lonelier, but that, after all, is the human fate."[14] With the death of

Natalie and soon thereafter the departure of their daughter, son-in-law, and granddaughter to Great Britain, Baeck remained alone to do the work that he felt it his duty to accomplish. To his old friend Hans-Hasso von Veltheim-Ostrau, he wrote at the end of 1939: "My days pass through steady scarcely interrupted work. Sometimes it gets a bit more difficult, but the old carcass must do it, which may perhaps be a quite healthy thing. And above all I experience the meaning of the expression . . . : 'Try to live as if you had a long, and as if you had a short, time to live.' That, too, is my intention for 1940."[15] Despite such intentions, a government document suggests that a year later, by early 1941, Baeck had reached the point of despair and may at least have been thinking about his own emigration.[16] Yet, in the end, his sense of obligation prevailed; despite the worsening conditions, he decided to stay.

If Baeck's work was at all bearable during his final years in Berlin, it was largely because of the equally conscientious labor of his associates. Otto Hirsch continued to be the full-time executive and as devoted to his tasks as was Baeck. When Hirsch was arrested in February 1941 and then brutally murdered in the Mauthausen concentration camp, Baeck was left without a capable colleague and without a close friend. Baeck wrote to Hirsch's son that his father was "filled with a genuine refinement, an aristocracy of thought and feeling. It was like a gift of Providence that in earnest times he entered our work in a leading capacity, and therefore the loss that we too suffer is so irreplaceable."[17]

Although the loss of Hirsch was indeed crippling for the RVe, Baeck was fortunate in still having a cadre of devoted workers to carry out specific tasks. Among them were Hannah Karminski, Cora Berliner, and Paula Fürst. They were not members of the Reichsvereinigung Executive, but they made its welfare and educational work, as well as its work of preparation for emigration, function effectively. All three perished in the Holocaust. Baeck had been entirely trustful of these women. He was especially close to Karminski, whose office at the RVe was next to his. Her presence brought him tranquility and joy.[18] After Karminski was deported in November 1942, he wrote of her and Cora Berliner: "All of us will miss Hannah, and, if I may speak for myself, I especially will miss her here every day. She was always the good spirit in the building, pure air surrounded her, everyone honored her and loved her. For some time we were in neighboring rooms in our place of work, and just to know that she was in the room next door was calming and pleasant. After the departure of our friend Cora, she was the only one with whom I could speak about everything that was on my mind."[19]

Sadly, Baeck could not say the same for others with whom he worked during the Reichsvereinigung years. Opposition to his leadership had not ceased. In particular, Heinrich Stahl continued to oppose Baeck. When the RVe was forming in the spring of 1939, Stahl sent a ten-page memorandum to the Gestapo in which he accused the earlier Reichsvertretung of having failed in its tasks. In conclusion, he proposed once again that the Berlin community be assigned the leadership of German Jewry. Baeck called the memo a denunciation and decided to break off the previous cooperation with Stahl. But due to Nazi support of Stahl, Baeck was nonetheless forced to endure his presence as deputy-president of the RVe until Stahl decided to leave the position a few months later.[20] A day or two before his later deportation to Theresienstadt, the authorities having turned against him, Stahl wrote a bitter letter to his family abroad that condemned the Reichsvereinigung, "whose president, now as earlier, is Rabbi Baeck and whose leadership is in the hands of obscure Jews distant from any religious outlook. Careerists—male and female—careerists and toadies . . . determine the fate of the Jews and allow the Nazis to dictate their measures." Stahl went on to claim that, unlike Baeck, he had never let the Nazis push their wishes on him, and for his opposition he had failed to receive backing from Baeck or Hirsch. Finally, Stahl went so far as to assert that when Eichmann ordered his deportation, this Nazi official was simply complying with a wish of the RVe itself.[21] Although that claim cannot completely be ruled out, no extant evidence supports Stahl's assertions.

In these years, another personality also embittered Baeck's life: Paul Eppstein, a sociologist and an intellectual, took over Otto Hirsch's duties after the latter's deportation in 1941. Like Hirsch, he was tasked with the contacts that had to be maintained with the Gestapo. Exercising his duties with alacrity, he was arrested numerous times, on which occasions he showed considerable courage in speaking his mind.[22] Unlike Stahl, Eppstein did not seek to displace Baeck from his position of leadership, though he possessed a high estimation of his own talents and might have thought himself a completely qualified replacement. The tension between the two men derived from a sharp difference of character. According to Herbert Strauss, who was acquainted with both men, they possessed such different values, talents, and personalities that a clash between them was unavoidable. On the one side stood the "grand *rabbin*," the esteemed rabbi, a product of Jewish tradition and Western idealism; and on the other side, the realist who had little regard for social taboos. According to Strauss, Eppstein aroused Baeck's displeasure because of the married man's intimate relationship with his beautiful, elegant secretary and because he was more concerned with the young, to the neglect of their elders.[23] The rabbi, the severe moralist, could not abide a man who did not take personal morality seriously. Baeck's distaste for Eppstein would only grow stronger when he later observed his behavior in Theresienstadt.

Transcending the Present

Throughout these difficult years, Baeck continued as rabbi and scholar/teacher. His religious and intellectual tasks required no confrontations but only a commitment to the spiritual welfare of fellow Jews, helping them transcend their persecution while seeking for himself to transcend subjectively the onerous and contentious work that often depressed him as head of the RVe.

In his personal life, Jewish holidays helped Baeck to separate a spiritual world from the mundane tasks of community leadership. Along with the other Jews still in Germany after the pogrom of 1938, he was forced to suffer numerous deprivations, including in the area of ritual practice, which became even more symbolically important at a time of dehumanization. He was fortunate that he had acquaintances who were concerned for his needs and whose benefits he could share with others. In spring 1940, he wrote to Rabbi Immanuel Löw in Szeged, Hungary, thanking him for the unleavened bread he had sent him for Passover: "With your shipment of matzah—all four packages arrived in excellent condition—you have given me great pleasure; I am truly touched by your kindness. Now I won't need to—as I had originally thought to do—number my matzot, 1 1/2 for each day, but will, thanks to you, be able to eat freely, with a contented feeling of surplus, and also be able to provide some for acquaintances."[24] The Nazis had not prohibited the Jews from observing their faith; they only made it more difficult for them to do so.

Upon the death of Claude Montefiore in 1938, Baeck became president of the World Union for Progressive Judaism. With all the good reasons for despair of the optimistic message of religious liberalism, he still clung to its principle that a better world was possible.[25] It was not only to set an example; it was Baeck's own philosophy, despite all the setbacks, to cast his eyes forward.

The present was surely dark and growing darker. The Jews who still remained in Germany felt trapped; there were no signs of any immediate salvation. So in addressing the German Jews, Baeck sent forth a message that avoided reference to the present by turning attention to the past and the future. History and hope were his antidote to present-day suffering. Looking backward, he recalled the Israelite experience in the desert. Like their ancestors, contemporary Jews were surrounded by wilderness. But the ancient Israelites had managed to hold out, and after forty years had reached the Promised Land.[26] For added perspective, Baeck recalled the persecutions that Jews had suffered in medieval times. They had always been encircled; that was not a new phenomenon. Their existence had been repeatedly endangered by the peoples in whose midst they dwelled even as, in their Jewish quarters, they dwelled apart. But their ancestors' situation had not been one of permanent distress. In a Jewish New Year message, Baeck recalled how "in all our generations that which seemed lost again became future, how our lives, which seemed to have reached their end, were renewed."[27] Moreover, in that earlier medieval situation, there was a blessing: being thus surrounded meant the persistent need for self-assertion. For Baeck, that self-assertion manifested itself through what he called *verpflichtendes Denken*, a mode of thought that entails the fulfillment of obligation, the moral obligation imposed by God.[28] "Behind us Jews lie far-off times of external non-freedom along with spiritual freedom within," he wrote. Later, in the nineteenth century, Jews gained freedom on the outside, but at the cost of that inner freedom. The external freedom was now gone, but its internal counterpart could return to what it had been centuries ago. Recalling the past, Baeck implied, could provide precedent and objective for the present.[29]

Relief from the weight of the present could also come if one thought not of the events of every day, the *Tage*, but of larger temporal units, which he called *Zeiten*, times or ages. In an essay that appeared in the *Schocken Almanach*'s last annual publication, 1938/1939, Baeck wrote of the person who looks to the ages: "He experiences how events and thoughts course through humanity; he lays hold of his days, and fate and error are also his. But he possesses the ability to raise himself up to the ages and ultimately always to hearken to the judgment of the Eternal."[30]

But what of the actual future? Did it make sense to hope? Baeck is ambivalent. Early in the Nazi period, he could write: "Destinies come and destinies go but justice remains."[31] He could even note obliquely with regard to the Nazi regime that although it represented the transformation from a world of light into a world of darkness, there could also be a retransformation.[32] Yet as the 1930s progressed, the Nazi-determined political destiny of Germany did not falter, making an argument for its evanescence less credible. It became necessary to put forth a different sort of view of the future, one that did not necessitate a political change that was beyond the Jews' control—not a change in the history of Germany but in the history of Judaism, which was still in Jewish hands:

> With regard to the future of our German Judaism, decisions are now being made. People are stirring and in motion in our communities, and a later day will reveal what they have accomplished. For there are two things that human beings give to themselves: a future and the lack of a future. The task and the person attract one another and it becomes determinative what they are to each other: the future is prepared when an ego wants to serve the task, the lack of a future when the task is to serve the ego. We German Jews have our history; we derive our existence from its yield. We German Jews have our task; our children will live from its fulfillment. With regard to the future of German Judaism, we are the ones who shall decide.[33]

If these messages were a way of transcending compulsions on the outside by focusing inward, they were inadequate without a larger vision that looked not backward or inward but far beyond, to the messianic goal of all history. In an essay that once again distinguished theologically between Judaism and Christianity, Baeck wrote in 1936 regarding Judaism that it rejected the notion of a completed world order and looked forward to a future that transcended the present. "Jewish thinking is not directed only to what is, not only to what had been, but, above all, to what will be, to that which summons the human moral will. . . . The Kingdom of God becomes the measuring rod for the order of creation, by which creation must prove and justify itself."[34]

The final transcendence for Baeck is, necessarily, to look not backward, or within, or far forward, but in these difficult times to look upward to God: "In easy times, everything is self-understood; satiety and habit can quickly become a wisdom that stretches itself out to unbelief. In difficult times, everything, all thinking and willing and doing, becomes a commandment to fortitude, to the task that is to be accomplished, and the person without faith is then without grounding or goal, without earth or heaven. Therefore the Jew can never be without faith, for from the beginning he has been the person of difficult days, the person forced to make decisions."[35]

Ultimately, human freedom is grounded in what the human being experiences within himself; it lies beyond all fellow humans and all events. It is not like the normal freedom of the human will, "something rational, but it is rather something irrational. It consists in knowledge of that which alone is real, the connection of the human with the divine. It is not a securing of the will but a certainty of human beings, their ultimate certainty and therefore their freedom."[36] Baeck uses the term *jenseits*, which has the sense of "beyond." It can mean life after death, but, in the case of Baeck, it symbolizes that which, though it frees from human affliction, points not to an afterworld but to the world of a God whose moral message is clear but whose essence remains a mystery. "We cannot experience God," he wrote in 1941, "but only the mystery that surrounds Him."[37] In this glance into the beyond, though it reveals no clear image, Baeck believes that the Jew is lifted above what surrounds and endangers him. By transcending the present in time, space, and dimension, the German Jews he comforted could carry on their lives without collapsing under the burdens imposed upon them.

Scholarship as Consolation

From early in Baeck's career, scholarship was more than an intellectual occupation or even a mission to bring understanding of Judaism to fellow Jews and non-Jews. In his last years in Germany, before his deportation in January 1943, scholarship became for Baeck also a consolation, a restoration of the spirit, and an expression of the higher self in search of truth. Even when communal responsibilities weighed heavily on his time, scholarship was an activity he was unable to neglect. But now it played an additional role in his life: it enabled him to concentrate energy away from the obligations of leadership. It gave him satisfaction that came from a different sphere of his personality; as he put it, scholarship provided "a path into the distance,"[38] the opportunity to shift attention to a broader perspective. It also supplied a diversion, a release from the enmeshing hostile environment, even a sort of personal transcendence. For Baeck, scholarship and personal virtue were intimately related. The ideologically tainted work of the Nazi scholars, which he could not specifically mention, was to his mind a corruption of Wissenschaft that was produced by a corrupted character. Scholarship reflected the person. In 1938, he wrote: "Every Wissenschaft requires moving forward toward a perfection of technique, but it is more than technique; it is the Wissenschaft of a particular person. As the person is, so is his Wissenschaft."[39]

Although he was fully occupied as head of organized German Jewry, Baeck was also a chief organizer of Jewish scholarly activities. Until the Nazi authorities put an end to it, he chaired the committee responsible for the multivolume jubilee edition of the works of Moses Mendelssohn; his task was to find funds to pay contributors and to urge the prompt submission of their work.[40]

During the Nazi years, Baeck continued to write about Christianity in relation to Judaism and its differences from it. In a lengthy essay, separately published as a small book in 1938 and dedicated to his recently deceased wife, he examined the Gospel as a source for the religious history of Judaism. He wanted to show how the oral traditions of the ancient Palestinian rabbis had channeled into the New Testament, resulting both in acceptance and rejection. At a time when Christian scholars, under the influence of Nazi ideology, were denying the Jewish basis of Christianity, Baeck was determined to "allow the Gospel to stand out as a piece of Jewish history, and not a minor one, as a testimony of Jewish faith."[41] It was a task not so different from the one that, in his youth, he had undertaken when he wrote against Adolf von Harnack. But in days that depressed the spirit, this new work was also intended to restore Jewish pride of possession, as Baeck made clear in the concluding paragraph of the first section, where he explained that the Gospel was a Jewish book "because the pure air that suffuses it, and in which it breathes, is that of Holy Scripture, because Jewish spirit, and it alone, holds sway in it, because Jewish faith and Jewish hope, Jewish suffering and Jewish distress, Jewish knowledge and Jewish expectation—they alone resound through it, a Jewish book amid Jewish books. Judaism must not pass it by, not fail to appreciate it or relinquish it. Here too Judaism should recognize what is its own, should know what belongs to it."[42] Baeck, who had held "romantic religion," as represented by Paulinism and Lutheranism, responsible for religion's failure critically to address state and society, here places the fundamental source of Christianity squarely within the Judaism of its time—and the two faiths not distant, but remarkably close to each other.

During the first year of Nazi rule, Baeck published a collection of his essays written during the previous decade. His *Paths in Judaism* covered the broad range of Baeck's interests during the Weimar period.[43] The subjects in the volume, some of which we have discussed earlier, included theology, mysticism, education, and personalities. Five years later, he completed a new volume, which he called *From Three Millennia*.[44] The title suggests a shift in Baeck's thinking: he no longer sought an essence of Judaism but wanted to display the variety of creativity produced over the remarkable length of Jewish history. Some essays in this new compilation appeared initially as early as the period before World War I, and others during Weimar; a few were written during the Nazi years. Among the later pieces are several of particular interest.

Although the newer essays are dominantly of a scholarly nature, they are not entirely devoid of contemporary concerns. In a set of three anonymous ancient Hebrew poems, Baeck finds a message of comfort. The poets sing of what in the face of wanderings and suffering still remains their possession and the basis for their renewed hope in an inimical world.[45] A theological essay on faith, once again seeking to distinguish Judaism as unique, understands faith not as vouchsafed by grace, as in Christianity; rather, for the Jew, faith is "a shift of stance that the human being, by virtue of his having been created by God and in the image of God, is able on that account to accomplish and, in spite of all that is transient and mundane, to reach the great 'And nevertheless,' the great constancy and unity of his life."[46] Here Baeck again uses the phrase "And nevertheless," which occurs frequently in his writings. It points to the article of faith, difficult to maintain at any time but especially in such times, that beyond the chaos and evil there is nevertheless a reason for hope.

Baeck continued to harness his scholarly work to his own philosophy of Judaism. A new article on a seemingly recondite topic, the early Jewish mystical book *Bahir*, stresses the cosmic optimism that penetrates the world and concludes with words about the book that could have been written in his own name: "A particular and especially Jewish spirit holds sway in the mysticism of the book *Bahir* as in the collective mysticism of Judaism. Here too is a mysticism of the task and of the turning, of the eternal mystery in which blessing, with its commandment, has its source."[47]

Excavating in the Jewish literature that he had taught for years, Baeck draws upon two familiar midrashim to comfort readers of the 1936/1937 *Schocken Almanach*. He takes note of the midrashic assertion that wherever Jews might be scattered, the *Shekhinah*, the indwelling female presence of God, accompanies them. Thus had She done for their ancestors in the past. Thus, by implication, might She do, as well, in the present. For, as Rabbi

Shimon ben Yochai taught: "Wherever the righteous go, the *Shekhinah* goes with them."[48] However isolated they might be, even in Nazi Germany, the Jews were not alone.

Scholarship was for the sake of knowledge, encouragement, and comfort; but in these times of intense, often frustrating, communal activity, scholarship for Baeck could also be a personal diversion. It could be a form of emotional escape and a way to restore his spirit. From 1933 to 1938, he found time in the early morning hours to translate the Gospels from Greek into Hebrew in a quest to determine their oldest elements. On a visit to London on behalf of Jewish emigration in 1938, he spent the extra hours unwinding in the Babylonian collection of the British Museum. To Ismar Elbogen, he wrote in 1940: "My work takes its accustomed course, and in my free hours Wissenschaft, with its path into the distance, provides its gratification."[49]

After the forced closing of the Breslau Jewish Theological Seminary in 1938, Baeck's institution, the Liberal seminary in Berlin—which, in 1934, was once again forcibly reduced from the high rank of a *Hochschule* to the lower one of *Lehranstalt*—took upon itself the burden of keeping Jewish scholarship alive. But the Nazi authorities would not allow it. In 1938, when Baeck published his second collection of essays, *From Three Millennia*, it was swiftly confiscated. Perhaps it was seized because it contained the essay "Romantic Religion," written back in 1922 and republished here, which could be seen as an indirect attack on dictatorship, or it could simply be that the very notion of Jews producing genuine scholarship ran counter to the darkening stereotype of the less than human Jew. Only a few copies survived.

Baeck now undertook publication of what would be the last issue of the *Monatsschrift*, the leading journal of Jewish scholarship. For him to publish that final volume was an act of self-assertion and honor that mattered deeply. In requesting an essay from Max Grünewald, he wrote that publication of the volume would be "a small testimony to how we here want somehow to remain subjects. . . . A final substantial issue, a small volume of the *Monatsschrift*, will show that we are departing armed."[50] In February 1941, Baeck could report to Elbogen that "the [current] volume of the *Monatsschrift* has been approved [for publication]" and that he hoped it would shortly appear.[51] The Reichsvereinigung contributed to the publication costs, and Baeck wrote a very brief philological essay, "Der Ibri" (The Hebrew), for the volume. Neither his piece nor the other essays seem initially to have been offensive to the Nazi censor, who, at first, approved publication.[52] We can only imagine Baeck's disappointment when that volume—which he had edited and which, he believed, represented purity versus propaganda—was, upon publication, confiscated by the Nazi regime, just as his volume of essays had been.

Along with scholarship went teaching rabbinical students at the Lehranstalt, which Baeck continued to do every semester until that institution was shut down by the Gestapo, in July 1942. When concern was raised that under Nazi domination and with decreased income, rabbinical education might suffer, Baeck was selected to head a commission that was delegated in 1936 to ensure the maintenance of standards and, insofar as possible, support comparable curricula among all three of the Jewish seminaries.[53] In 1940 at the Lehranstalt, even after five students had been able to leave in order to continue their studies at the Hebrew Union College in Cincinnati and some faculty members had received teaching positions there, new students were still joining the classes in Berlin. Auditors, as well, came to Baeck's lectures. Among Baeck's students, and then on the teaching staff, was Abraham Joshua Heschel, who would later gain renown as a Jewish religious thinker in America. According to Heschel, Baeck was "the most educated man" he had ever met.[54]

In 1942, only three students remained, but for their sake—and his own—Baeck continued to devote time to them. Ernst Simon, a member of the German Jewish intellectual circle and a Zionist educator, conjured up an image of the Lehranstalt's last days: "Leo Baeck is sitting and 'learning' with three students in the midst of the massive madness of the Second World War! In historical perspective, the picture that these words conjure up recalls the worst times of the Middle Ages; in a perspective that transcends history, they vouch for the endurance of Judaism as a movement of spiritual resistance, of the 'eternal nonconformity,' as Baeck himself characterized it."[55]

One student during these years, Nathan Peter Levinson, recalled his experience sitting in Baeck's classes. Among the courses that Baeck taught was the skill of preaching in the synagogue. On Friday mornings, he held a homiletical practicum attended by students as well as practicing rabbis looking for ideas for their morning sermons the next day. Baeck's critiques of student sermons were, as a rule, kindly but could also be stinging. In response to a practice sermon by Levinson, he allegedly said: "My dear young colleague, you possess excellent diction, but why must you say everything you know? I could with ease have made ten additional sermons from your one."[56]

For the students at the Lehranstalt, Baeck was far more than a teacher. After most of his colleagues had left, he was still present, a symbolic figure of endurance to whom students could bring their needs—a pillar of strength amid chaos. Another student, Herbert Strauss, saw him as "the

Figure 5. Leo Baeck, seated at the far right, at a farewell party with Lehranstalt students in 1939. Courtesy of Leo Baeck Institute, New York.

last overarching representative of free Jewish thought, on whom all our dilemmas could be projected, as if, father-figure by style and choice, he could have transcended the iron limits imposed on the rest of us by the powerlessness that imprisoned him as well."[57] Strauss described Baeck as "a tall, slim man whose white beard would underline his dignified distance." He venerated him for "his command of the universe of European humanism" and saw character traits in his teacher that he believed epitomized the German Jewish symbiosis. His presence provided a sense of spiritual and emotional security. "That the Hochschule had become a symbol of stability and pride in ourselves was to an eminent degree a projection of Leo Baeck's attitudes," Strauss wrote after the war.[58] The students could feel that the seminary was "an island," somehow able to repel the poisonous winds blowing in from outside its walls.[59]

At the Lehranstalt, Baeck taught the first female rabbinical student, Regina Jonas. In 1941, he would attest to the accuracy of a translation of her ordination certificate from Hebrew into German, apparently for some official purpose. Baeck, who had earlier encouraged a number of women to study at the Lehranstalt, sympathized with Jonas's intent. When she received ordination in 1935, he congratulated his new "colleague" and wished her that "in the position that you have reached—indeed, practically conquered—may you always be able to possess satisfaction and fulfillment of your hopes."[60] Assigned mainly to pastoral work, Rabbi Jonas would typically introduce herself: "My name is Miss Regina Jonas. I am not the wife of a rabbi, but a rabbi. What can I do for you?"[61] Later, Rabbi Jonas would join Baeck in Theresienstadt, doing pastoral work similar to his own, before being sent to her death in Auschwitz.

As a teacher, Baeck was invariably punctual and polite. He genuinely cared about his students, meticulously preparing his lectures to them, seeking their personal welfare. When the Lehranstalt finally closed, he wrote a personal letter of recommendation for each student attesting to his rabbinical qualifications.[62] Tragically, most of the students in those last years did not survive. An effort to transfer the Lehranstalt across the channel to Cambridge or London faltered partly on account of Baeck's unwillingness to leave his flock in Germany, even for the sake of ensuring the institution's continuity. After the war broke out, the plan became totally unmanageable.[63] Still, Baeck told a student as late as December 1942: "If we survive the war, I shall see to it that the work of the Lehranstalt be continued in England."[64] But that envisaged revival did not occur; the remaining members of the faculty scattered or did not survive.

Although Baeck was not the only leader of German Judaism who passed up multiple opportunities for refuge in Great Britain or America, and although he may at one point have considered emigration, he persistently refused all offers. He rejected an invitation to join the rabbinical staff at Rockdale Temple in Cincinnati; he turned down offers to be a congregational rabbi or a university professor in England. Given his theology, leaving his flock behind would have been a self-inflicted blow to everything he stood for: Baeck's God, the God who commands moral action, does so even in extremis. In medieval times, Baeck noted, massacred Jews thanked God for the opportunity to be among the few who were given the privilege of performing the mitzvah of *kiddush hashem*, the sanctification of God's name through martyrdom. Already in the spring of 1933, he had spoken about the power of martyrdom as "this gift which was not received from God above, but is the potential task of every individual."[65] Persistently, Baeck stressed the commandment of obedience to God, an obedience that allowed no compromise. Martyrdom, in fulfilling God's command, was for Baeck the highest form of heroism. Just as the Prophets, whom Baeck so greatly admired, had not compromised in the face of tyranny and present danger, he, as a latter-day leader of his people, could do no less. To his mind, Jewish thought that did not carry consequences in the world of action was not genuine. In 1935, he wrote: "Jewish thinking has its opposite in the thinking that obligates to nothing, a thinking of the kind that people experience again and again in their tranquil minds, in pleasant dreams, in nonparticipatory glances. That is not Jewish thinking and not Jewish existence. Jewish existence is the thinking that obligates, obligates every single individual and at all times. You can't be a Jew in your head and something else in your heart, and also not a Jew in your heart and something else in your head."[66]

To split thought and deed was impossible for Baeck. To have left his community in need would have meant destroying the unity of his own being. One could not merely reflect on the divine imperative; one was commanded to live it. And if the response of remaining in Germany for the sake of others meant martyrdom, so be it.

Helping the Desperate Depart

The most urgent need for Baeck to stay in Nazi Germany was now, above all, to assist others to leave as soon as they possibly could. That objective was what the remaining German Jews now cared about—almost to the exclusion of everything else. The revival of interest in Jewish culture that, thanks to an extensive system of adult education, had provided renewed content for an externally imposed Jewish identity, was giving way to a dominant concern with means for leaving Nazi Germany behind. As early as 1937, Rabbi Joachim Prinz noted: "Thus the dream of renewal came to naught. Our people, who in 1933 eagerly took in everything called Judaism, have today abandoned it. Being Jewish is no longer a challenge but a [constricting] form of life. Having become bored with it, they leave the courses and the lecture halls and often also the schools and don't perk up their ears until they hear the words 'certificates for entry to Palestine, affidavits [for entry into the United States].'"[67]

The Jews remaining in Germany lived in the hope that somewhere there would be a place to which one could escape. Ironically, as the Nazi regime increased economic pressure, further impoverishing the Jews, it made it more difficult for them to have the financial capacity for a successful emigration. A plea by the Reichsvertretung to cease shrinking their professional opportunities went unheeded.[68] For the Nazis, that would have been a step backward. They determined instead to nurture the idea of emigration through increased, not decreased, pressure, intending "to undermine ever more any idea of Jews possibly remaining longer in Germany."[69] That policy of pressure, along with purposeful impoverishment, made Baeck's work more difficult. Even more so did the negative attitude of those countries that could have served as places of refuge but refused to do so.

In January 1938, still months before the November pogrom, the RV, under Baeck's direction, issued a declaration that included these words:

> The Reichsvertretung sees it as its duty to bear responsibility for speeding up emigration. But it finds it necessary to warn against exaggerated expectations. The possibilities for emigration don't depend only on its intentions and the work of the emigration organizations but, rather, above all, on the readiness of the other lands to hold open their gates for the Jews from Germany as well as from Eastern Europe. In that area, the Reichsvertretung possesses no defined influence. It can't perform miracles and it is not able to alter the conditions that stand opposed to its work. . . .
>
> The Reichsvertretung at this hour directs an appeal to the government in Palestine not to block the path of the Jews in Germany, above all of the trained young people who want to devote themselves to building up Palestine. It directs its appeal [as well] to the lands overseas, in particular to those with thinly settled areas, that through the promulgation and implementation of immigration laws, they adopt a greater number of useful immigrants.[70]

Whatever the nations' attitude toward accepting Jewish immigrants, the burden of facilitating their emigration remained on Jewish shoulders alone, especially on Baeck and his associates. They called their task the "last phase in the process of dissolving German Jewry."[71] However, bearing that burden, Baeck believed, did not weaken the German Jews but rather strengthened the community. At the premiere of a film that the Reichsvertretung produced a few months later, *Creative Will—Jews Become Craftsmen and Farmers*, he expressed a characteristic sentiment that the imposed task had transformed the German Jews from a community of fate into a community of will. Preparation for a new life outside Germany, or assisting others in that preparation, was the collective imperative for all Jews that made them, at least in one hopeful respect, masters of their fate.[72]

That July, at Évian-les-Bains, a French resort town on the shore of Lake Geneva, a conference took place that was intended to deal with the situation of the Jews in Germany and, hopefully, to find places of refuge for them. Convened by the United States and attended by representatives from thirty-two countries, as well as by Otto Hirsch representing German Jewry, the results were disappointingly minimal. With the exception of the Dominican Republic and Costa Rica, no promises were made. Both the Nazis and the German Jews were unhappy with the results. The Nazis realized that they could not quickly be rid of their unwanted, though they could now persuasively claim that they were not the only ones who didn't want the Jews. Évian had confirmed their ideology. For their part, the Jewish leadership had to recognize that the nations were abandoning the German Jews to their fate. The United States refused to increase its small quota, did not even fill it until the last years, and laid stumbling blocks in the paths of those seeking visas. Great Britain severely limited the number of certificates it parceled out for Jewish immigrants to Palestine, and in 1939 issued a white paper that allowed for no more than fifteen thousand per year. It was an increasingly desperate situation.

Of the more than half-million Jews who lived in Germany at the beginning of the Hitler regime in January 1933, fewer than two hundred thousand remained following the November pogrom. Of these, some 164,000 were still in Germany when the deportations began in October 1941. They were approximately one-third of the original Jewish population. Of that number, scarcely more than ten thousand would escape deportation, some surviving in hiding until the war's end, others captured and murdered.[73] A similar number chose to end their lives by suicide, preferring death by their own hands over continued suffering and deportation.[74] Following the November pogrom, reported suicides accounted for more than half of Jewish burials.[75] At that time, Mahatma Gandhi suggested that the German Jews should engage in mass suicide, on a single day at a single hour, as a spectacular collective act of protest; then would the European conscience awaken.[76] But such a proposal, which Gandhi made to a friend of Baeck's visiting in India, was fully at odds with Baeck's—and Judaism's—reverence for life. Baeck's friend Hans-Hasso von Veltheim-Ostrau did not dare at that time to convey the message to Baeck.

That the number of those ultimately deported was not greater than it was must be attributed in no small measure to the work of the Reichsvertretung and its successor, the Reichsvereinigung. Along with their subsidiary and associated organizations, they worked at preparation and facilitation of emigration to Palestine or to other countries. As conditions grew ever worse, the pressure on the leadership and its workers mounted exponentially. The priorities were clear: the young people had to be given preference. Not only were they the most eager to leave and had the most shallow roots in Germany; properly trained, they, more than their elders, could hope to find gainful employment abroad. The emigration of the youth was a mixed blessing, for their departure left behind a dominantly aged population largely without employment and often ill. As early as 1936, half the Jews in Germany were older than forty; of these, many were in need of assistance. A poster issued by the RV at that time spoke of the increasing obligations: "Few young people, a relatively thin layer capable of making a living, and an excess of old people characterize the [current] state of things. This picture is becoming ever more unfavorable due to the emigration specifically of the young and employable."[77] Yet emigration meant salvation. After Leo Baeck realized, as he stated following the war, that "we could not hope for any change in the near future in the Nazi regime of violence," he proposed that "we should therefore start taking our youth to other countries, and that the older folk should meanwhile stand fast and hold on to their positions as far as possible, in order to facilitate the youth emigration."[78] By 1938, numerous young Jewish emigrants had succeeded in establishing new homes in many lands. In Baeck's eyes, their success became their obligation. He believed that the fortunate emigrants now had the duty to assist those left behind through their financial contributions and through securing a viable income for members of the older generation when the latter would be able to join them.[79]

The children constituted a separate category. Once it became uncertain if their parents would find an emigration possibility, the question arose as to whether there was a moral obligation to undertake a special effort for the children. They would have to be unaccompanied by their parents, who might perhaps be able to join them later—or perhaps not be able to join them at all. Initially, Baeck was opposed to the idea. When it was proposed, as early as 1933, that children might avoid the torments of life in Germany by finding placement with Jewish families associated with B'nai B'rith in America, Baeck offered his view that children up to the age of fourteen, unless there was a compelling reason for the separation, would be better off remaining in the circle of their families. He thought that "it seemed substantially more important for young people of school age to receive an orderly education for the sake of the future."[80] At that time, Baeck apparently believed that such an education would still be possible in Germany.

By the November pogrom in 1938, Baeck's opinion had clearly changed. England now offered to accept unaccompanied Jewish children as part of an operation that became known as *Kindertransport*, the children's transport. About ten thousand children, predominantly Jewish and from Germany and Austria, were brought to the United Kingdom and placed in foster homes in the months following the pogrom. Among them, in January 1939, was Baeck's own granddaughter, Marianne, whom he had personally given Hebrew lessons every Friday night before dinner. Her parents were able to join her two and a half months later, though her father, Baeck's son-in-law, along with other Jewish immigrants, was soon subjected to internment—ironically, on account of his being German.[81] Other children never saw their parents again. After he was convinced that it was necessary, Baeck was actively involved in the *Kindertransport* project, struggling to push it forward. In August 1939, together with Otto Hirsch, he accompanied one of the transports on its way to London. Only a few months later, with the outbreak of war on September 1, this project—which, even with the poignancy of parents separated from their children, had been a ray of light—came to an end.

Palestine was the other goal of emigration to which Baeck devoted himself. In February 1935, together with Natalie, he embarked on the maiden voyage of the steamship *Tel-Aviv*, bound for Haifa. Interviewed upon his return, he closed his remarks with a memorable statement that, typically, stretched into the religious: "If there is anything in the history of the Jews which shows that Providence reigns over us, if the ancient talmudic saying ever proved true, that God brings forth healing ahead of suffering, then it is the historical fact that a Jewish Palestine is today once more a reality: a land that month after month and year after year, in increasing numbers, is able and willing to take in Jews."[82] In a speech on the boat, Baeck cited in Hebrew a phrase from the hymn that would become the Israeli national anthem, declaring that "our hope has not been lost." "Whenever we hoped, our hope was never in vain."[83]

During his visit to Palestine, Baeck was not, of course, able to alter British policy regarding the limitation of Jewish immigration; such decisions were made in London. But that was not his purpose. Aside from a personal desire to visit the Land of Israel, he was there to inquire about the welfare of the Jewish emigrants from Germany and thus perhaps derive lessons as to how those who had the good fortune to receive certificates for immigration to Palestine might be better prepared for their new environment.[84] In 1935, the RV had decided to make Palestine the focus of its emigration activity.[85]

In the years following his trip, Baeck engaged in a correspondence with Chaim Weizmann, the international Zionist leader and later the first president of Israel. In 1936, he suggested to Weizmann a plan regarding the native Arab population. It maintained that the historical and legal right of the Jewish people to immigrate to Palestine should be limited only by the absorptive capacity of the land. Regarding relations between Jews and local Arabs, Baeck suggested the formation of labor organizations that would include both groups. If that were done, he believed, perhaps naively, it would lead to common achievement in place of antagonistic competition. When in 1939 the British government issued its white paper severely limiting further Jewish immigration, Baeck wrote again to Weizmann, this time noting that the German Jews had learned of it "with deep dismay." He added: "The white paper wants to obstruct immigration to the Jewish national home at a time when maintaining and increasing the possibilities of immigration for the Jews of many lands is a life necessity."[86]

Despite their urgent need to leave Germany, Jewish emigrants were fearful as to whether they could adjust to radically different physical and cultural surroundings, especially in a Hebrew-speaking Palestine. Baeck saw it as his task to reassure them that it needn't mean a complete abdication of self. Settling in the Land of Israel—or any other country—did not have to imply exchanging their identity for a radically new one. German Jews in Palestine would remain culturally German Jews, able to bring along their German Jewishness, as it had been shaped before the Nazis. Moreover, it was hardly the first time in their history that Jews had been uprooted and still carried along something of their place of origin. In a positive sense, they were like colonists. Baeck wrote: "Today fate has again led us out into the world. Colonists, settlers, are marching out. Colonies are being established that will remain when the mother community disappears. Jews from Germany have always and everywhere been builders of communities, builders also of houses of Jewish scholarship. So shall it be again today. . . . Something of the music of eternal revelation will continue to resound in their hearts, connecting the scattered, uniting the distant."[87] However different the lands of their dispersion, the spirit of German Jewry would be a binding force. Baeck was assuring those departing Germany that emigration might mean giving up individual space, but it did not require breaking the old religious and cultural bonds. The new lands could become *Heimat*, the homeland that Germany could be no longer.[88]

Even as Baeck sought in vain to increase opportunities for Jewish emigration, he and other members of the RVe leadership felt compelled to remain at their tasks despite the deprivations and dangers. Of Baeck, we know that by winter 1940, he had to make do "without coal or heating material of any kind" while Hirsch offered an indigent Jew a suit and a pair of boots, of which he was himself in need.[89] Baeck was deeply appreciative of those who, like himself, felt it a duty to remain in order to serve fellow Jews. In particular, he praised rabbis who gave up opportunities for emigration in order to counsel and comfort their flock. At the end of 1939, thirty-six rabbis remained in Germany, twelve of whom served in Berlin. However, most of the better-known rabbis had fled Germany following the November pogrom a year earlier or were compelled by the Gestapo to abandon their congregants, leaving them without spiritual guidance and thereby serving to increase their anxiety about an emigration that so often could not be realized.[90]

Baeck distinguished between those rabbis whose lives were in danger—who had been threatened that if they did not leave they would be sent to concentration camps; and those who, at least for the present, were still relatively safe. On the one hand, he expressed his gratitude to Chief Rabbi J. H. Hertz of Great Britain for his efforts in finding employment for German rabbis who had been able to enter his country.[91] But on the other hand, he had high praise for Manfred Swarsensky, among the younger rabbis, and Max Dienemann, among the older clergy, because, at some risk to themselves, they gave priority to their rabbinical duties in Germany.[92] There was also a third category, one that Baeck held in contempt: those German rabbis who, for whatever reason, were not in immediate danger but nonetheless chose to abandon their flock. To his mind, the decision to run away from fellow Jews who depended on them went along with what we have earlier called the Weimar morality that Baeck so despised. In an unusually angry and revealing letter, addressed to Lily Montagu in London, Baeck wrote regarding Max Nussbaum, later a Reform rabbi in Hollywood:

> We have in the last decade in Germany had several talented young rabbis—Dr. N. belongs to them—in whom the striving for dramatic and rhetorical effect was stronger than their moral qualities, and

> where their appearance counted for more than their work. It was as if the dandy and the comedian had become the ideal and even religiosity was only role-playing. Also their moral conduct did not match the demands that must be placed upon a rabbi. The sermons of these rabbis for a time enjoyed a significant vogue, but seen in their totality, they brought more damage than blessing. . . .
>
> Today the community requires a rabbi more than ever. Dr. N. is likely the rabbi in Germany who is least in danger since he is a Romanian citizen and enjoys the protection of the Romanian legation; he is the only rabbi here under the age of sixty years who was not arrested [during the November pogrom]. It is painful that in these days, in which the pastoral counseling of the rabbi is called upon every day, in these days when the integrity of the rabbi should prove itself, he has already been absent for three weeks. The way the rabbi should be we see in the example of Dr. Swarsensky, whom you know. Immediately after he was released from the concentration camp, where he had manifested exemplary behavior, and despite physical complaints, early until late he tirelessly carried on the duties of his office.[93]

Baeck also carried on his own duties from early until late—not only as a pastor but more crucially, as the respected leader of all German Jewry, who, in these last years before his deportation, was forced to make exceedingly difficult and controversial decisions.

Resistance

It can be argued that Baeck was engaged all along in a form of opposition to the Nazi regime that has been called "spiritual resistance." Many of his writings during the Nazi period can rightly be called that. But what of resistance that went beyond the spiritual—that was directed at obstructing the deadly plans of the regime? And what of the burden of sharing or not sharing what Baeck knew of such plans?

Leo Baeck was not a proponent of violent resistance by Jews against the Nazi regime. When a Communist resistance group, consisting of Jews and named after its leader Herbert Baum, in May 1942 set fire at night to an anti-Communist exhibit sarcastically called "The Soviet Paradise," Baeck could not sympathize with the effort, for at least three reasons: his long-standing revulsion against Communism, his realization that such actions could have little effect, and, most important, his awareness of the revenge that the Nazi regime would take not only against the instigators but, more broadly, against the Jewish population. During the arson attempt, the perpetrators were apprehended; a few days later, Baeck and the collective Jewish leadership were summoned by the Gestapo, where they were held responsible for what had occurred. They were forced to stand against a wall for four hours, with only Baeck and one leader of the Vienna community allowed to sit for a quarter of an hour. They were then told that, as retribution, five hundred Jews would be arrested, one hundred for each of the five Jewish participants. Of these, 250 would be shot and 250 deported. They were also told that they should expect further, even more extreme, responses in case another act of sabotage should occur in which Jews were involved. Relatives and members of the Jewish leadership were forced to witness the murders that followed in the SS barracks just outside Berlin and in the nearby Sachsenhausen concentration camp.[94] The Reichsvereinigung had no choice but to draft a proclamation impressing upon the Jews still in Germany that their acts had implications for the entire community. When an approach to the remnants of the Baum group failed to persuade them to cease activities that endangered all Jews, Baeck supposedly said: "Quite frankly, I have never believed that under these circumstances, reason would prevail. What they have undertaken was pure madness from the outset. Now at least we know it. There is nothing that we can do."[95]

Initially, Baeck preferred simply to issue protests to the government regarding its various actions against the Jews. Although the protests proved futile, self-respect required them nevertheless. When, in 1934, an issue of the notorious Nazi newspaper *Der Stürmer*, complete with vicious cartoon drawings of Jews, was devoted to alleged Jewish ritual murder, Baeck sent a telegram to Hitler on behalf of the Reichsvertretung, condemning it.[96] Seeking support for his protest, he wrote to the highest Protestant authority in the country, the *Reichsbischof*, for support, "certain that the profound indignation that we feel will be shared by every believing Christian."[97] No written response from Hitler or from the bishop has come down to us, although, fearing it would provoke what at that point was considered undesirable uncontrolled violence against individual Jews, Hitler ordered confiscation of the remaining copies of the newspaper. Correcting lies, it became increasingly clear, had little impact; and Baeck did not really believe that it would. Rather, the only readily realizable goal was internal. As he put it in a response to a vicious antisemitic attack by the Nazi editor of *Der Stürmer*, Julius Streicher: "In defense of our honor, we have no choice other than solemn protest!"[98]

A more effective means of exercising pressure on the Nazi government, some believed, was the boycott of German goods abroad. But this effort, at least initially and officially, was opposed by the Jews in Germany. They feared that, on account of their connections with fellow Jews, especially in America, the regime would hold them responsible for the boycott and that they would reap the consequences. When in 1937, the Nazis decided to dissolve B'nai B'rith, they arrested Baeck and eighty other RV officials, apparently on the suspicion that this international organization, led in Germany by Leo Baeck, served as a conduit whereby German Jews encouraged coreligionists in America to maintain the boycott. On behalf of the Reichsvertretung, Baeck and Hirsch had no choice but to declare that they had not promoted it, but rather had suffered from the diminished purchases of German goods no less than had non-Jews.[99] Moreover, the boycott worked against their emigration efforts. German Jewry entered into a "Transfer Agreement" with the Nazi regime by which Jewish migrants to Palestine could use what remaining assets they had for the purchase of German goods delivered to them in their new home. Whereas that agreement would benefit the German economy, it would also help the emigrants. A difference of opinion soon emerged between the German Jewish leadership, especially the Zionists,[100] and Jewish leaders in America who were urging economic boycott as the best means for bringing down the Nazi regime. Abba Hillel Silver, the Cleveland Reform rabbi and, ironically, a leading Zionist, severely castigated the German Jewish leadership for what he believed to be their shortsightedness. In his eyes, they were "cowardly"; though they might suffer, German Jews would do better to remain in Germany and not undermine the boycott, lest their purchase of German goods abroad damage an economic venture that he believed would "weaken and finally crush this bloody foe of civilization."[101]

Between the November pogrom of 1938 and the comprehensive deportations beginning in October 1941, Baeck and his associates were in sporadic forced contact with the Gestapo and other officials who now more directly intervened in Jewish affairs. In meetings of whose content we know little and within the bounds of the possible, Baeck proved himself a shrewd and steadfast political tactician. His five brief imprisonments were apparently intended to "soften him up" and, by placing him in jail cells with informants, to get him to speak unguardedly. But that underestimated Baeck's intelligence.[102]

Grudgingly, he became known among officials and colleagues as "the old fox."[103] In the course of time, the atmosphere in these contacts became increasingly hostile. Early on, government officials held over from the Weimar period were at least cordial. But one by one, they retired or were replaced by younger men, many of them deeply imbued with Nazi ideology.[104]

Gradually, the Gestapo not only increased its interference in Jewish affairs but sought to humble Jewish officials—and Jews, in general—by making them act against their religious conscience. The order given in autumn 1939, shortly after the outbreak of war, that all Jews had personally to turn in their radios at a police station, stipulated that this must be done on the Day of Atonement, the most sacred day of the Jewish liturgical year. Failure to comply would be severely punished. Nonetheless, Baeck did not comply. Only after the conclusion of the holiday did he turn in his radio. As he arrived, he heard one police officer say to his colleague, "Didn't I tell you that Rabbi Baeck wouldn't turn up on his holy day?"[105] Apparently, the police did not report his act to the Gestapo, and the rabbi received no punishment.

Baeck sought support wherever it might be found. Via the Jewish theologian Hans-Joachim Schoeps, he reached out to the anti-Nazi Confessing Church, though we don't know that it bore any practical results.[106] If Baeck was disappointed by the church leadership, he was heartened by courageous individuals. Average Germans deeply opposed to the regime may have been few, but they did what they could to show their concern for men and women who, until the Nuremberg Laws, had been—at least officially—fellow citizens. Often they had also been their neighbors. Sometimes such men and women provided food for Jewish acquaintances, since rations for Jews were more severely limited than those allotted to non-Jews. Helping Jews was, in fact, a form of resistance on their part. Even strangers, at risk to themselves, sometimes engaged in acts that demonstrated their abhorrence of the Nazi discrimination. In autumn 1941, shortly after all Jews, including Baeck, were required to wear the yellow star, the Gestapo once again summoned Baeck to its office. As he was about to leave, one official mockingly said to him: "Now, Dr. Baeck, you, as well, certainly can't deny that the entire German people stands behind the actions of the Führer and therefore also behind his policy toward the Jews." Baeck later recalled that he responded: "That is a question I do not wish to address, but I do want to say this: When I now walk home from here, . . . I am completely certain that nothing bad will happen to me. On the contrary, here and there someone—a stranger—will try to get close to me, will somewhat fearfully look around, and will then shake my hand. Perhaps he will also slip an apple into my pocket, a piece of chocolate, or a cigarette. That is all that will happen to me. I don't know whether the Führer, were he in my position, would have a similar experience."[107]

Non-Jewish friends whom Baeck had known earlier did not abandon him in the Nazi years. Their visits to his home required some courage, since multiple regulations strictly prohibited non-Jews from meeting with Jews. According to a decree of October 24, 1941, such contacts were punishable by imprisonment and internment in a concentration camp. Nonetheless, they came, among them the German aristocrats whom Baeck had befriended during the Weimar years. Their willingness to stand up for principles and not be carried away by demagoguery endorsed an opinion that Baeck had long held: "Democracy cannot be based on the masses but only on an aristocracy."[108] Count Hermann Keyserling, Baeck later recalled, remained loyal to their friendship "even during the evil years, when so many sought to avoid me."[109] Clearly concerned for his friend's physical and spiritual welfare, Hans-Hasso von Veltheim-Ostrau, as late as 1942, visited Baeck repeatedly, together with two of his disciples who were serving in the German army. Along with food, Veltheim on one occasion brought a volume of subversive antiwar poems by Reinhold Schneider, whose publication had been banned in Nazi Germany. Thanks to one of the young soldiers, Cramer von der Laue—for whom, because he was actively serving in the Wehrmacht, meeting with a Jew was even more daring—Baeck was able to remain informed as to what was happening in the East as well as to receive food. In conversations in the privacy of Baeck's home, matters were discussed that could not be mentioned in letters, since Baeck's mail was subject to special oversight. The two younger visitors were deeply impressed by the embattled Jewish leader. One of them felt that Baeck possessed a remarkable charisma, an aura that stayed with the visitor after his departure. Following a conversation with Baeck, he wrote to Veltheim: Baeck "is an unbelievably serene patriarch! For me it was a moving experience."[110] The baron's cousin Elizabeth von Thadden was likewise concerned for Baeck's welfare. Unlike Veltheim, she was active in the political resistance, which she ultimately paid for with her life. It was probably she whom Baeck later mentioned as the countess who "came to my apartment every Friday and left vegetables that were not on the Jewish ration card."[111] Another visitor was Gertrud Luckner, a Catholic social worker who organized relief for Jews deported to Poland and, with Baeck's help, also for the Jews still in Germany. She, too, was eventually arrested by the Nazis and sent to the Ravensbrück concentration camp, where she was fortunate to survive. Baeck believed that, in whatever the land might be, few were her equal.[112]

Through these contacts, Baeck was able to receive reliable information about what was going on in the war. A major in the artillery, who had good connections, drew maps illustrating the current situation of the opposing forces, which the Jewish archivist Jacob Jacobson brought to Baeck, who tucked them away in a biblical concordance under the Hebrew entry *milhamah*, meaning "war."[113] The Reichsvereinigung also maintained a "black box," from which money was surreptitiously given to some of those Jews who, once the deportations began in 1941 and further emigration was prohibited, chose to live in Germany illegally.[114]

During his final Berlin years, Baeck established a relationship with two wealthy and powerful individuals who opposed Hitler, Robert Bosch and Carl Goerdeler. His contact person in the one case was Hans Walz, CEO of the Robert Bosch Works in Stuttgart, with whom a relationship had begun in 1934. Walz gained Baeck's full trust after he learned that Walz was the author of a statement in which, in the wake of the Great Depression, he demanded that Jews be placed at the head of any effort to reconstruct Germany, "since otherwise Germany would politically and economically collapse."[115] Walz first met with Baeck in 1935 and visited him repeatedly in Berlin, beginning in 1939. Like Bosch, he had long been acquainted with Otto Hirsch from the time that Baeck's associate had been a high government official in Württemberg. Now he sought to assist the Reichsvereinigung with financial contributions from the funds of the firm. These funds, which were held secret, were used to assist endangered Jews trying to flee or to survive in an underground existence. When Hirsch was arrested, Bosch sought in vain to secure his release. Hirsch was soon thereafter murdered in a concentration camp.[116]

Through Bosch, Baeck established contact with Carl Goerdeler, a prominent conservative politician, onetime mayor of Leipzig, and sworn opponent of Nazism. Bosch served as an adviser to Goerdeler and supported his efforts at resistance, which ultimately led to Goerdeler's hanging following the July 20, 1944, plot's failure to assassinate Hitler. But even had that well-known plot succeeded, there were very few Jews still remaining in Germany who might yet be saved. After the war, Baeck recalled that he had met with Goerdeler during the early Nazi years and had attended some meetings of the militant resistance. He had hoped that an early violent overthrow of the government would put an end to persecution of the Jews. But he realized that the Jews scarcely had the means to do so themselves. He therefore apparently placed his faith in Goerdeler and those associated with him. He regarded this right-wing politician highly and, after the war, expressed his belief that Germany would one day fully appreciate him and his supporting circle. The goal "for which they had staked their lives," he was convinced, "will be recognized in its full dramatic greatness."[117]

Yet it is unlikely that, had the anti-Nazi conservatives succeeded in gaining power, they would have restored the full emancipation that Jews had enjoyed from 1871 to 1933. Only a few among the resisters favored that objective.[118] Scholars have therefore doubted a recollection that Baeck put forward after the war: that in 1942, Goerdeler had asked him to prepare a manifest titled "To the German People" that would be publicized after the regime's collapse.[119] Baeck further recalled that his draft of the manifest, in competition with others, was accepted by the organized resistance. Whether Baeck actually did prepare such a manifest remains questionable because such a document has not come to light and because it seems incredible that German conservatives should have asked a Jew to prepare a manifest projecting a future for the entire German nation. Nonetheless, in 2001, Goerdeler's daughter expressed the firm opinion that such a request from the conservative circle would have been possible.[120] Baeck later promised to write about his relation to Goerdeler, but never got around to doing so. Perhaps the requested work was an informal document intended more for advice regarding the position of the Jews after a successful putsch than a comprehensive plan for all Germans—and, following the failure of the resistance, it had been destroyed. However, given the lack of clear evidence, the matter must be regarded as unresolved.

Another enigma likewise concerns an assignment given to Baeck. In this case, the document is extant—in multiple copies—but the source of the commission and the circumstances are wholly unclear. In 1955, Baeck related to friends in London that it had been suggested that he write a book "on the development of the Jews in Europe for the information of the public after the liberation."[121] He worked on the project from 1938 to 1941, especially during the morning hours, beginning at 4 A.M. To accomplish the task, which ultimately comprised five volumes of typescript, he was assisted by two co-authors and two secretaries.[122] There were four copies, he said, though later a fifth was discovered. The title of the manuscript was "The Development of the Legal Status and the Place of the Jews in Europe, Primarily in Germany, from Antiquity to the Beginnings of the Age of Enlightenment."[123] It ran to 1,245 pages.

The unresolved question is the source and date of the assignment. Was it, as Baeck suggested, the organized resistance that had requested it back in 1938, or was it some branch of the regime at a much later date, in March 1942? Following the recent discovery of Gestapo files relating to the document, it is beyond doubt that the Reich main security office was involved in the project, supervising it and urging its speedy completion.[124] The extraordinary permission that Baeck received to withdraw books from the Prussian State Library is further evidence of state control over the project. Notably, the names of Jewish authors cited in the manuscript are marked with a red letter "J," as was the case with other Nazi documents that cited Jewish authors. But how could Baeck and his associates have managed so large and comprehensive a manuscript in the mere seven months from March 1942 to the date of its completion in October? Barring further new evidence, the issue cannot be finally resolved; but it seems conceivable that the assignment came originally from the resistance—and that the Gestapo learned of its existence and decided to take advantage of it,[125] perhaps with the same intent that induced it to preserve Jewish ritual art objects: as testimony to the existence of a culture that had been destroyed.

The important question is the content of the manuscript. In no sense does it contain a historically documented self-accusation regarding sins that the Nazis and earlier antisemites had laid upon the Jews. Quite to the contrary: it is a solid scholarly work that leaned, if anything, toward apologetics rather than confession.[126] It was Baeck, the scholar, along with his associates, writing Jewish history in an academic tone.

More questionable is Baeck's decision not to inform Jews of what awaited them in the East and to encourage fellow Jews, among them students of the rabbinical seminary, to participate in the process of deportation. Baeck learned of Nazi atrocities in the East when they were in their initial phase, when carbon monoxide from a vehicle's exhaust had been directed inward to asphyxiate all those inside. After the war, he told Eric Boehm:

> I got the first indication of the scope of the Nazi bestiality in the summer of 1941. A Gentile woman told me that she had voluntarily gone along with her Jewish husband when he was deported. In Poland, they were separated. She saw hundreds of Jews crowded into buses, which were driven off and came back empty. The rumor that the buses had a gassing mechanism was confirmed by the apparatus attached to all but one of them. That one carried a

group to bury those who were gassed; afterward the gravediggers were shot. Similar stories were told by soldiers who came back on furlough. Thus I learned that the lot of Jews shipped east was either slave labor or death.[127]

This knowledge placed Baeck before a severe dilemma. Should he inform at least some of the community, so that they might consider going underground? Herbert Strauss, a student at the Liberal seminary at the time, would later question why, during personal meetings, Baeck kept him in the dark, even after Strauss had gone into hiding. Strauss, who greatly admired Baeck, wondered, "Would his making public what awaited us in Eastern Europe have saved lives, even if it would have cost him his own?"[128] On the other hand, revealing what he had heard could also have had the negative effect of multiplying suicides and would be a denial of the possibility that some, despite all odds, might nonetheless survive in Germany or in Poland, or even that the Nazi regime might come to an end before a particular individual was put to death. Although the mostly older and infirm Jews remaining in Germany might live under an illusion, Baeck may have thought that was better than being reminded daily that they were destined for death. Moreover, there was almost nothing they could do about it. Here was a dilemma where moral arguments could be made for either side.

A second decision was forced on Baeck and his associates when the mass deportations from Berlin began in October 1941 and emigration was no longer allowed. According to one recollection, the Gestapo placed a stark choice before the Jewish leadership: The "resettlement" of the Berlin Jews was beginning, and the Jewish community had to cooperate. Otherwise, the operation would be carried out by the SA and the SS, and "you know what that would mean."[129] In other words, the Gestapo was saying: If you refuse to assist us in the process of notification and collection of the designated deportees, we will do it ourselves—and in a far less kindly manner. Since it was clear that the Reichsvereinigung did not have the possibility of resisting the deportations, should Baeck therefore have allowed men of the Gestapo to rough up the Jews who had been selected for deportation, even before they reached the collection station? Would not making possible even a brief moment of empathy at the start of a cruel process be a moral act? On the other hand, would such participation be a form of collaboration with the Nazi aggressor? But collaboration with aggressors implies sympathy with their purpose, which was obviously not the case. Rather, the employment of

Jews could be seen as a humane act, as it was by one participant who had briefly served as a "helper." He later testified to how appreciative the deportees were of the Jewish helpers' presence. "They esteemed the fact that it was we who helped them to pack, shared the last meal in their homes, gave them advice, and sought to comfort them—we, and not a couple of SS men."[130]

Baeck decided that among those sent to the homes of the unfortunates to inform them of what would occur or to accompany them to the collection points would be rabbinical students from the Lehranstalt whom Baeck was still teaching. Among them was Ernst Ludwig Ehrlich, who related that Baeck gave him three names and addresses. When one notice that he delivered provoked a suicide, he refused a second bundle of names that Baeck's secretary was planning to give him. When he then met with Baeck and told him of his decision, his teacher accepted it and the matter was closed. Ehrlich, who survived and, after the war, served as a rabbi in Switzerland, continued to admire Baeck greatly after the Holocaust. He believed that his teacher's controversial decision reflected the pastoral orientation that Baeck frequently displayed, which was beyond critique.[131] After the war, Baeck himself gave voice to his thoughts at that time: "I made it a principle to accept no appointments from the Nazis and to do nothing that might help them. But later, when the question arose whether Jewish orderlies should help pick up the Jews for deportation, I took the position that it would be better for them to do it, because they could at least be more gentle and helpful than the Gestapo and make the ordeal easier. It was scarcely in our power to oppose the order effectively."[132]

Nonetheless, when an earlier regional deportation to a camp in France took place in October 1940, the Reichsvereinigung did not sit idly by. It did what little it could. Jewish officials warned coreligionists, who were subject to deportation but away from their homes, not to return. Otto Hirsch lodged a protest with the authorities and demanded the return of the deportees. Wanting to demonstrate their extreme opposition, members of the board of the Reichsvereinigung threatened to resign collectively. Secretly, they informed the foreign press. In addition, a circular letter proclaimed a day of fasting as an act of protest incumbent on the entire staff of the Reichsvereinigung throughout Germany. Special prayers and sermons were to be devoted to the subject on the following Sabbath. But the Reich main security office forced the Reichsvereinigung to rescind its instructions. Julius Seligsohn, an RVe high official much admired by Baeck, was responsible for the circular letter; he and Baeck's closest associate, Otto Hirsch, were arrested thereafter and ultimately murdered. It thus became clear that such acts of protest were not only worse than useless: they would bring swift retribution.[133]

Baeck's last years in Berlin were lonely. He was without the comfort of his beloved wife; and his only grandchild, and shortly thereafter her parents, were now in England. Frustrating disputes with Heinrich Stahl and Paul Eppstein wore him down. After Otto Hirsch and Julius Seligsohn were executed and some of the women devoted to serving the community were deported, Baeck remained with fewer confidants and friends in the Reichsvereinigung. He sat alone in one of its dingy offices. Fortunately, he was able to continue teaching at the Lehranstalt, which was a godsend. He developed close relations with the students, whom he continued to teach until the summer of 1942. At the seminary, he was able to convey a Judaism that, in his optimism, Baeck believed would somehow survive the darkness. This faith found expression not only in his teaching but also in his new writing project, which would combine Jewish history and theology. On November 9, 1941, Baeck reported to Veltheim that he was sending him biblical sections of a new manuscript, for safekeeping.[134] Other portions followed. It was a project he would continue to pursue in Theresienstadt and later in London. It would mark a shift from religion to religious peoplehood, from an essence abstracted from history to a lived existence within history. After a long gestation, it would finally appear, first in German, with the title *Dieses Volk: Jüdische Existenz* (This people: Jewish existence).

If scholarship in these times provided a few rays of light, performance of what Baeck believed to be his duty toward fellow Jews was likewise life-sustaining. For him, duty always came first, and that was now the case more imperatively than ever. Much, perhaps most, of his time during these final years in Berlin was spent as a pastor to men and women overcome by anxiety, not knowing what would become of themselves. However difficult and even implausible it might be, Baeck had to give them some hope for a future as their world crumbled into chaos. In return, providing psychological assistance to persons sorely in need of it gave him some sense of purpose. In an appeal to fellow Jews in June 1942, now signed as Leo Israel Baeck, he said that "the Jewish community today, more than ever, means: a community of those who help. Helping, with whole heart and soul, with all of one's means is *Jewish obligation*."[135] But that required a high degree of commitment, especially from

Baeck himself. To a former member of the Reichsvertretung who had recently arrived in Palestine, he wrote in 1939: "We here are determined to remain within the 'And nevertheless,' and, as you said months ago, 'to ward off the specter of chaos.' It often rests heavily on head and shoulder."[136]

To another friend, who had been able to flee to Argentina, Baeck, normally remarkably reserved, poured out his agonies—though not without adding that something positive remained: "What shall I tell you about myself? The circle has grown smaller and more lonely. I occupy myself with daily labor in order to help and be of use where it is possible to do so, and I am thankful whenever I can do something for a fellow human being. I am deeply grateful that I regularly receive good news from my children and my granddaughter. And I'm thankful too that I can be satisfied with my health."[137]

What Baeck called, in another letter, "work that was often so difficult and futile" was redemptive, for it repeatedly brought "good and happy moments when it becomes possible to help people and to stand by their side."[138] That letter was one of the last he composed in Germany, written little more than a month before his work in Berlin was forcibly brought to an end.

In September 1941, German Jews were required to mark themselves with a yellow star sewn onto their garments; mass deportations, announced for Berlin on the Jewish Day of Atonement, began a month later. Once gathered at a collection point, designated victims were herded onto trains, mostly cattle cars, and sent eastward, not knowing where the trains would take them. Euphemisms veiled the impact. The deportations were called "relocation" or "evacuation" or even "emigration." As a destination, one spoke only of "the East." The pressured work of the Reichsvereinigung to facilitate emigration had lasted less than three years, from the November pogrom to the prohibition of all emigration and the subsequent deportations.

Baeck's own turn arrived on January 27, 1943. They came for him early in the morning. Later, he recalled: "I was fully dressed when the bell rang at a quarter of six. Only the Gestapo would come at that hour. My housekeeper let in two men in civilian clothes. One of them addressed me: 'We have orders to take you to Theresienstadt.'"[139] Baeck did not resist. He must have expected that sooner or later, that day would come. But once again, he refused to be simply an object, passively drawn into their hands. He insisted on permission to write letters to relatives and friends and even made a request that some critics later thought displayed an obsessive clinging to bourgeois norms but was a way of raising himself morally above his captors: he would not go until he had paid his gas and electric bills.[140] Then he went along to the collection center on the Große Hamburger Straße. The building was formerly a Jewish boys' school in front of which a bust of Moses Mendelssohn once stood, and it was not far from the first Jewish cemetery in Berlin, dating from 1672. The following day, Baeck boarded a train headed south. His role as titular leader of German Jewry, resident in Berlin, had come to an end. The tasks now before him would take place within physical confinement.

Chapter 7

Theresienstadt

The Place

In a memorable passage of recollection, Baeck described Theresienstadt and its conditions:

> What was the first thing you felt when you entered there, when you were driven inside through the fortress gate, between the bastions and ramparts, and then a fateful gate was shut behind you, perhaps forever? You were locked in. And inside you were even more shut off—a portion of the fortress town, the better and healthier part, was set apart as the zone of the SS. In a space that was earlier intended to accommodate scarcely more than 3,000 persons, closely domiciled in military fashion, nearly 45,000[1] were often squeezed together here in barracks and other housing tightly next to one another and packed closely on top of each other. When the sun shone, thick dust, which the high ramparts prevented from dispersing, hovered above the streets. When rain or snow had fallen, there was the deep, heavy mud, which seemed to expand daily. And from everywhere and to everywhere came the vermin, the great host of the crawling, jumping, and flying against the host of the walking, sitting, and lying, the hungry against the starving—a persistent battle day and night. Month after month, year after year, that was the world. The mass swallowed the individual, who was locked into the multitude even as he was encased by confinement and dust and mud, by the swarming hordes of insects . . . , by hunger that seemed never to

want to end—concentrated in a camp where you could never be with yourself alone.[2]

Today known by its Czech name as Terezín, Theresienstadt lies in a fertile plain broken by nearby hills, forty-four miles northwest of Prague, near the Ohre River. The town was originally a fortress, built in 1780 by the Habsburg emperor Joseph II and named for his mother, the empress Maria Theresa. It consisted of a small and a large fortress, the latter having an area of seven hundred by five hundred yards. When Nazi Germany acquired the Sudetenland portion of Czechoslovakia in 1938, Theresienstadt became German territory. Two years later, the Gestapo began to remove the civilian population that had settled in the town and transformed Theresienstadt into a ghetto for Czech, German, and Austrian Jews. Among the more than 140,000 Jews sent to the ghetto from its beginning to its end, all ages were represented; 15,000 of those confined were children; 42,000 came from Germany. Of those who entered the ghetto on transports from their homes, fewer than 6,000 were alive at the end of the war; the rest died in the ghetto of hunger or disease (33,000), or were shipped to one of the death camps, mainly Auschwitz (88,000). Most of those alive when the ghetto was liberated by Soviet troops in May 1945 were recent transfers from camps in the East.[3]

The great majority of inmates were housed in eleven enormous, poorly heated, overcrowded barracks. A few were given space in what had been family homes. In the barracks, men, women, and children were forced to live separately. Private space was limited to a bed and a suitcase containing a few personal items. The results endangered not only the body but also the soul. Baeck recalled, perhaps with some exaggeration: "More and more people were crammed into a small, ever-shrinking space, so that each person was constantly bumping into and rubbing up against everyone else; as intended [by the SS], all manner of selfishness and greed blossomed and all decency withered away."[4] By contrast, the well-furnished headquarters of the SS, which adjoined a grassy, tree-lined main square, were comfortable and roomy. Across the river loomed the Small Fortress, the dreaded site of incarceration, torture, and execution.

Although some writers, including Baeck, have called it a concentration camp, Theresienstadt lacked most characteristics of the concentration and death camps. There was no electrified wire and there were no gas chambers. Residents did not wear striped uniforms, and they enjoyed a measure of freedom inside the ramparts that was not true of the camps. Although, as in the camps, the scanty meals were prepared and distributed centrally and the inmates were perpetually hungry, those fortunate enough to have connections with the outside world could receive food parcels sent by private individuals or agencies. Religious services, even weddings and bar mitzvahs, were permitted, along with a variety of cultural activities. Under strict SS supervision and control, inmates were allowed self-government by a Council of Elders. Yet the watchful SS was always ready to punish every violation of its harsh rules, resulting, where there were major infractions, in execution in the Small Fortress; minor infractions resulted in caning by a fellow inmate who was forced to do so. Attempted escape always meant death. Hard labor, mostly in support of the Nazi war effort, was required of everyone healthy enough to perform it, including children above a certain age. As in ghettos in the East, many died of hunger and disease; and, like those ghettos, Theresienstadt was not the final station but a transition point on the way to a death camp. Survival in the ghetto required daily combat with conditions that could diminish an inmate's desire to live. Dysentery was common, resulting in long lines of impatient sufferers at an inadequate number of latrines. Baeck was among the many affected by the disease. In response, he fasted for three days, and considered himself fortunate to have recovered.

Most German Jews were not sent to Theresienstadt. The great majority, especially the young who had been unable to obtain a visa to settle abroad, were deported directly to a camp in the East—toward the end, primarily Auschwitz. Those who, before boarding a train, were presented with a "T," for Theresienstadt, were relieved that it wasn't an "O," for *Ost*—that is, the East. Although the deportees did not know what exactly their fate in the East would be, they did know that Theresienstadt was the better place. Those receiving the "T" were especially the elderly (the Nazis even liked to call it an "old-age home"), wounded or decorated Jewish soldiers, and employees of the Reichsvereinigung. They were allowed to travel in passenger trains; each was given a transport number, though it was not tattooed on the arm, as was done in Auschwitz; Baeck's number was 187894. As he said later, it now became his ongoing struggle to remain, at least in his own eyes, more than a number, never to capitulate to the filthy surroundings, and always to safeguard his self-respect.[5]

Authority in Theresienstadt lay in the hands of the SS commander, in charge of a population comprising Czech Jews of all ages and German and Austrian Jews, most of whom were elderly. Subservient to the commander was a Jewish self-administration headed by an "elder of the Jews," chosen by the Nazis but given a measure of freedom in matters of day-to-day life. For most of the period that Baeck was in the ghetto, this position was held by Paul Eppstein, a competent executive but, as we have seen, a man whose personal behavior in Berlin had not been to Baeck's liking. The elder was assisted by two deputies and advised by a council, on which Baeck served and which he chaired, beginning in December 1944, when there were no further transports to Auschwitz. His particular responsibility was for the Welfare Department, which was tasked with caring for the special needs of old and young.

As former head of the Reichsvereinigung, Baeck was given a more favorable status and a better living situation than most other German Jews arriving in Theresienstadt. As one of 114 *Prominente*, notable Jews who had held high positions or enjoyed fame in Germany, he was not settled in the barracks; rather, after several weeks, two relatively large rooms were found for him in one of the houses that had earlier been occupied by the civilian population of the town. It was the house assigned to prominent Jews who were religiously observant. His former housekeeper lived in the second room.[6] A visitor recalled that his room had "a real bed" as well as a table with a pair of chairs and—most extraordinarily—even an oven for heat in the winter.[7] Here he could meet with old friends and acquaintances and talk about life before Theresienstadt, including the Lehranstalt and its students.[8] What made Baeck different from the others who were given prominent status was that, unlike most of them, he did not set himself apart from those who were not raised to that category. On the contrary, he felt what might be called a sense of noblesse oblige: his position made it possible for him to help others with their physical and spiritual needs. Whether by intention or not, he could serve as an example.[9]

The prominent persons were divided into two categories, A and B. Only the former, who were designated as such by the SS, possessed the additional advantage of being protected from deportation eastward; the latter, selected by the Jewish authorities, did not enjoy that protection. Baeck was in prominent category B.[10]

Upon arrival at the train station in Bauschowitz, everyone faced a long trek by foot to the gates of the ghetto. Each physically able person was initially placed in a labor battalion before being given permanent work. At first, inmates could rest on the Sabbath; but once the war effort required it, Jews were forced to work every day, including the High Holidays.[11] Among the chores that Baeck, aged sixty-nine, was given during his first weeks was to pull hearses, used as carts to carry bread, potatoes, or other items through the ghetto. He refused any special treatment. After the war, he told the Jewish philosopher Emil Fackenheim, who had been his student at the Lehranstalt, that using the occasion to discuss Plato and Isaiah with a fellow wagon-pulling Jew made the heavy physical labor quite bearable.[12]

Rabbi in the Ghetto

When Leo Baeck reached the ghetto on January 28, 1943, his arrival made an impact, not alone among those inmates who had earlier known him, or at least heard of him, in Germany. Broader circles were aware that an extraordinary man had arrived, someone they could trust in their time of need.[13] He could make them feel that they were more than the transport number they had received upon deportation—that they had names, they were persons, and their outer servitude did not preclude a measure of inner freedom. Baeck later recalled that it was a continual struggle to create moments when an impersonal mass of people became, at least for a time, a connected community. Whereas it was the policy of SS guards to destroy solidarity and stir up mutual animosity among the inmates, especially in their struggle for a bit more food, Baeck strove, as best he could in that antechamber to hell, to reverse the process and create *Gemeinschaft*, community.

Much of Baeck's time in Theresienstadt was devoted to rabbinical functions, not unlike those he had exercised in Berlin. Along with other rabbis, he conducted religious services on the Sabbath, which one survivor described as "more than full and sustained by a genuine need to feel close to God in prayer."[14] Another, himself a rabbi, compared the services held in attics and basements to those held long ago in the catacombs of Rome and remarked that they made a powerful impression on the worshiper and on the rabbis who led them.[15] Not long after his arrival, Baeck officiated at a wedding, solemnly held in the attic of the Magdeburg barracks.[16] Sometime later, he conducted a funeral for the daughter of Theodor Herzl, the founder of political Zionism. On that occasion, he supposedly said: "If we had listened to the words of the father of this unfortunate woman, we would not all be here today."[17] Again and again, Baeck had to lead the kaddish memorial prayer over stacks of sheet-wrapped bodies. He composed a simple eulogy that was read at all funerals, in German or in Czech.[18] Later, he described his attempt on these occasions, as long columns were winding their way through the ghetto, to recognize the dead not by their transportation number but by their name and individuality. It was a difficult and all too frequent scene:

> The mortuary was a deep dark passage within a fortress rampart, itself like a mass grave. There were days when more than a hundred persons had died. The shabby coffins of the dead stood in a very long row, always two or three, one over the other. The names were read and the ancient prayer for the dead, millennia old, was spoken. Then the coffins were lifted and carried out while a psalm was sung that for generations had accompanied the dead on their last journey: "You who dwell in the shelter of the Most High," down to its conclusion, "I will show him My salvation" [Ps. 91:1, 16]. It was like a demonstration, a piece of freedom within the slavery. Outside, huge heavy wagons waited, and the coffins were loaded onto them. It was permitted to follow for fifty paces until the edge of the camp was reached. [From there] only the dead continued on to the place of cremation.[19]

Jews, newly arrived and assigned to physical labor, were given the task of burying the remains.

It is not, however, for his performance of ritual functions that survivors especially remembered Baeck the rabbi; rather, it was for his pastoral work. Once he was settled, Baeck would make it a practice to meet new arrivals at the "lock-gates," greeting those he had known in Berlin, comforting them and making the place seem a bit less strange.[20] Just as he had visited wounded soldiers when he served as a chaplain in World War I, he now visited the sick and depressed in the ghetto, those who had no one to look after them. Such visits enabled him to converse with fellow prisoners and be helpful to them. To the comforted, the visits seemed like personal points of light, making bearable, at least for a few moments, the surrounding darkness.[21] He also brought small gifts, especially food items from packages that, on account of his being better known than others in the outside world, had reached him in relatively large numbers. He became, according to one survivor, "the outstanding benefactor of the ghetto's distressed." He seemed less the official who conducted welfare than its personal practitioner, "the embodiment of the good spirit of a religiously oriented Judaism. . . . He was concerned for young and old, the neglected and the disabled."[22] Baeck did not distinguish between Jew and non-Jew in the ghetto, attempting to serve everyone in need. For H. G. Adler—poet, scholar, and Theresienstadt survivor—Baeck embodied the conscience of the ghetto.[23]

When he was not serving the physical needs of the least advantaged of the ghetto dwellers, he was striving to raise inmates' spirits. In a lecture after the war, the poet Ilse Blumenthal-Weiss described her occasional meetings with Baeck, when she could leave her cramped barrack and, sitting in his room, direct her thoughts away from present travails: "Those were festive hours that I spent with Baeck, hours when all frights, fears, and privations seemed not to be present. For never, really never, did we speak about the horrific situation in which we found ourselves. Don't regard me as effusive if I compare those hours to a high-altitude flight of the spirit. For Baeck understood how to convince me more than ever that even under the most humiliating circumstances it is possible to remain faithful to the true values of life."[24]

Baeck would occasionally gather a small circle of six to eight people in his room for a discussion led by one of the invitees on a topic of his or her choice. Baeck commented only at the end, but what he said was regarded as the highlight of the evening. No matter what the topic—science, art, or politics—he had something to offer. One of those attending, Edith Kramer, a physician, deemed these evenings "among the few bright spots of Terezín life."[25]

Baeck was well aware that whether a person survived physically depended on circumstances beyond the individual's control: whether one was struck by deadly disease, subjected to torture, sent to the Small Fortress to be murdered, or was able to avoid all these. But as he had in Berlin, Baeck distinguished the outward fate that lay beyond free choice from the inward attitude that remained in one's own control. To remain inwardly strong, he believed, required two qualities: patience and imagination. Patience meant a resilience that did not allow the will to live to give way. Imagination meant the vision that allowed one, despite everything, to see a future. Each quality required the other. Patience without imagination could sink the ghetto dweller into an acceptance of the slavery imposed by the environment; imagination without patience could become a personal daydream, a dangerous turn away from everyday reality. For Baeck, in characteristic fashion, both qualities were linked to the moral sphere: moral patience made it possible to hold on to fellow human beings and not allow the bond between self and others to be severed; moral imagination enabled persons to see themselves in the place of others and to feel with them both their grief and their happiness.[26] Baeck's own moral imagination was a response to the urgency of empathy when it was required more than ever.

In Baeck's rabbinical eyes, Theresienstadt was a horror not only on account of its imposed deprivations; it was also a place that offended his acute moral sensitivities. Paul Eppstein, the intellectual who had aroused Baeck's displeasure in Berlin, was sent to Theresienstadt, together with his wife, about the same time as Baeck. Earlier, he had seriously considered leaving Nazi Germany.[27] Shortly after his arrival, the SS assigned Eppstein the position of elder of the Jews, the highest Jewish authority in the ghetto, which Eppstein then used for personal advantage. The elder, it was later claimed by H. G. Adler, was known to have pushed people onto transports to the East only because they, though Zionists like himself, dared to speak the truth about the corruption that was all too rampant in the Jewish ghetto's administration. When the inmate Vladimir Weiss sent a long memo to Eppstein detailing what amounted to robbery in food distribution, Weiss, with wife and child, disappeared on the next transport.[28] Baeck, who saw the first edition of Adler's book on Theresienstadt and wrote a foreword for it, was clearly aware of Eppstein's actions and appalled by them. It was not only the questionable performance of his formal duties that distressed Baeck—and not Baeck alone. It was also a question of moral sensitivity: on one occasion, a group of inmates, with no binding objection from Eppstein, held a masked ball on the very day that a transport was loading for the East.

Perhaps above all, Eppstein's private life is what vexed the rabbi. Unlike Baeck, Eppstein obtained special favors from the SS—most notably, the right to bring his grand piano into the ghetto and place it in a room large enough to accommodate it. And he had no compunctions about a well-known intimate relationship with a woman other than his wife, for whom he obtained private quarters. The survivor Vera Schiff recalled of Eppstein that "a friend of mine, Helen, a woman of unusual beauty and charm, became his mistress. . . . Though she loved Eppstein passionately, [even] she had a few qualms about his character."[29] That Baeck's aversion for Eppstein was largely in relation to his personal life is attested by another survivor and, in general, a defender of Eppstein. Jacob Jacobson was convinced that Baeck's disgust was based on Eppstein's "actual or suspected, perhaps also exaggerated, straying from the straight path that was expected of a married camp leader." Although Jacobson, unlike Baeck, was reluctant to judge Eppstein, he concluded that "it must be admitted, it would have been better if he, in his position as elder of the Jews, had given no cause for rash critique of his personal behavior."[30] When Jacobson sought to reconcile the two men, Baeck supposedly responded that should both he and Epstein survive, he would refuse ever to work with him. The elder simply did not measure up to Baeck's personal standards. In the end, Eppstein became a tragic figure, murdered by the SS in the Small Fortress on the Jewish Day of Atonement in 1944, after he had proven himself not fully amenable to their will.[31]

Eppstein's personal behavior was not atypical for inmates of Theresienstadt. Although the sexes were, for the most part, segregated, there was ample opportunity for young people to engage in trysts. As one survivor put it, "Morals went to hell here."[32] She told of a youth club that admitted young women only after they had slept with all its male members. Another told of what was happening in younger families: following the evening meal, "each went his own way, the wife to her lover—frequently, someone else's husband—the husband to his mistress."[33] As Zdenek Lederer understood the scene: "Only the present was real, and the best way to fight its depressing effects was by the pursuit of pleasure, in particular sexual pleasure."[34] But for the straitlaced Leo Baeck, such behavior, even if understandable, further polluted an atmosphere that was already deeply unpleasant on account of its many deprivations and the storm clouds of an uncertain future. Fortunately for him, and partly by his own actions, there was also another culture in Theresienstadt, as there had been among the Jews of Weimar, which did not rest upon momentary physical pleasure but instead imbued the atmosphere with activities that could inspire the spirit and raise it above a painful reality.

The Lectures

Although inmates of Theresienstadt worked long days and almost always felt hungry, there was time in the evenings when those who were interested and physically able could participate in educational and cultural events on a remarkably high level. The ghetto's diverse population included composers, musicians, actors, university professors, and almost every other sort of artist and intellectual. They managed to pull together sufficient energy to stage musical and dramatic productions as well as lectures on a broad variety of topics. Educating children was formally prohibited, but the children and those dedicated to caring for them succeeded in staging an original children's opera, *Brundibar*, which enjoyed more than forty performances. Classical musical works, familiar from a happier time, were performed in the ghetto, as well as original compositions. In addition, there were performances of cantorial music drawn from the synagogue. Only a portion of the ghetto population was able, and sufficiently interested, to participate in these artistic offerings. We do not know the extent, if any, to which Leo Baeck had a part in them. According to one account, he "boycotted" the ghetto band's afternoon concerts, perhaps because the tunes were linked to a culture that was not to his taste. It is known that Eppstein was more closely involved in this aspect of cultural life in Theresienstadt than was Baeck.[35] The rabbi's efforts were directed toward the other branch of the organized free-time activity: academic and inspirational lectures.

The presentation of formal lectures began in the summer of 1942, six months before Baeck's arrival, and continued until May 1945, the month of the ghetto's liberation. According to one tabulation, there were a total of 520 lecturers and at least 2,430 lectures.[36] Inmates who had led intellectually rich lives before their deportation longed for at least a partial restoration or connection with their earlier lives. The Nazi authorities frowned upon such lectures, for Jews were not supposed to be capable of expressing profound truths. But since the lectures were generally held late at night and not out in the open, and because they were useful when their taskmasters were trying to show off the ghetto as a beneficent place of residence, they did not prevent them.[37] All his life, Baeck later recalled, he had loved the light. But in Theresienstadt, light and life arrived only when darkness fell. "There," he concluded, "I learned to love the dark."[38]

The lectures were frequent, and audiences could be quite large. Even the elderly were willing to stand at length in cramped quarters, generally far up in one of the barracks. According to one description, bitter cold could not deter scores of men and women from climbing dark stairs to an attic, where an icy wind blew through the slits in the roof.[39] In some weeks, nearly a hundred lectures, some on more elevated and some on more popular topics, would take place. Whatever the topic, the lecturer was likely, before arrival in Theresienstadt, to have been an expert in that field. If necessary, the lecturer could draw upon the sizable Theresienstadt library for advance preparation. The director of the lecture project recalled that it was extraordinarily moving when "on the evening before a catastrophic transport eastward, organizer and public sought solace and support, and they obtained it from offerings of a genuinely artistic or intellectual nature."[40]

Given what we know of Baeck's long-standing refusal to use gimmicks when he delivered sermons or lectures, as well as his weak, rather high-pitched voice and unwillingness to diminish a topic by oversimplification, it is remarkable that not only did his lectures draw crowds that filled the available space, but he was judged to have become "the most popular speaker in Theresienstadt." The memoirist Norbert Troller, a Czech Jew, called Baeck's lectures "wise and brilliant."[41] Philip Manes, organizer of the lectures, who perished in Auschwitz but whose diary survived, recorded that Baeck's lectures were "models of crystal-clear exposition. It is a pleasure to listen to him":[42]

> The first time I heard Dr. Leo Baeck speak I was astonished by his transformation since Berlin. He had changed completely; he was easy, fluent, and pleasant to listen to. His demeanor was quiet and calm, and he spoke convincingly, without pathos, forcefully and memorably. This was how we imagined a philosopher to be, at the evening of his life, having gathered the harvest of many decades and generously giving of his wisdom. We rushed to his lectures, which he delivers without the slightest sign of fatigue. . . . He made such a deep impression that he had to repeat the Spinoza lecture.[43]

For the five-hundredth lecture, Manes chose Baeck to deliver it, on August 6, 1944, for he judged him "the worthiest speaker we have in this ghetto—in which we have an abundance of good orators." Obtaining a ticket for this occasion was no easy matter, as the designated space was limited.[44] Baeck spoke on a topic in which he had long been interested: "The Epochs of Life."[45] Once again, Manes was extravagant in his praise: "Dr. Baeck spoke standing up with captivating warmth and generosity. For over an hour he held us under the spell of his words; a life blossomed before us, the life we all share, and he gave us the motto, 'one does not become old if one does not forget one's childhood.' The skill with which Dr. Baeck developed this theme and wove it together gave us a rare experience. The audience listened with bated breath to the seventy-one-year-old speaker, whose youthful exuberance corroborated and demonstrated his theme. The appreciative applause did not want to end."[46] The day after the lecture, Manes met Baeck, who, in typical fashion, thanked *him* for the evening, thereby testifying to the modesty that continued to pervade Baeck's character.

Figure 6. Leo Baeck, wearing a Jewish star, attending a lecture in Theresienstadt in 1944. Courtesy of Leo Baeck Institute, New York.

Manes was not alone in his high evaluation of Baeck's Theresienstadt lectures. Interviewed after the war, Trude Simonsohn, who had been quite young at the time, shared an equally ecstatic memory: "I cannot forget how in the attic of a barracks, Leo Baeck spoke on Judaism and Hellenism. For me, those two hours were as if I were in a university and not in a camp. You submerged yourself so much in the spiritual that you forgot you were freezing, that you were hungry and standing in an ice-cold attic."[47]

Given the divisiveness of the ghetto, Baeck's ability to address most everyone was surely a reason for the popularity of his lectures. In more than one respect, they served as a bridge: between Jews from different countries; between religious Jews, secular Jews, and Jews only by racial definition; and between European culture and the Jewish heritage.[48] Ruth Klüger, later a prominent literary scholar, was only eleven during the year she spent in Theresienstadt. But she attended Baeck's lectures and especially remembered how he was able to connect seemingly obsolete biblical myths, such as the story of Creation in seven days, with modern scholarship. The measure of biblical days was not the same as modern measurement, he had said, and the sequence of the Creation did correspond very well with modern science. Baeck "gave us back our heritage," she wrote, "the Bible in the spirit of the Enlightenment; one could have both, the old myth and the new scholarship." She added: "Baeck must have been a highly talented preacher—how else would I have remembered all of this?"[49] Jacob Jacobson went further: Baeck's "earnest moral challenge, his profound discipline of thought and the charm of his personality could not but inspire reverence; and, in revering Dr. Baeck and his words, reverence was, in fact, shown to the very essence of Judaism."[50] For his part, astounded by the size of the audience at his lecture on Plato, Baeck was moved to ask himself: "Is there another such people on earth which has such a deep and true connection to the spirit that, although it is facing humiliation and danger, it asks for the word of the philosopher?"[51]

Baeck delivered lectures on at least thirty-eight topics during his time in Theresienstadt. Some were historical, some philosophical, some on general topics, some on Jewish ones; others seem to have combined more than a single subject. Topics in the historical realm included "The Religion of Primitive Peoples," "The Messianic Idea," "The Age of the Maccabees," "The Talmud," "Life in a Medieval Jewish Town," "The Jewish Mystics of the Middle Ages," "The Transition from Medieval to Modern Times," "The Enlightenment," and "Great and Small Nations." His portraits of individual significant figures dealt exclusively with men of the spirit, both Jewish and Gentile: Plato, Maimonides, Galileo, Spinoza, Moses Mendelssohn, Kant, and Hermann Cohen. One lecture must have been of particular relevance in Theresienstadt, where Jews who had earlier engaged in white-collar professions had been forced into physical labor. It was titled "The Worker in Jewish Teachings."[52]

Baeck was clearly aware that the topics he chose and the way he dealt with them were not determined by academic considerations but by spiritual ones. Why had he chosen the ancient Greek philosopher Plato as one of his subjects, he was asked after the war. He replied: "People in distress should be helped to expand their brains and to think of something other than the present." His listeners needed to raise their spirits to a Plato—an idealist and a visionary. Like the lecture on Plato, about half the others focused on non-Jewish thinkers and topics. It was a way of attracting listeners for whom figures and subjects from general history and philosophy were more familiar than Jewish ones. They could more easily feel, as one of them said, that "for a moment, it was the way it used to be." But that is not to say that Baeck neglected Jewish worthies or that his lectures, even on non-Jewish topics, could be called secular. Giving a lecture without a religious element in it would not have been Baeck.

Regrettably, the text of only one of Baeck's lectures has survived: *Geschichtsschreibung*, "The Writing of History," was delivered on June 15, 1944, at the Theresienstadt Community House.[53] Baeck introduces this lecture with some basic assertions: history is not meaningless; it is not composed of scraps that need to be patched together. Rather, it represents a continuity from past to present and on into the future. The possession of history is the mark of a civilized humanity. To write it requires the knowledge of the scholar and the skill of the artist. Baeck proceeds historically, beginning with a critical analysis of the Greek historians Herodotus and Thucydides, and going on to the Hellenistic Polybius and the Roman Tacitus. While he admires the Greeks, Baeck is critical of Polybius for his subservience to the Roman conqueror and of Tacitus for his utter lack of a sense of justice. How different in this regard, Baeck notes, was Tacitus's historiography from an opposing genre of historical writing: that of ancient Israel. "For the Israelite-Jewish historiography," Baeck maintains, "justice is the ultimate meaning of history. Were justice to perish, it would be meaningless any longer to live on earth." In words clearly intended to sustain his listeners, he continues: "True history is the history of the spirit, of the human spirit, which may sometimes seem powerless, but which in the end remains superior; which survives because even if it does not possess power, nonetheless it possesses strength, strength that can never cease."[54]

Baeck goes on briefly to discuss modern historians, including Gibbon and Macaulay in England, Niebuhr, Ranke, and Mommsen in Germany, and he concludes with generalizations that must have been poignant for his listeners. A people dies, he suggests, when its spirit dies. Without being explicit, he intimates that such a death has afflicted Germany, and, he stresses, the German historians failed to take note of it; they chose instead to remain silent. In Baeck's eyes, it was the task of the historian to be the conscience of his people and thereby take up the challenge that had already been posed by Israel's prophets: to reach out beyond the narrowly national to the universal, to engage in the broad vision that can revive a moribund spirit. "That today," Baeck concludes his lecture in Theresienstadt, "remains the great assignment of historical writing. The rebirth of many a people could thereby be brought about, a discovery of the great connections of life, a universal finding of self, aimed at a single humanity."[55] Was Baeck thinking of pre-Nazi Germany when he spoke of a spirit that could yet be reborn, or was it a rebirth of the Jewish people? We cannot know; Baeck avoids specificity. Nevertheless, the hopeful conclusion was not only characteristic for Baeck but perhaps also a fragile consolation for his listeners.

Among the other lecturers in Theresienstadt was one of Baeck's students from the seminary in Berlin, the aforementioned Rabbi Regina Jonas. Her topics were listed as "Lectures of the Only Female Rabbi." Whereas Baeck concentrated on the abstract and ideal, Jonas focused on the substance of Jewish religious traditions. He spoke as the rabbi who was also an intellectual; she spoke strictly as the rabbi. She preached on religious duties, the joys of Sabbath observance and Hanukkah celebration, mothers and fathers in Jewish tradition, Jewish prayer, and why religious services were necessary—perhaps especially in Theresienstadt. We have no complete texts of her lectures, but it is known that on one occasion, she said: "Man and woman, woman and man, take on this duty [the moral tasks of the Jews] equally, with equal Jewish humility. Our serious, arduous task in Terezín also serves to fulfill this ideal." At least six of her talks were devoted to the Jewish woman—her role in the Bible and in Jewish law, Jewish culture, and Jewish history. Altogether, Jonas delivered forty-four lecture-sermons. When she was not speaking publicly, Jonas visited Jewish women in the houses and barracks, convincing them of the meaning that Judaism might have for them, even—or perhaps especially—under the present circumstances. Jonas was sent to Theresienstadt a few weeks before Baeck; unlike him, she did not survive. Together with her mother, she was deported to Auschwitz on one of the last transports, on October 12, 1944.[56]

Survival

Conditions in Theresienstadt varied; sometimes they seemed to improve but then would deteriorate again. When a few hundred Danish Jews arrived in autumn 1943, it soon became clear to the authorities that representatives from Denmark would want to view the ghetto and that they would have to make it seem presentable. When the inspection team, composed of the Danish Red Cross, arrived the following June, the SS had completed a "beautification" project that made the ghetto appear like a resort community or, as the Germans called it at the time, a "Jewish Home for the Sick and Aged." The visitors, who spent eight hours there, were led through the ghetto by SS officers. Upon their return home, they reported—falsely—that they "had been able to talk with everyone" and that they had come to believe that "Theresienstadt is not a transit camp." To the members of the delegation, "the inhabitants looked healthy and not undernourished"; they claimed to have seen no lice or other insects.[57] But perhaps they were not entirely fooled. One ghetto survivor thought that the fresh paint on the houses and the forced artificiality of the general appearance must have hinted at the true story. What is beyond doubt is that the visit brought little permanent change for the better. Baeck recalled the deep disappointment he and others felt that the charade had been so successful. "It looked as if they did not want to know the truth," he recalled. "The effect on our morale was devastating. We felt forgotten and forsaken."[58] Months later, shortly before liberation, a different Red Cross delegation arrived. This time, it was Baeck who led them around the ghetto and pointed out what it was really like. The pavilion for children that had been proudly shown on the earlier visit, Baeck explained, had in fact never been used.[59]

The beautification was not the only attempt by the SS to convince the world of Theresienstadt's beneficence. To further camouflage its horror, they produced a film that included a scene showing inmates bathing in the nearby river—which they had never been allowed to do. The film also depicted one of the lectures, with Leo Baeck, perhaps better known to the intended audience outside the German orbit than any of the others, with the Jewish star on his coat, listening attentively in the first row. The film was never shown.[60] The transports eastward continued.

Among the decisions that Baeck was forced to make in Theresienstadt, some were intensely personal. In the ghetto, it was not unusual for persons of influence to obtain exemptions from deportation for friends and relatives—someone else then being substituted to fill the quota. When such a case arose affecting Baeck's family, he was constitutionally unable to make a moral compromise and refused to intervene. As a result, a niece and nephew boarded a transport headed for a death camp.[61] Other relatives died in the ghetto or were sent directly to the East. Baeck lost four of his sisters in Theresienstadt, three of them before he arrived, and the fourth shortly after his arrival. Both his brothers perished in a death camp. These personal losses were among the painful memories that underlay Baeck's reluctance in later years to recall his ghetto experience.[62]

Oddly, the Nazi authorities thought that Baeck himself was no longer alive in the ghetto. Apparently, a Rabbi Beck from Moravia had died, and the matter had become public. The assumption spread that it was Rabbi Leo Baeck who had succumbed. Among Baeck's few public recollections of Theresienstadt was a verbal exchange a few weeks later, in April 1945, while he was in one of the ghetto offices:

> The door opened and an SS officer entered. It was Eichmann. He was visibly taken aback at seeing me.
>
> "Herr Baeck, are you still alive?" He looked me over carefully, as if he did not trust his eyes, and added coldly, "I thought you were dead."
>
> "Herr Eichmann, you are apparently announcing a future occurrence."
>
> "I understand now. A man who is claimed dead lives longer!"[63]

The all-too-clear hint in these words of Adolf Eichmann, the high Gestapo official whom Baeck had already encountered in Berlin, convinced him that his demise in one form or another was imminent. Nonetheless, he refused to be intimidated. When Eichmann blocked the door, Baeck simply put his hand on Eichmann's arm just below the shoulder, lightly pushed him aside, and passed through the doorway. As he walked down the street, Baeck could feel Eichmann's astonished glance following his departing steps.[64]

Baeck now immediately wrote farewell letters, said good-bye to friends, and made himself ready for whatever might come. But, as far as we know, his number did not come up for transport to Auschwitz. If it had, Baeck would surely have forgone seeking out a substitute. Judging by what he had written earlier, he would have regarded it instead as an opportunity to perform the commandment of *kiddush hashem*, of martyrdom, a self-sacrifice in preference to a self-preservation at the cost of another person's life. Fortunately for Baeck, he had no role here (as he had in Berlin) in gathering individuals for the departing trains. The SS provided a quota and decided on particular age groups and gender. Then the Jewish administration, which Baeck had chosen not to head up until the last of the transports departed, was required to compile lists of selected individuals.[65]

As we have seen, in Berlin Baeck had been constrained to make two highly controversial decisions: whether to urge participation in the process of rounding up the intended deportees; and whether to tell future victims what he had reason to believe lay at the end of their journey. In Theresienstadt, the first matter was out of his hands; but the second reemerged with even greater urgency and agony. Having learned—at the latest, in August 1943—of the ill fate that awaited those loaded into the cattle cars exiting Theresienstadt, should he make his knowledge public?[66]

Following the liberation of the ghetto, Heinrich Liebrecht, a former inmate who had survived Auschwitz and returned to Theresienstadt, encountered Baeck on one of the ramparts of the fortress. They recognized and embraced each other, grateful that they had survived. "In my case, as for everyone in Theresienstadt," Baeck supposedly said to the new arrival, survival "hung by a single silken thread."[67] Liebrecht used the occasion to question Baeck regarding his decisions. During the conversation that followed, Baeck first recalled that he had rejected the possibility of physical resistance, which Liebrecht had earlier proposed to him. Baeck mentioned to his interlocutor the fate of his brave close associates in Berlin when they had so much as aroused the suspicion of plotting physical resistance. Nonetheless, as the so-called work transports departed the ghetto in October 1944, he had seriously considered physical resistance, only to reject it once more. Nazi retribution in Theresienstadt would have been massive and brutal, as it had been in Berlin. Then Baeck went on to speak of what he did and did not know:

> I did not know whether [the transports were going] to Auschwitz. But that the intention was probably to murder immediately whoever was not fit for hard labor and to let those who were capable of working for the war machine eventually perish from hunger and deprivation—that I knew was the Gestapo's goal. At the time, I was caught up in pangs of conscience: Should one shorten the agonies of those destined for departing transports through a self-initiated massacre or give some, even if only very few, a chance for survival? I finally said to myself: Even if only a single person will survive, we may not sacrifice that person.[68]

When, after the war, Baeck learned that some Theresienstadt deportees had indeed survived the death camps, his conscience was at least partly assuaged and he became convinced that he had made the right decision; a mass suicide prompted by despair would not have been a better outcome.

Some agreed with Baeck's decision to remain silent. Among them was Paul Eppstein, the man for whose character Baeck had so little regard. Like

Baeck, Eppstein feared that if knowledge of what awaited in the East became public, a catastrophe would have threatened the nearly 35,000 inmates of the Theresienstadt ghetto.[69] It was better that only a small number knew the truth. The few who were still alive in the ghetto at liberation also felt that it was the right decision. Charlotte Opfermann recalled: "We did not want to know . . . so many suicides already."[70] The survivor Ruth Bondy remembered: "We knew that transports meant severance from family, exile to the unknown, starting all over again, more arduous conditions. Had we known what they really meant, we would not have been able to endure." But she added: "Those who went to the gas chambers not knowing were unable to give their opinion."[71]

Among those who, after the war, disagreed with Baeck's decision was Paul Tillich, a friend and admirer of Leo Baeck. Whereas Baeck's defenders might have believed that he had rightly opted to be compassionate by not adding anxiety to deprivation, Tillich thought that Baeck should have revealed his knowledge. According to this prominent Protestant theologian, "the full existential truth" should have been made available to all, "just as the incurable patient should always be told the full truth."[72] In those days, however, it was the common practice to save terminally ill patients the agony of knowing what almost certainly awaited them. In withholding knowledge, quite apart from the possibility that death was not an absolute certainty as well as what Eppstein had called the "catastrophe" that such knowledge would unleash, Baeck was following a morality not only his own but one regnant in his time.

In December 1944, knowledge of the concentration camps became widespread in the ghetto as some four hundred Slovak Jews, well-informed about Auschwitz, arrived from a camp in Slovakia and reported what they knew.[73] But now, the Allied victory seemed closer than ever. The Russian army was no longer far away, and German authorities were more worried about how the ghetto would look to the world. Yet they also wanted to reduce the number of Holocaust survivors by "natural" means. They sent to Theresienstadt some fifteen thousand starving and deathly ill inmates from labor and concentration camps in the East. Utterly exhausted and looking like skeletons, they could not eat the food offered them. Many simply collapsed and died. They brought a spotted-fever epidemic that soon ravaged the ghetto. Baeck recalled that the last few weeks before liberation, which finally came on May 10, 1945, were among the worst: "From everywhere those ill from spotted fever were brought to Theresienstadt in open freight cars—from one train we carried away more than a hundred persons who had died on the way. It was like a lottery who would be infected, but the plan was clear—to 'liquidate' the camp."[74] In May, when the disease was rampant, 730 people died, some before and some after the liberation. The ghetto's remaining inhabitants now turned to stubborn endurance until medical salvation would arrive and people would be sufficiently healthy to walk out of the ghetto.

Once again—this time, following liberation by the Russian army—Baeck gave up the opportunity to run away from a responsibility that had recently been cast upon him. During these last days, having finally agreed to participate actively in making ghetto decisions, his duties had become formal. He traveled for a day to Prague, where, in the service of the afflicted, he picked up medicine that had arrived from America. While in the Czech capital, the American major Patrick Dolan, who had brought the medicine, told Baeck that he was authorized to fly him to England, where his family awaited. Characteristically, Baeck refused the offer. He still required four or five weeks to help the sick and healthy survivors in the liberated ghetto to get well and to find a passage to elsewhere. Only a month later, at the end of June, when the major returned to fetch him, did he go along. On July 1, Baeck recalled, a large American Flying Fortress brought him to Paris. From there, an English warplane took him on to London, where his daughter, son-in-law, and granddaughter eagerly awaited. For the rest of his life, Baeck would feel grateful for his personal salvation from what, after Eichmann's veiled threat, had seemed a certain death.

When the victorious Soviets occupied the ghetto, they urged the rescued victims to take vengeance on their oppressors. Some survivors of the Holocaust were doing just that. But Baeck would have no part of such actions against the perpetrators. Eric Warburg, who participated in efforts to evacuate Theresienstadt, reported his words at the time: "Don't touch them; ignore them. It's not our task to repay one injustice with another."[75] Vengeance, Baeck believed, citing the New Testament, belonged only to God.[76]

But he could not shake off the lasting effect of his Theresienstadt experience. Despite his efforts to consign it to the past, it continued to haunt him: "Every so often the shadows arise before me, the shadows of those who perished, the shadows of those who condemned them to death. Hardly a day passes that an image doesn't confront me or a tone enter my ear: the sudden throbbing or ringing when the myrmidons, as on many a day, demanded entry in order to haul me off to this place or that. A friend here [in London], whose father and I were close, is accustomed to saying "time is a good healer." Is he right? It is difficult to be completely restored from a difficult time, and perhaps sometimes the recuperation lasts as long as the sickness."[77] Nevertheless, Baeck refused to live in the past. Once in London, even though he looked back in anger, he also looked forward, even hopefully, toward the future.

Chapter 8

Reality After Catastrophe

Glancing Backward and Forward

When Leo Baeck arrived in London on July 5, 1945, he looked emaciated, after nearly thirty months of deprivation, resulting in a weight loss of seventy pounds. Now, at last, he could relax in the simple pleasures of family life. In Theresienstadt, he had dreamed of that salvation, longing for a day when he could see a meadow, a field, or even a forest, when he could fall asleep without hunger. He had imagined what it would be like to be once more among the living and no longer in the midst of death.[1] To a colleague, he wrote shortly after his arrival: "After all the dread and the pain that had surrounded and accompanied me, here I was met with joys, the joys of every day, of being with my children and [my granddaughter] Marianne."[2]

The final decade of Baeck's life now began. It was not spent in extended recuperation but in an astonishing flurry of Jewish activity similar to what had engaged him during the Weimar years. Once again, he was the holder of several high offices in the Jewish community. He resumed his presidency of the World Union for Progressive Judaism, adding to it the presidency of the Association of Synagogues of Great Britain and the Jewish Society for Human Service. He presided over the Council for the Protection of the Rights and Interests of Jews from Germany and, on a visit to Germany, chaired a meeting of the European Rabbinical Association. He had become a symbolic figure who enjoyed the utmost respect and even reverence in every circle of which he was a part. As in the past, the organizational activity occupied only a portion of his remarkably busy schedule. These years were, as well, once again an intellectually productive period, during which he could devote himself to writing and teaching, now for a readership and audience that stretched to the old and new centers of Jewish life in Europe, America, and Israel. In all of them, he hoped to implant what was best in the heritage of German Jewry. Old and new relationships included Christian individuals and groups to whom he now stressed those elements that united the two faiths, though not forsaking his earlier stated differences between them.

On December 21, 1945, only a few months after his arrival in London, Baeck stepped off a plane in the United States, where he was greeted by numerous dignitaries. It was the beginning of a three-month fund-raising venture on behalf of the United Jewish Appeal, which wanted to exploit his stature to assist impoverished Jews in Europe and Palestine, many of them survivors of the Holocaust. The German Jewish newspaper *Aufbau* used the occasion of his arrival to ply Baeck with questions about Germany. Casting his glance backward, he was dubious as to whether the land of his birth, a land to which he had once been deeply attached, could recover its moral stature. But he distinguished between age groups: "The older generation of Germans, those over forty-five years, had not seldom behaved decently," he replied. "But the youth, and especially the Hitler Youth, was made rotten through and through and perverted. It is so corrupted that I do not see how reeducation can help here. A new education of the Germans really makes sense only for children under the age of six."[3] Upon his arrival in London, Baeck had warned of the danger of failing to impress their deeds upon the German people by delaying punishment. He counseled severity. Democratic methods, he believed, were not effective when dealing with democracy's enemy. Only in conjunction with a merciless extirpation of the ill parts of the German body politic could the healthier portions be allowed to recover.[4]

At this point, Baeck held the entire German nation responsible for what had happened to its Jews. The Germans had taken pleasure in their crime and sought to derive benefit from it. They "condoned it and would have applauded the criminals had they been victorious."[5] Above all, Baeck lodged responsibility with the university intellectuals who were so ready to render obedience to the regime. But he did have a degree of appreciation for the pressure that the Nazi regime had placed on individuals. On a visit to Switzerland after the war, the influential non-Jewish psychoanalyst Carl Gustav Jung visited Baeck, pleading that the rabbi have some understanding for Jung's initial support for the Nazi regime. He claimed that, given the new prospects for Germany in 1933, he had "slipped" (*ausgerutscht*). Baeck clearly thought this a very lame excuse; but since Jung was apparently repentant, a relationship between the two men, which had formed at Keyserling's School of Wisdom, was restored.[6]

Baeck was similarly pessimistic regarding the future of a German Jewry restored in its former land. Vehemently, he denied that possibility, recalling that he had lost faith in its future years earlier. "No!" he exclaimed. "The history of German Jewry is decisively at an end. The clock cannot be turned back. I recognized that when I was still in Germany. When, at that time, I gave the German Jews the advice 'Send out your young people first; you older people, hold out until you are able to follow,' I was decried as a defeatist. . . . Too much stands between the German Jews and the Germany of the period 1933–45—so much murder, theft, and plunder, so much blood and tears, so many graves. That cannot be erased. . . . The nurturing layer of soil is no longer there."[7] As Baeck saw the situation in 1945, there was no immediate hope for a polluted land, or for a survivor community in its land of origin. Three years later, in 1948, he was still of the opinion that the Jews presently in Germany should not want to remain there. "It would be like living in a cemetery of their own brothers and sisters."[8]

Baeck was severely disappointed when, even after the destruction of the Jews became well known, leading German intellectuals failed to condemn it outright. In 1946, when Friedrich Meinecke, Franz Rosenzweig's teacher and a highly regarded German historian, published the book *German Catastrophe*, it contained nothing of "the bankruptcy with which he should be especially concerned, the bankruptcy of the universities," Baeck noted with great regret. Moreover, in considering the factors that led to the rise of Nazism, Meinecke remained silent regarding the long history of German antisemitism. He also passed over the enormous guilt of the silent churches and the literary intellectuals. Although Baeck had been a disciple of Wilhelm Dilthey, who stressed that the historian's job was to "understand" historical phenomena sympathetically, the Holocaust set a limit to such understanding. In criticizing Meinecke's work, he condemned his historicism, which, in seeking to understand all, had enabled him to excuse all; it was simply a comfortable and convenient escape for those unwilling to face up to the past. In the process of writing understandingly, one could easily justify "obedient cowardice" by arguing that such base conduct was simply a necessary occurrence in the historical process.[9]

Absent as well, Baeck noted, in the writings and speeches of German politicians in the years immediately after the war, was any recognition of the contributions that Jews had made to German society and culture. His conclusion approximated the Kabbala scholar and Jewish intellectual Gershom Scholem's controversial assertion that the German Jews' love of their country had been wholly unrequited by the non-Jewish public. Baeck now leveled a critique on himself and others who had been blind to the dark spots in the Weimar reality. He reflected on "how lonesome we Jews were among all of the people in the German land, and we ourselves were scarcely aware of it."[10] The myth of "the German Torah," the racist doctrine, Baeck wrote to Scholem, was canonized and taught in German schools and universities, the myth of the all-encompassing totality of the worldview of the *Volk*, of the German people minus the Jews.[11]

During his first few months in London, Baeck sought to suppress the recent past. It was painful to recall, and even more so to write or speak of his own experience. He had lost so many who were close to him. Drawing upon a passage in Psalms, he wrote: "I have made myself to be silent."[12] But personal obligation forced him to glance backward. Multiple letters regularly besieged him, seeking information about relatives and acquaintances whom he had known in Berlin or with whom he had been in contact in Theresienstadt. Baeck was waging what he later called "a daily battle with a correspondence" that he felt obliged to undertake.[13] In response to a letter from a widow, he wrote: "I was often together there [in Theresienstadt] with your departed husband. . . . I soon found him and he told me about you and your sister." It had been a joy for Baeck to converse with him and "to allow a beam of the past to shine into the present." He related the sad tale of his former esteemed associates Hannah Karminski and Cora Berliner, informing his correspondent that the first, in a condition of sickness, had been deported to the East, where she died after a few days; the second had similarly been deported, but, not knowing of her fate, Baeck continued to hope (in vain) that he would see her again one day.[14] In another letter, he wrote: "One must not give up all hope. Again and again signs of life appear from the East."[15] Baeck himself refused to give up hope. Although both his brothers had been deported to the East and disappeared there, he wrote in 1946: "I know how thin and perhaps without substance this hope is, but I cling to it firmly, [that] perhaps one day, nevertheless, [I will be able] to hear from them and to see them once more."[16]

There were also requests for references that might protect individuals whom Baeck had known earlier from the suspicion of having aided the Nazi cause. In response to one such request, Baeck wrote a lengthy "To Whom It

May Concern" letter for Hans Walz, director of the Bosch Werke, who had supplied funds for Baeck's work during the Nazi period. Walz was, wrote Baeck, a man of pure character who rejected National Socialism.[17] He received a similar request for a reference from his old friend Hans-Hasso von Veltheim-Ostrau. In this instance, it was necessary to justify Veltheim's becoming a "candidate" for admission to the Nazi party in 1937, supposedly as a necessity in order to receive a passport for international travel. Veltheim claimed that he had helped many Jews escape Germany and settle abroad.[18] Now it was Baeck's turn to help. A longtime admirer of those German nobles who were not antisemitic, he became this German aristocrat's patron and protector after the Holocaust.

For a long time, Baeck had doubted the notion of steady moral progress. In 1945, he explicitly denied its existence, distinguishing it from technical advance, which could move forward into the future, unaffected by history. By contrast, "moral progress," he now held, "must always be striven for anew."[19] Returning to the feelings he had after World War I, Baeck once again believed that a catastrophic conflict would bring the nations to their senses: "The sovereignty of the state is now being restricted to something relative, in favor of a higher common interest. . . . The idea of 'national' has lost considerably in value, and the idea of 'international' has instead gained value and substance, even though the old idea here and there still possesses its convulsive spasms."[20] He invoked earlier forms of united existence—the United Kingdom and the United States—as models for the idea of a "United Nations." The new community of nations, Baeck hoped, would create a different world, based not on "the satan of *raison d'état*" but on a broad concept of humanity. The nations would become "nations of human beings" who would think in universal rather than in national terms. Together they would create "a culture of humanity."[21] Yet in the Cold War years that followed, Baeck's hopefulness turned to doubt. Even after 6 million Jews and many million non-Jews had lost their lives, the lesson had not been learned. In his final major work, titled in its original German edition *Dieses Volk: Jüdische Existenz* (This people: Jewish existence), he asked: "Is this the beginning of a humane epoch, an epoch at the beginning of which the affliction of this [Jewish] people stood as 'a sacrifice for many'?" He concluded evasively: "Those who come later will hear the answer."[22]

Baeck's hoped-for culture of humanity required a shift away from the concept at the middle of the spectrum of political organization—the state—and toward the individual human being on the one end and humanity on the other. The Weimar Republic had prided itself on laws "in which the idea of freedom inhered." Its founders and representatives thought that its political framework would prevent intolerance and persecution. But that expectation had proven false. It had been, Baeck now wrote, "but a brief dream, to be followed inevitably by a gloomy awakening." It is not the state but those who compose and serve it that make the difference, he believed. "It is men of justice that count. The essential course is the education of just men." Not merely by reshaping laws but by also reshaping a different sort of individual could further catastrophes be avoided, especially in the new Germany.[23]

During the last decade of his life, Baeck repeatedly stressed the individual as the irreducible and "ineffable" constituent of humanity. The right to diversity among individuals was inalienable, not to be infringed upon by any grouping of community or state. The goal of justice, for which Baeck fervently argued, was by itself insufficient. Humanity had to be added to it, and that required recognizing individual difference. As he put it: "Justice measures everyone by the same standards. Humanity, however, indicates that those who are measured are different human beings. Each of these is a world unto himself."[24] Both, he believed, were required. In sum: "Justice is the foundation; upon it, and upon it alone, can and should humanity be built, in order that human society may be firmly founded, a society in which all shall have their place to live for the high tasks for which the Creator has made them, each with his individual nature, each with his unique personality."[25] Moreover, it is not justice alone that depends on the humane individual; the same is true for peace. An ideal of world peace is ultimately not dependent on nations but, like justice, on individual human beings. The task is to educate men and women who will embody that ideal.[26] To do so requires a struggle against what Baeck now regards as an initially nonmoral human nature. In a scholarly lecture that he gave at the prestigious Eranos Society in Ascona, Switzerland, in 1947, bearing the Latin title "Individuum Ineffabile," Baeck argued that, by nature, the human being is not unselfish, just, truthful, or loving. Nature stands outside morality. It is only the one God, mysterious in essence but knowable through the moral commandment, that transforms the creature of nature into the moral person, thereby fulfilling that person's individuality.[27]

Because of their prophetic heritage and the suffering that they have experienced from the world's lack of these three values—justice, humanity, and peace—the Jews bear a special obligation to urge advance on the path toward them. Small in numbers, they are not in a position to affect major political and economic circumstances, but, according to Baeck, they can affect the inner life of individuals. And, as Baeck noted, that inner life is the ultimate basis for the realization of moral goals. Echoing what he said to console the Jews of Germany in his public prayer of 1935, Baeck reiterates that Judaism "stands upright in the current of historical events."[28] Its task is to serve as the conscience of humanity, to work at building that awareness of evil which Baeck terms "the public conscience, the awakened world conscience."[29]

To arouse the conscience of humanity, Baeck maintains, will require the daring to speak out. Addressing the delegates at the first World Union for Progressive Judaism conference after the war, held in London in 1946, he urged involvement in world affairs:

> We must not, as Jews, remove ourselves from the problems of the time, nor hide ourselves as Jews. . . . We are Jews also for the sake of humanity; we should be there, quite especially in this world after the war; we have our questions to raise and have to give our answer. To rouse the conscience of humanity could here be our best title-deed. Surely we will then often have to speak a No to much that happens on earth and that rules on earth, to speak a No for the sake of our great Yes, of our great demand. We shall often have to accuse for the sake of justice and love, for the sake of the promise; say No and accuse, because we are what we are and should be, the Lord's most loyal opposition on earth, the steadfast and stubborn for God's sake.[30]

According to Rabbi Caesar Seligmann, who had been the spiritual leader of the Liberal Synagogue in Frankfurt am Main and had fled to London, one of Baeck's favorite citations from Jewish literature was the imperative *letaken olam be-malkhut shadai*, to set the world aright under the sovereignty of God.[31] This phrase, shortened to *tikun olam* and representing God's social commandment, was to become an ever more popular Hebrew phrase in all forms of Liberal Judaism.

The Heritage

At least initially, Baeck had his doubts that a healthy Jewish community could be reestablished in the new Federal Republic of Germany; but he was certain, from the start, that the spiritual and intellectual legacy of German Jewry was worth preserving, wherever German Jews might now be scattered. In "The Idea Remains," an essay published in a periodical by surviving members of the non-Zionist German Jewish fraternity (Kartellconvent deutscher Studenten jüdischen Glaubens, or K.C.), he recalled a pre-Nazi Germany that had seen itself as part of the world, especially the Germany of the classical period, the time of the great poets, musicians, and thinkers.[32] That Germany, Baeck noted, had been praised even outside its boundaries—for example, by Thomas Carlyle in England and Ralph Waldo Emerson in America. It had meant even more to Jews than it did to others. It was the land of Moses Mendelssohn's friend Gotthold Ephraim Lessing; of the champion of the improvement of Jewish political status, Christian Wilhelm Dohm; and of the Humboldt brothers, who had favored the Jewish cause. It was on German soil that Jewish critical scholarship had been born. And it was the classical spirit of those days, the spirit of the German Enlightenment, that had stirred Jewish souls, though making many think that, in return, they were required to give up something of their Judaism. Only gradually did German Jews learn that their greatest contribution was not their submergence in the surrounding culture and society but rather the display of their own particular talents.

In the course of time, however, it became clear where Germany was headed. Instead of seeing itself as part of Europe, Germany, tragically, turned from its neighbors and from its own humanistic tradition. Antisemitism was the first symptom of that separation and soon became its driving force. Finally, Germany disengaged both from humanism and humanity. But the Jewish community remained attached to those values. Its Judaism, linking internalized values to those that were once at home in Germany, was an idea, Baeck argued, that would remain. Over the years, German Jewry produced outstanding individuals whose lives Baeck recounted in a series of lectures he delivered in Germany during the last months of his life. He began with premodern figures such as Josel of Rosheim, the sixteenth-century champion of Jewish interests, and then focused on four individuals representing variant types of Jewish consciousness: the philosopher Moses Mendelssohn; Moses Hess, the socialist and precursor of Zionism; Walther Rathenau, the tragically assassinated diplomat; and Baeck's personal friend, the theologian Franz Rosenzweig. Baeck dedicated these lectures to "the memory of that former German Judaism and its great spiritual history."[33] Wherever German

Jews would now live, their noble heritage, combining Jewish with Enlightenment values, would continue, in new places and in new forms.

In other articles, Baeck became more specific about the nature of the German Jewish heritage, which he believed worthy of transplantation to other lands. German Jews, he argued, had a talent for organization that enabled them to form effective Jewish communities; they displayed deep appreciation for education and for the obligation to engage in philanthropy. And, from the first, they included strong women. To Ottilie Schönewald, the last president of the Jüdische Frauenbund, Baeck wrote: "In the history of Judaism in Germany during the great generation before the coming of darkness, the Frauenbund possessed its unique place and its unique paths." During the Weimar period, it had overcome the romanticism of the general women's movement and successfully bound together activity in three vital areas: the spiritual, the social, and the political.[34] In the Nazi period, the women's strength became yet more apparent:

> What the Jewish women achieved in those years, in that time of peril, no words can do justice. Few other examples equal what these women displayed in terms of self-sacrifice and courage. Whoever saw how in Berlin after the conflagration of the synagogues, when the men were dragged from their homes and brought to the camps, the Jewish women stormed—that is the right word—the central police station in the Alexanderplatz, how they declared there that they would not withdraw until their husbands were returned to them or they at least would be told where they had been taken—that witness experienced a great historical event and will never forget it.[35]

It was also the Jewish women who carried their husbands, as it were, on their backs, out of Germany and to lands of freedom. Once again, Baeck specifically mentioned Hannah Karminski and, this time, along with her, Martha Hirsch, wife of his former associate Otto Hirsch. "Whoever had been with her [Martha Hirsch] in the final hours before her deportation [as clearly Baeck must have been], received a lifelong blessing."[36]

This was the heritage that Baeck wished to preserve, both the legacy of German Jewry as a whole and the legacy of its individual members. He hoped that it could be revived, noting that "during the last decades before the Jewish catastrophe, there were symptoms of a nascent Jewish renaissance in Germany. These forces are not extinct, and it is up to us to develop them anew. Just as the heritage of Sephardi Jewry is still a reality, the achievements of Ashkenazi Jewry, from Strasbourg to Lemberg, from Prague to Scandinavia, will continue to play their part in Jewish life."[37] But Baeck realized that for such a renaissance to occur, two elements were necessary: a source of financial support for the impoverished German Jewish emigrants and books to sustain the intellect. He was determined to obtain both.

The Jewish refugees from Germany, who were beginning new lives in the United States, in Great Britain, South America, and elsewhere, had been deprived of most or all of their wealth before their departure. Some were not in a position to become self-supporting; the elderly required old-age homes for their final years. Property belonging to Jewish organizations and institutions, like the B'nai B'rith in Germany, had been confiscated and needed to be restored. As president of the Council for the Protection of the Rights and Interests of the Jews from Germany, centered in London, Baeck sought to recover what had been lost. He became the German refugees' and survivors' chief advocate, but he achieved little success. In 1950, he urged the American Jewish Joint Distribution Committee to act quickly to obtain restitution funds, believing that "what sense of responsibility for the crimes of Nazism existed at all has greatly vanished, owing to old German self-pity and new German self-importance."[38] For years, he attempted to convince the Jewish Restitution Successor Organization (JRSO) that "20 percent of the net proceeds from the realization of heirless and unclaimed Jewish property in the U.S. Zone of Germany should be allocated by the JRSO to this council" for distribution among the organization of Jewish refugees from Germany all over the world.[39] Baeck continued to press his case for five years, but without success. The leaders of the JRSO would not allocate a defined percentage of restitution funds to any one group. They insisted on controlling all distributions themselves, some of which, they claimed, had, in fact, gone to German Jewish refugees.[40] Finally, Baeck wrote a letter of deep disappointment to Monroe Goldwater, president of the JRSO. He recognized the importance of dividing the available funds among Jewish refugees and survivors everywhere but regarded the refusal to allow a definite amount to be allocated to the German Jewish refugees as inherently unfair: "The funds which were to be disposed of were funds earned by the parents, the ancestors, and the relatives of those Jews who had lived in Germany and were granted refuge in various countries. These people, who through their industry and talent had acquired these funds, had a very fine record of social feeling and were always prepared to help Jews in distress, regardless of where they lived."[41] Now that the former benefactors were in need, their requests were being denied. Baeck felt that he had no choice but to withdraw the council from the JRSO.[42]

In addition to the conflict over the distribution of restitution funds, an argument ensued over who would receive the Jewish books that had belonged to German Jewish individuals and institutions. On this subject, a tug-of-war erupted between America, represented by Salo Baron, a noted Jewish historian; Israel, by Gershom Scholem, scholar of Jewish mysticism; and the United Kingdom, represented by Leo Baeck. Each wanted some share of the confiscated books, and ideology underlay the conflict. American Jewry was the largest, had significant institutions of Jewish learning, and, simply on that basis, claimed entitlement to the lion's share. But Israel, in Zionist perspective, was seen as the great spiritual center of the Jewish people worldwide. Surely, it should have the benefit of the necessary tools to sustain it. Scholem wrote to Baeck: "The view of the [Hebrew] University holds that Jerusalem is to be regarded as the central spiritual heir and successor of those institutions of Central European Judaism that perished in the catastrophe of our people."[43] The argument for England, as presented by Baeck, was the weakest. It was based mainly on the presence there of a large number of German Jews, who wanted to continue the German Jewish intellectual and scholarly traditions through new institutions of Jewish learning that they had already founded or would establish in the near future.[44] Baeck recognized the centrality of the Israeli claim and also that America had a right to some of the volumes. He argued only against a monopoly. To Salo Baron, he wrote that the former German Jews "ought to receive a share in the cultural property, which for a long time belonged to their congregations and institutions. Nor is this claim a merely sentimental one. It expresses the fact that the bonds still exist, and with them, a deeply felt consciousness of their heritage."[45]

In 1947, German Jews in London created a Society for Jewish Studies, which met weekly for lectures and was steadily growing. Soon it instituted regular academic courses. The society was much in need of Jewish books, having to rely on the relatively small library of one of the local congregations. Baeck, who had lost his own library when he was deported to Theresienstadt, was chosen to be the society's president and principal. He was also its most popular lecturer, drawing as many as 150 attendees whenever he spoke there. Especially on account of the society, Baeck was fervently interested in obtaining surviving volumes from the Lehranstalt in Berlin, where he had taught for so many years and whose books would be venerated and used by German Jews in England. He believed that, as the last survivor of the seminary's faculty administration, he should have a special say in the books' distribution.[46] The efforts in this area were at least partially successful: the society received confiscated books from the continent, thanks to the work of the Committee for Restoration of Jewish Books, Museums and Archives.[47] In 1956, the hoped-for successor to the Berlin Lehranstalt was established as a rabbinical seminary in London, which came to serve both Liberal and Reform Judaism in Great Britain, as it still does today. When Leo Baeck died later that same year, it was given the name Leo Baeck College.

A New Germany

For Leo Baeck, the fact that Chancellor Konrad Adenauer was willing to pay reparations to the State of Israel and to persecuted Jews everywhere was an indication that Germany was beginning to accept responsibility for its crimes. It was not simply a matter of money; rather, the willingness of the German people to make reparations, Baeck told the *Aufbau*, was an important indication of how the new Germany related to the value of justice.[48] But that was insufficient reason for Baeck to forgive the German people for its crimes. He made his view clear that forgiveness is something carried out solely by one individual with regard to another. As for himself, "I am personally ready to forgive the evil that was done to me personally. But to forgive a people—that right belongs to God alone."[49] Baeck did not believe in collective guilt, but he did insist that the German people as a whole had a collective responsibility for what had occurred.[50] In a private letter, he distinguished, with uncharacteristic sarcasm, the perpetrators from their few active opponents. He did not deny that there had always been—and that there were now—morally conscientious people in Germany, but they were few: "I myself have valuable friends there, with whom I maintain an ongoing connection. I am not well versed in the literature on cannibal tribes, but perhaps even among them there were isolated admirable people who abstained from the preparation and enjoyment of human flesh."[51] However, by 1952, the year in which Martin Buber received the Peace Prize of the German publishers in Frankfurt, Baeck had begun to speak of reconciliation between

Germany, the Jewish people, and the State of Israel—as long as such reconciliation was not accompanied by forgetfulness. There were many reminders. Writing in a postwar German periodical, he noted that the shadows of the dead were ever present. "They walk with every Jew and remain with him when he steps on a new soil. In the Land of Israel the watchword is 'gathering in the scattered.' The shadows too are gathered in there. They too demand to speak." Baeck does not mince words about the past readiness of the German people to submit to its worst elements. But reconciliation—peace between the Jewish and German peoples—is possible, if the unfettered nationalism and deification of the state that reigned in the past would give way to a new humanism in the future. In typical fashion, Baeck concludes on a hopeful religious note: "It can be of significance for humanity if this peace, regarded and prepared honestly—and that means also without forgetting—is, God willing, finally concluded."[52]

Following the Holocaust, many Jews refused to have any contact with the new Germany. For years, the Leo Baeck Institute, named in Baeck's honor, declined any representation there. Rabbi Alexander Schindler, later president of the congregational arm of American Reform Judaism, questioned Baeck's touching down in Germany. "The hand you shake there," he told Baeck, "may be the hand that held a dagger."[53] Nonetheless, Baeck chose to visit the new Germany in September 1948, close to six years after his deportation from German soil. It would be the first of a half-dozen such trips. During the initial journey, which lasted some three weeks, he traveled from city to city, beginning in Hamburg and concluding in Frankfurt. People who had known him, Jewish and Christian alike, sought him out to exchange a few words. For a man of seventy-five years, his schedule was astonishing. He lectured and preached, all without a text or even notes and, according to his guide, without repeating himself. In Hamburg, where he spoke in the auditorium of the university, his topic was "Thou Shalt Hope." In the philosopher Leibnitz's town of Hannover, he spoke on the future of Europe; in Düsseldorf, where he had once served as a community rabbi, he discussed the meaning of history; and at the University of Cologne, he devoted his remarks to the essence of democracy. Wherever he spoke, the halls were more than filled. Jews who had somehow survived came to hear him, as did government representatives, members of the occupation forces, and leaders of the churches. In Bremen, he delivered a Jewish New Year sermon to local Jews, and in Frankfurt, a Day of Atonement message to its new Jewish community. It was his longest trip to Germany. Not willing to elide the past,

Baeck used the trip for a shattering visit to the site of the Bergen-Belsen concentration camp. Later visits were not as extensive and were devoted to dealing briefly with one or another specific task.[54]

On one such later trip to Germany, in summer 1954, Baeck chose to speak on Moses Maimonides, commemorating the 750th anniversary of the death of the great medieval Jewish legist and philosopher. The lecture was held in Düsseldorf in the plenary chamber of the state parliament of North Rhine-Westphalia. In the audience, aside from the Jewish community, was an array of prominent individuals drawn from politics, diplomacy, and academe. Non-Jews filled the hall to capacity, wanting to hear a leading Jewish thinker reflect on the most important Jewish intellectual of the Middle Ages. What Baeck especially emphasized in his lecture was Maimonides' remarkable independence. In a time of upheaval, the Rambam, as Jewish tradition calls him, had succeeded in remaining loyal to the principles of his faith while participating actively in the Islamic intellectual world of his environment. He had been both a man of science and a man of faith. For Baeck, Maimonides was a model of integrity, a scholar and community leader who had withstood the pressure of external forces and preserved his Jewish identity. Thus, Baeck held, Maimonides' life could serve as a challenge for the present. He concluded: "That was this man, Rabbi Moses ben Maimon, the Rambam. Recalling him implies directing a question to ourselves."[55]

Among those in attendance at Baeck's Düsseldorf lecture was the president of the Federal Republic of Germany, Theodor Heuss. As Heuss descended the flight of stairs from the building after a reception following the lecture, he clasped the hands of the Jew and the Christian who were accompanying him and said: "This lecture by Dr. Baeck was for me one of my most beautiful experiences." And, noticing hundreds of Düsseldorf citizens waiting outside to see him, he added: "But just as great is my joy at seeing that so many Germans have been standing on the street half the night to await their government officials, although they know that they have just been with the Jews."[56] In the 1930s, Heuss was a passive opponent of Nazism; now he sought to shape a very different Germany. It had become one of the president's objectives to accept a "collective shame" with regard to Germany's recent past and to deter all those who sought to suppress that ignominy. Baeck had fleetingly made Heuss's acquaintance before the war, thanks to Otto Hirsch, Heuss's friend during their years together as university students in Württemberg. At that time, Baeck held more profound conversations with Heuss's dynamic wife, Elly Heuss-Knapp, who was well versed in

Figure 7. Leo Baeck (right) with Theodor Heuss, first president of the Federal Republic of Germany, in 1947. Courtesy of Leo Baeck Institute, New York.

Christian theology. After the war, at the president's invitation, Baeck regularly visited Heuss at his home during trips to Germany, and they developed high regard for each other. To Ludwig Meidner, an artist friend who had painted Baeck's portrait in 1931, he wrote: "It is, if I may say so, a piece of history for the German people that this man is the president of the West German Republic."[57] Baeck and Heuss found that they differed on whether Christianity was, as Baeck had held, a form of romantic religion. But their relationship developed an openness to the point that Baeck, with obvious reference to the 1930s but also as a veiled warning for the present, could, in honor of Heuss's seventieth birthday, write forthrightly to the president about how the German people had allowed bourgeois morality all too easily to decay into immorality. When called upon to act, people had become frightened. Fear had replaced independent thought, community given way to the mass.[58] As a result of their relationship, Heuss came to see Baeck as a modern Nathan the Wise,[59] while Baeck, in turn, regarded Heuss as a hopeful indicator for the new Germany. When Heuss nominated Baeck to receive in London the German government's highest civil order, the Great Cross of Merit, Baeck did not refuse the honor.[60]

Baeck came to believe that, under the aegis of men like Heuss, a new Jewish community in Germany might, after all, be able to develop, even if he did not believe that it could flourish to the same degree as it had in the past. In any event, Jewish communities were being established in both West and East Germany, and Baeck felt obligated to assist them in any way that he could—without returning to live there himself.[61] The small new Jewish communities, Baeck noted on his visits and through correspondence, were very different in religious orientation from what he had known before the war. Earlier, German Jewry had comprised mostly liberal and moderately conservative Jews. Now the majority were either adherents of Orthodox Judaism or "indolent" individuals, perfectly happy to leave the communities under Orthodox control.[62] Moreover, the earlier class of educated Jews was missing. Many congregants were now of Eastern European origin, lacking any direct connection to the traditions of German Jewry.

Not all were either fully observant or indifferent. There was also a minority of non-Orthodox Jews, some of them served by rabbis who had been Leo Baeck's students at the Liberal seminary in Berlin. They now called upon their former teacher to advise them about practical problems that they encountered in leading their congregations. Though he lived abroad, Baeck was the authority to whom they turned. Their principal concerns related to the religious status of non-Jews. Should non-Jewish wives be buried in a Jewish cemetery? Who was to be considered Jewish, with regard to marriage with a Jew? Was a conversion necessary for someone who had been baptized under duress?[63] Baeck's responses made considerable reference to the traditional literature of Jewish law as he searched out rabbinic prooftexts for his views and looked for examples of ancient practice that did not offend his conscience. He was sufficiently conservative to urge one disciple to cover his head when engaged in religious teaching, not only when leading a worship service. On the matter of separating the sexes during worship, Baeck's views had not changed since the Weimar years. Once again, giving expression to his concern with inappropriate verbal intercourse between the sexes, he wrote that "customs and forms belong to the things that are a useful brake in revolutionary times. The separation of the sexes in the House of God, which, by the way, can also be found here and there in the Calvinist domain, lends the service a completely unique dignity."[64] His recommendation was the same as it had been earlier: most desirable was to create a section for those worshipers who sought mixed seating and another for those who did not.

A principal religious issue causing conflict between the Orthodox authorities in Germany and the Liberal rabbis was the question of conversion to Judaism, which the former discouraged. Writing to Rabbi Steven Schwarzschild, then a Liberal rabbi in Berlin, Baeck argued that subjective factors, not only legal ones, should play a role in deciding whether to accept a prospective convert:

> I have often encountered cases regarding which, from the standpoint of religious law, I could have no hesitation about accepting a certain individual but I declined to accept him because factors of sexual morality arose against the acceptance. On the other hand, occasionally I had no hesitation about accepting someone, although I had to give the regulations of religious law a wide interpretation, because the personal human impression I received said to me that it is necessary to do so. . . . When I was in Germany last year, I always answered the manifold questions that were directed to me in this regard to the effect that the person and his experience should be taken into consideration and that the decision that followed should be rendered accordingly.[65]

Baeck, who eschewed dogmatism in theology, similarly opposed rigidity in practice.

America

The status that Baeck enjoyed in postwar Germany had its parallel in a community where his name had been known by very few before the war: among the Jews of the United States. As early as 1945, and only months after his reunion with his family in London, Baeck, as noted earlier, came to America to raise philanthropic funds for the United Jewish Appeal. On that trip, the Jewish Theological Seminary of America, the rabbinical school of American Conservative Judaism, presented him with an honorary degree. His sponsor was Abraham Joshua Heschel, Baeck's former student at the Lehranstalt, who was soon to become a prolific Jewish theologian. Baeck was pleased to learn that Heschel had found a productive role for himself in American Jewry.[66] What set the two men apart was that whereas the thirty-eight-year-old Heschel's fame as a religious thinker and civil rights activist still lay in the future, Baeck had become a sort of celebrity, enhanced by an aura that surrounded the courageous survivor. And Baeck was more than willing to let his celebrity be used for those causes in which he believed.

No group was more eager to take advantage of his fame than the Union of American Hebrew Congregations, the collection of synagogues now known as the Union for Reform Judaism. Its enterprising president, Rabbi Maurice Eisendrath, decided, in the first months of 1948, to lead an "American Jewish Cavalcade" from city to city to build support for Reform Judaism. With Leo Baeck as its principal speaker, this religious revival of sorts would draw attention wherever it went. And so Eisendrath invited Baeck to make a second trip to the United States. He would participate in his official capacity as president of the World Union for Progressive Judaism, the international organization of which the UAHC was a constituent. Impressed by the vigor of American Jewry, Baeck suggested that, although the headquarters of the WUPJ had been in England since its founding in 1926, he was hopeful that soon it would be transferred to the larger and more dynamic Jewry of America.[67]

In the United States, Baeck managed an extraordinarily busy schedule, just as he had in Germany. Undeterred by his heavy accent, people came as much to see as to hear him. In New York, he gave a series of lectures at the Jewish Institute of Religion, the rabbinical seminary that had been founded in 1922 by the Zionist leader and "Liberal" (a term he preferred to "Reform") Rabbi Stephen Wise. From New York, Baeck went to Florida and California; then to Detroit, Pittsburgh, Chicago, Boston, and other cities—a total of eleven cities from coast to coast. On this trip and on others, he enjoyed visiting Albert Einstein at Princeton, who, over the years, had become a very close friend. Baeck's purpose on the 1948 trip, as he wrote in a letter, was both public and private: "to quicken the spiritual heartbeat of American Israel" and also "to see again the people from the dear old forgotten Jewish communities of Germany."[68] Those former German Jews, now in America, were as grateful for such reunions as their counterparts in England had been when Baeck first arrived there from Theresienstadt. The *Aufbau* reported that Baeck's talks and lectures showed no trace of his ghetto experience. His speech sparkled, his gaze was bright and clear, and his gait was upright and energetic.[69]

Baeck greatly admired the spirit of mutual respect that reigned among the major political parties in American elections, a quality that he found extraordinary. Whereas Weimar had failed as a democracy, America had succeeded in enshrining it in its political ideology. He was deeply impressed that a disputed election could be followed by an honest working together. "Here it is not a matter of mere form that the losing candidate is the first to congratulate the victor; the opponent remains a fellow citizen."[70] In an interview with a reporter from an American weekly, Baeck expressed his regard not only for the Jews of America but also for what the United States had represented during the Nazi years and what it could become in the future. America, he said, meant something special "to all of the Jews of Europe who at one time or another, like me, were imprisoned and held in the clutch of despair. To me, America has always meant hope. We could live without food and without clothes, but we could not live without hope, and so long as there was an America, we knew that it would be our salvation. And on this visit of mine to America, the first feeling that came to me was that America had become the center of the world. Perhaps even more than that, it had become like an Atlas and was carrying the world on its shoulders."[71] Baeck had praised Woodrow Wilson's unsuccessful attempt to bring the United States into the League of Nations following World War I; he now expressed appreciation for America's willingness to dedicate its strength and its idealism to the idea of the United Nations.[72]

Baeck's status was such that prominent American politicians and public figures were eager to meet with him. On February 11, 1948, after laying a wreath at the grave of Franklin Roosevelt at Hyde Park, he was the luncheon guest of his widow, Eleanor. At New York's City Hall, he was received by Mayor William F. O'Dwyer, to whom Baeck expressed gratitude for the overseas relief that the mayor had directed in the early days of liberation from the camps. He held a lengthy conversation with President Truman, who impressed Baeck with his profound piety and an idealism that Baeck likewise attributed to some of the former presidents of the United States.[73] He urged the current president to do what he could to alleviate the plight of the displaced persons, the homeless following the war. The suffering of Jewish DPs

Figure 8. Leo Baeck delivering the invocation at the United States House of Representatives on February 12, 1948. The chaplain of the House is standing behind him. Courtesy of Leo Baeck Institute, New York.

had become another of Baeck's moral concerns: "Bring the displaced Jews out of the camps in Germany and make them 'placed' persons in Palestine or in other countries," he urged. "Give them a place of their own right, and a right to their own place."[74]

The greatest honor that accrued to Baeck during his visit was the invitation to deliver the opening prayer at a session of the U.S. House of Representatives. Although more than fifty rabbis had preceded him (the first being in 1860), it was a privilege not previously bestowed upon a non–North American rabbi.[75] It was especially meaningful to Baeck that the date chosen—probably by chance—was the anniversary of Abraham Lincoln's birth. Baeck had long admired the American Civil War president for his integrity and courage. When he visited Washington in 1930, he declared the Lincoln Memorial the most beautiful site in the city. While in New York, he spent some time in Harlem, "the local Negro area." In 1940 in Berlin, he had read anew Lincoln's "magnificent" Gettysburg Address, and had noted in a letter that at its end, Lincoln expressed the hope "that this nation, under God, shall have new birth of freedom." To which Baeck added, with scarcely veiled reference to Germany: "The question is there. The answer?"[76] Now he was given the opportunity to express his great respect for Lincoln and at the same time to include in his prayer a central element of his own religious philosophy:

> Our Father, our God, we pray unto Thee on this day on which six-score and nineteen years ago was born that man who came to be Thy servant, "the man in whom is the spirit," and who for the sake of this land became witness and testimony of humanity, herald of Thy command and Thy promise, to the everlasting blessing of this country and of mankind. . . . Almighty God, Thou choosest people and selectest nations "to bring them into the place which Thou hast prepared"; Thou changest the times and the seasons; Thou makest history enter the world. Thy servant, Abraham Lincoln, in a message to Congress, said, "We cannot escape history," so help us, O God, that we may not evade history, but may we be granted history.[77]

Encapsulated in this invocation is Baeck's conviction that a transcendent element is always present as history's driving force for good, though the source of that force be shrouded in mystery. In Baeck's words: "It is not that which is limited, that which arises from the human world, but rather it is the divine that makes history."[78] According to Baeck's interpretation, when Lincoln said that "we cannot escape history," he was saying in essence that we are unable to evade the divine moral imperative that, through responsive human action, drives history forward. After the tragedy that the world had just experienced, Lincoln's words that we cannot escape history served Baeck as a prelude to his own fervent hope for a divinely inspired history that would move humanity toward a better time.

Baeck's 1948 visit also brought him to Hebrew Union College in Cincinnati, the rabbinical seminary of Reform Judaism, established by Rabbi Isaac Mayer Wise in 1875. There, during regular semester-long stays until 1953, he was able to resume the teaching without which his life seemed incomplete, and also to have sufficient time for his scholarship, which was

Figure 9. Leo Baeck with Eugen Täubler to his right, Selma Stern Täubler to his immediate left, and Manja Guttmann, wife of Professor Alexander Guttmann, with the three Guttmann children in Cincinnati (1948). Courtesy of Leo Baeck Institute, New York.

greatly assisted by the college's outstanding Jewish library. In Cincinnati, his pace was relaxed, since he was required to give only a single weekly lecture course for the seniors. The college supplied him with a comfortable suite in the dormitory, where students would frequently come to engage him in conversation on all manner of subjects.[79] But few students were able to relate fully to his lectures. He was a figure to be admired, but his insights were lost on all but a small cadre, some of whom were themselves from Germany and who became his disciples. Baeck was pleased that several American university professors, apparently more easily capable of following his trains of thought, were drawn to his course, as well.

Baeck had more in common with the German Jews who had settled in Cincinnati than he did with most of the American students. Among them

Figure 10. Leo Baeck with young people at Hebrew Union College in Cincinnati (undated). Courtesy of American Jewish Archives, Cincinnati.

was Franz Landsberger, a historian of Jewish art, who was one of eleven German Jewish scholars, including Heschel, whom—despite severe opposition from the U.S. State Department—Hebrew Union College had brought to Cincinnati, thus saving them from likely death at the hands of the Nazis.[80] Landsberger, who was director of the Jewish Museum in Berlin until it was forced to close, was sent off to the Sachsenhausen concentration camp following the November pogrom of 1938. While in Cincinnati, he published his groundbreaking *History of Jewish Art.* A great admirer of Baeck, Landsberger spent many hours with him in Landsberger's Cincinnati home.[81] Selma Stern, an outstanding historian of German Jewry and the wife of Eugen Täubler, a historian of ancient Rome, was another valued acquaintance. Baeck had known and admired her in Germany. Now, having escaped from Germany at the last minute, she was living with her husband in Cincinnati, still doing research and publishing important work while employed as an archivist at the American Jewish Archives on the Hebrew Union College campus. During his stays in Cincinnati, Baeck was a regular guest in her home, saw her often on the street, and visited her at her desk in the archives. Stern greatly admired Baeck for his steadfastness in Nazi Germany. Of her conversations with him in Cincinnati, she wrote: "I can discuss everything with him, personal, human, scholarly. . . . These talks . . . have repeatedly lent me strength."[82]

A personal joy for Leo Baeck, who was regularly accompanied to Cincinnati by his granddaughter, Marianne, was that during her stays there with him she met a rabbinical student, A. Stanley Dreyfus, who would soon become her husband and carry on the Baeck family's rabbinical tradition.[83]

Israel

In addition to traveling to Germany and America following the war, Baeck visited Palestine in 1947—and, four years later, the new State of Israel. In the summer of 1947, he spent seven weeks traveling about the country. Over the years, he had become an enthusiastic cultural Zionist and ever more cognizant of the role that the Jewish settlement in the ancient land would play in the Jewish world. Shortly after the establishment of the state, he put it most strongly: "The destiny of Palestine will be our destiny. We are connected with a Jewish Palestine. It is our future which we build up there."[84] He could rhapsodize over what had been accomplished and, though with hesitation, see the return to Zion in religious terms. It was "as if ordained by Providence" that "the old soil of the fathers, the land of Israel, has become Jewish soil, not only a place of refuge, but a site for building and at the same time, as it were, a place of world history."[85] In Baeck's eyes, the Zionist project was rational in purpose but also mystical in significance, a refuge for the survivors and at the same time a hope for the future. "There cannot be Jewish hope, spiritual, moral, messianic hope," Baeck told the twenty-fifth-anniversary conference of the World Union for Progressive Judaism in 1951, "without embracing Israel."[86] A year later, he wrote to Lily Montagu that, while in Israel in 1951, he had emphasized the intention to establish a rabbinical seminary in Jerusalem. But he warned that it "must be the concern of the whole of Jewry" and not "ensnared by political orthodoxy, and quite especially [not] by American Jewry."[87] Likewise, he thought that someday someone would courageously urge that the World Union be centered in Israel.[88] But he also expressed displeasure over the discrimination that Progressive rabbis in Israel suffered at the hands of a politically controlling Orthodox rabbinate. The state did not—and still does not—recognize marriages conducted by any rabbis not authorized to do so by Israel's chief rabbinate. Asked to render a written opinion on the subject, Baeck warned of the severe damage that such a policy rendered to Jewish unity. If the policy were not revoked, it would lead to a profound schism within the Jewish people, not unlike what had occurred between the Hasidic movement and its opponents in the eighteenth century.[89] In a personal letter, he condemned the refusal of the Israeli Orthodox rabbinate to apply Jewish law flexibly for the sake of allowing oppressed women, the so-called *agunot*, to gain divorces from their recalcitrant husbands.[90] But these limitations did not diminish Baeck's positive feelings for Israel and for Zionist attachment to it. When, after the establishment of the state, he detected a waning of Zionism among young Jews in America, he urged initiating new ties that could bind the next generation to their brothers and sisters in Zion.[91]

Baeck's 1947 trip took him throughout the country, from its northern border to the Negev in the south. Necessarily, he visited those places, such as the collective settlement of Shavei Zion ("Returners to Zion") and the kibbutz of Hazore'a ("The Sower"), where German Jews had settled. As he traveled, he recalled his earlier visit in 1935 and its bittersweet memories. On that trip, his wife, Natalie, only two years before her death, had accompanied him, "and now it always seemed as if she were with me once more and was speaking to me."[92] In keeping with Zionist ideology of the time, Baeck argued that reclaiming "desert, swamp and rocky desolation" entitled Jews to the land that they had made fertile. It was nothing less than "a commandment of life to give life to the soil."[93] What especially impressed Baeck about Israel was its pioneering spirit and its social structure, the willingness to engage in hard labor to fructify the soil and establish a utopian form of socialism that was not based on class conflict. He compared the settlers to pilgrim fathers; like them, the Jewish agriculturists sought to implant a new spirit in the land, a social idealism that transcended political differences.[94] Baeck went so far as to suggest that the State of Israel was not a state in the old European sense, but in a new one: it was a social community, a "socialism in freedom," as envisaged by the German Jewish sociologist Franz Oppenheimer. Nothing was forced on anyone, and everything was accomplished voluntarily within the framework of the collective.[95] Within that context, the Jewish settlers pointed toward a future that moved away from the state domination that had been so destructive in the European past and toward the individual, the communal, and the universal—values that Baeck hoped would everywhere characterize the period after the war and the Holocaust.

But would the State of Israel meet the test that Germany had failed? Would it become a state that transcended state-oriented interests for the sake of human ones? Baeck put it this way: "Now on the old holy soil there is the State of Israel. Where there is a state, there may appear the head of that demon of state interest, of the reason of state. Thus it shall be shown whether there too, and there foremost, Judaism proves to be universal religion."[96] If the extant report can be believed, on at least one occasion Baeck expressed the wish to "spend his remaining years in the Holy Land."[97]

It is not surprising that among Zionist leaders, Baeck favored the moderation of a Chaim Weizmann to the aggressive statism of a David Ben-Gurion, as well as preferring the diplomatic approach of a Stephen Wise to the militancy of an Abba Hillel Silver.[98] Speaking to reporters in New York a few months after his 1947 visit, he glowingly described the relations between Jews and Arabs in a manner reminiscent of Theodor Herzl's utopian novel *Old-New-Land*. When a young reporter asked: "How are the Jews going to get along with the Arabs in Palestine?" Baeck responded:

> They will get along with them if they are left alone, because 95 percent of the Arabs in Palestine are satisfied to have the Jews in Palestine and happy that they are there. This past summer, whenever I visited a Jewish colony, the first question I asked was: "how are your relations with your Arab neighbors," and the answer was always—yes, always—"our relations are good," or "of the best." Let the Jews and the Arabs alone and they will live together and be friends. You must know that there is one reason why all people should help the Jews in Palestine, and that is because what they are trying to do is to create not in theory but in actuality a true fraternity of mankind in Palestine—a real democracy.[99]

However, Baeck was not so naïve as to believe that what he may have heard from some of the rural settlers and wished to convey to an inquiring reporter represented the full reality. A month later, shortly before Israel's Declaration of Independence, he joined his long-standing acquaintance Albert Einstein in an appeal sent to the *New York Times*. It deplored the fact that "both Arab and Jewish extremists are today recklessly pushing Palestine into a futile war." At a time when Arab contingents and members of the Jewish Irgun were both engaging in acts of terror, the signatories said that it was their duty "to declare emphatically that we do not condone methods of terrorism and of fanatical nationalism any more if practiced by Jews than if practiced by Arabs." Baeck associated with men living in Palestine who sought reconciliation between Arab and Jew. Among them were Judah Magnes, president of the Hebrew University; Martin Buber; and Kurt Wilhelm, rabbi of the Liberal congregation in Jerusalem. Their appeal insisted that "Jewish immigration into Palestine must be permitted to the optimal degree." But it did not insist on a separate Jewish state.[100] Baeck thought that the partition of Palestine into a Jewish and an Arab state meant balkanization—two small states, neither of which would be wholly viable. Nevertheless, shortly before the positive partition vote in the United Nations in November 1947, he realized that the time had come to acquiesce. If mutually beneficial, economic cooperation could be established, the effects of balkanization could be minimized.[101]

Following Israel's successful War of Independence in 1948, Baeck remained deeply attached to the Land of Israel and to its Jewish inhabitants. But he refused to close his eyes to what he regarded as a tragedy that occurred in the process: the displacement of hundreds of thousands of Palestinian Arabs. It was, he maintained, his deep love for the land and its people that forced him to see the situation clearly. He wrote: "There is a proverb that love makes people blind, but if ever a proverb was false and deceptive, it is that one. It is not love that makes people blind, but coldness, indifference, hate. Love makes one see. One must see with the glance of love in order to understand, to reach the truth. Whoever sees in this way recognizes that something great is being accomplished here [in Israel], that a new society is being created. Certainly we must also look upon much that was unjust, un-Jewish, much from which we have to turn away in deep pain. It is love which sees that, too, and sees it with the pain of love."[102] The question was what the Jews, many of them refugees, should be obliged to do about the Arab refugees produced by a war that the Arabs had themselves initiated—but for whom, Baeck believed, the Jews bore some responsibility. There could be no peace with the Arab world surrounding Israel, without "a sensible and prompt solution of the refugee problem."[103]

A small circle of British Jews, including Leo Baeck, set out to see whether, at least in some limited fashion, they could alleviate the suffering of the Palestinian refugees. They adopted the name "Jewish Society for Human Service" and within it created the "Committee for Relief in the Middle East." Baeck served as president of the society. Its chairman was Norman Bentwich, a lifelong, moderate cultural Zionist who was, for a time, attorney general in British Mandate Palestine and was professor of international relations at the Hebrew University. The third central figure in the leadership was the left-wing humanitarian and publisher Victor Gollancz. At the group's first meeting, in the spring of 1948, Baeck called for action. A pamphlet soliciting donations announced the intended evenhandedness of its objective: that it was the committee's purpose to aid both Jews and Arabs who were in need. "We did not and do not think that Arab suffering is in any way more 'important,' or calls for greater effort to alleviate it, than Jewish suffering, which indeed for nearly two thousand years has surpassed all bearable measure. It was rather that we could not and cannot feel that the suffering of Arabs, or of whatever other people, is in any way less important than the suffering of our fellow Jews."[104] The committee intended to assist Jews and Arabs in the State of Israel and then to extend relief to Arab refugees beyond its borders. For Baeck and the others, it meant the application of Jewish universalism in a Jewish national context. According to Bentwich, Baeck expansively said to the group: "This is the Jewish rule: we cannot stand by the Kingdom of God without standing for human need. Helping distressed people, we help our soul as well as all mankind."[105] Messianic hopes, however much Baeck cherished them, were not to overshadow immediate needs. Twice the leadership sought funds through letters in the *Jewish Chronicle*, Britain's leading Jewish newspaper.[106] But the results were meager, and what relief work could be undertaken was limited to Jews and Arabs within the borders of the Jewish state. In any case, Arab governments surrounding Israel would not accept refugee relief from a Jewish source.

On his two trips to the Land of Israel following the war, Baeck was well received, especially by old friends and acquaintances who sympathized with his universalistic outlook. In 1951, Gershom Scholem greeted Baeck at the airport and hosted him in his Jerusalem home, where he also held a farewell for him at the end of his stay; at Passover, Baeck was the Scholems' guest for the seder.[107] Much of Baeck's time during his two trips was taken up with speeches and lectures. In 1947, he spoke to university students in Hebrew and to new immigrants in German. In 1951, the Hebrew University invited him to deliver the Orde Wingate Lecture, named for the senior British army officer who had assisted the prestate Jewish military. Baeck, who gave his talk, "The Psychological Root of the Law," in English, stressed the importance of law as the element that provides continuity and stability in society as well as in religion: "Law is the continuing and lasting element in virtue of which creation remains creation, and revelation remains revelation, and the covenant remains the covenant." Law provided the negative moral command, "the great 'thou shalt not,'" the essential predecessor to the "thou shalt," which is its consequence.[108]

With all of Baeck's love for Israel and his hopes for it, he had to recognize that the ancient homeland was not, at least demographically during the years immediately following the war, the single spiritual center of world Jewry. It was apparently the Jewish philosopher and historian Simon Rawidowicz who first came up with the idea that the Jewish people had figuratively assumed the shape of an ellipse, which has not one focus but two: the Land of Israel and the Diaspora of Israel.[109] It is unclear whether Baeck adopted this idea from Rawidowicz or came to it on his own. In either case, the notion of a people with two foci, each having a particular vocation, became a key element in Baeck's Jewish worldview. In a lecture delivered in New York in 1950, he argued that such a division had characterized Judaism frequently in the past, in ancient and in medieval times. Now an ellipse was again present, with its revived ancient focus being the Land of Israel and its new one being the Jews of America. Each of the two, Baeck argued, had its particular function: American Jewry to assist Israel "to keep the breadth of horizon, the universality of thought and outlook"; and Israeli Jewry to maintain the essential "strength of peculiarity" within its borders and beyond. Together the two centers could safeguard the Jewish heritage of revelation everywhere and retain a sense of the great task of bringing that heritage to actuality.[110]

Rethinking Christianity

In the wake of the catastrophe that devastated Jews in almost every country that fell under Nazi control, in countries long devoted to Christianity, whether Protestant or Catholic, Baeck could not declare Judaism's daughter religion free of guilt. With more courage and more religious regard for Jews and Judaism, the churches might have prevented, or at least mitigated, the disaster. But, except for a few individuals, they chose to remain silent, thereby seriously damaging the stature of Christianity. A few months after his liberation from Theresienstadt, still stunned by the catastrophe, Baeck wrote of Christianity: "A religion which in days when force rises up against the idea, the denial of morality against the moral law, absolute obeisance to man against the fear of God, a religion which in such days wants to stand outside the battlefield, to hesitate and to follow the time, has buried a part of its soul. A religion which, in days that demand the word of religion, is silent has denied itself. . . . A religion which in earnest days did not call the world to account will sooner or later be called to account by world history."[111]

Baeck had long believed that Christianity, understood as a form of "romantic religion" that focused on the individual soul, was dangerously subservient to the state. He could scarcely retreat from that position after the support that some church leaders had given Hitler while others had chosen to remain silent when they learned of Jewish persecution.[112] It was not until April 1950 that the Evangelical Synod, meeting in Berlin-Spandau, passed a resolution expressing a measure of guilt. It stated: "We declare that on account of omission and silence before the God of mercy we have been complicit in the crime that was committed by members of our people against the Jews." Baeck thought that this statement represented a leap forward, even if it came five years later than it should have. It deserved appreciation, he thought, since—citing the English expression—"better half a loaf than no bread [at all]."[113]

Yet some Christian leaders clearly passed the test, and Baeck was pleased to spend time with them on his visits to Germany. In 1951, his former rabbinical student Peter Levinson, who had returned to Berlin as a Liberal rabbi, gave a reception for his teacher, attended by two prominent members of the anti-Nazi clergy: the Evangelical bishop Otto Dibelius, a leader of the independent Confessing Church; and the Reformed theologian Heinrich Grüber, who had been denounced for showing sympathy to the Jews.[114] When Cardinal Michael von Faulhaber of Munich died on June 12, 1952, Baeck published an appreciation of this Catholic opponent of the Nazi "deformation movement." Although Faulhaber had at one time been under the influence of the Christian religious doctrine that proclaimed God's curse upon the Jews, Baeck chose to accent the positive. He praised Faulhaber's command of the Hebrew language, but especially the willingness he had expressed to keep up friendly relations with the Jewish community even when it had become dangerous to do so. "His untiring voice, manifesting both his moral and his intellectual power, was heard. He never lost courage."[115] Following the Holocaust, Faulhaber vowed to do all in his power to tear antisemitism from the hearts of the Bavarian Catholics whom he served. During the last months of his life, Baeck developed a high regard for Albert Schweitzer, the great Lutheran scholar, theologian, and physician who had established a hospital in Africa and coined the expression "reverence for life." Baeck, who had at least one personal conversation with Schweitzer, admired the Nobel Prize winner, especially for his energetic personality: for the fervor that imbued his life and made his accomplishments possible.[116]

In these years, Baeck's scholarship, which had initially been largely polemical and apologetic, gradually became more balanced with regard to Christianity and Judaism and to the ties between them. He hoped that on the moral level, the relationship between the two faiths would become reciprocal: "To each other Judaism and Christianity will be admonition and warning: Christianity becoming Judaism's conscience, and Judaism Christianity's."[117] In London, it was not unusual for Baeck to attend Anglican services, where he found the sermons much superior to those he had heard delivered by Christians in Germany.[118] His goal was mutual respect arising from an understanding of one's own religion and appreciation for that of the other: "The more Judaism understands itself, the more it will realize the greatness which is in Christianity. The Christian Church should never forget that for her there can be no Bible without the Jewish Bible."[119] Whereas his earliest writing had stressed the Hebrew Prophets as models of unconditional commitment to morality, Baeck's later scholarship focused equally on the ancient Rabbis and then, in his last years, broadened to include a more sympathetic understanding of Paul.

An apologetic element indeed remained in Baeck's popular study of the Pharisees, which first appeared in 1927 and was reissued in an expanded form after the war. Like Abraham Geiger in the nineteenth century, Baeck wished to show that the Pharisees were not as pictured in the New Testament—that they were not detestable hypocrites but should, rather, be understood as they were described by Josephus and especially as they appeared in their own literature. They were, Baeck argued, a community that valued saintliness and committed itself to the teaching of the Oral Law; they were not a sect or a political party but "a movement within the Jewish people,"[120] the very terminology he had used to describe modern Liberal Judaism. Like the Prophets, the Pharisees were not enthusiasts for the ancient sacrificial service; for them, prayer could be its substitute and the synagogue a replacement for the Temple. Their designated opponents were not the followers of Jesus but rather the priests, a hierarchy that protected its own interests and resisted removing the teaching from their control and anchoring it—as the Pharisees sought to do—more broadly, in the people. Pharisees indeed prayed for the rebuilding of the Temple, a dream for which Baeck employs his favorite term of disfavor: "romanticism."[121] But more broadly, they set their eyes on the hoped-for and striven-for Kingdom of God. Their conviction that that kingdom had not yet come was the crucial point of their difference from Paul, whom Baeck now wanted to reconsider.

In 1952, in a Jewish journal, Baeck published an erudite article in English, which he called "The Faith of Paul." In sharp contradiction to Baeck's earlier treatment, Paul does not appear here as the source for a dangerous "romantic religion." Instead, he is presented as a Jew of his time, with all the sympathy and understanding for historical characters that Baeck long ago learned from Wilhelm Dilthey. If there was a polemical purpose in this study, it was to oppose the divisive tendency that had been fiercely displayed by Nazi theologians who sought to cut Paul off from his Jewish environment. For Baeck, Paul's separation from Judaism did not come from within but from influences originating outside ancient Palestine. Hellenistic thought, which flourished in Tarsus, and especially the widespread mystery cults of the time, made these influences felt. "Paul was carried away by them far outside the Jewish boundaries." Although he did not deny the validity of the Jewish law, he came to believe that the days of the Torah, which were to end upon the arrival of the Messiah, were concluded with the arrival of Jesus and that the days of the Messiah had begun. Thus, unlike the Jews of his time, "Paul did not preach expectancy of a future age. By proclaiming the resurrected Christ he proclaimed the presence of God's kingdom."[122] That separated him from his Jewish origins. But, Baeck stresses, he did not therefore despise his people. He finds the eleventh chapter of Paul's Letter to the Romans, which indicates Paul's belief that God did not reject the Jews, to be deeply moving. "The sincerity of this man, the depth of his feeling rooted in his Jewish people, are all revealed here."[123]

Earlier, to keep German Jews within their community, Baeck had stressed how Judaism differed from other faiths; now he balances the desire to point out his own faith's uniqueness with a new emphasis on what other religions have in common with it. Baeck notes that Judaism and Christianity possess the common heritage of the Hebrew Bible as well as the common hope for a better time, understood in Christianity as the Second Coming of the Messiah and in Judaism as an event that has not yet occurred. As for Islam, little separates it from Judaism, as medieval Jewish thinkers gladly acknowledged.

Both religions stress the oneness of God. However, Baeck notes, Islam and Judaism have become estranged because of the conflict in the Middle East. He concludes: "Everything depends on whether, even as in the Middle Ages it became a blessing for both, [so likewise today] a way be found from Islam to Judaism, from the Arab world to the Israeli world, a way from Israel and its religion to the Arab world and its religion."[124]

Baeck also notes that Islam has been remarkably successful in spreading its faith to others. In recent years, it had enjoyed great success, especially in Asia and Africa, just as Christianity had greatly increased its numbers in earlier times. Although missionizing remained an essential of the faith for many Christian groups, contemporary Islam was now proving to be more successful in this regard than Christianity or Judaism. Unlike other Jewish leaders, especially in the State of Israel, Baeck recognized and respected the urge to proselytism in Judaism's two daughter faiths, and he did not seek to set his own faith apart from them as more tolerant by its rejection. Proselytism, he believed, was the prerogative of every religion and an indication of the fervor with which its faithful adhered to it. It was dishonest to arrogate the right to proselytize only to one's own religion, but it was also a denigration of one's own faith if one believed it lacking in broader appeal.[125] Such turning away from the missionary task was an indication of "inner weakness and indolence or even a self-centeredness contradictory to the religious way."[126] Baeck had always been an advocate of converting non-Jews to Judaism—and more so now, after the losses sustained in the Holocaust. "We are in need of expansion for our own sake," he insisted.[127] But he was no longer convinced that the message had to be presented with an apologetics that omitted less palatable elements. As he wrote to a former student: "Only if we present our Judaism inclusive of its rough and sharp edges will it make an impression on persons of honest intent."[128]

People of the Commandment

The last years of Baeck's life did not represent a sharp break in his religious philosophy. He continued to believe in the twofold link that bound the individual to God: an awareness of the transcendent God whose essence remained mysterious; and the ineluctable moral commandment that issued from that God in every generation and to every person. But he also had new thoughts and—unavoidable for Baeck—engaged in new endeavors to instill

Figure 11. Leo Baeck (left) with Lily Montagu and Martin Buber (probably 1951). Courtesy of Leo Baeck Institute, New York.

his ideas in the minds of fellow Jews, as well as in those non-Jews who might be drawn to the message that Judaism had to offer.

The principal audience for his ideas now, as in the past, comprised those individuals who were serious about their Jewish faith but spiritually removed from its orthodox expression. Although he was hesitant to assume the responsibilities involved, Baeck continued as the titular leader of religiously progressive world Jewry for almost the entire remainder of his life, until frailty caused him to pass it on to Lily Montagu in 1953.[129] In the summer of 1946, he once again exercised his earlier role as president of the World Union for Progressive Judaism when he gave the principal address at the WUPJ international conference that year in London. In his address, Baeck expressed, more explicitly than he had in the past, the importance of tradition for Liberal Jews, even if official Orthodoxy had, to some extent, distorted it. The task, as he understood it, was neither finding fault with tradition nor agitating for further religious reform, but rather critical appreciation. Speaking in English, he said: "Tradition should not be a mere word for us. Jewish tradition stands on sacred soil; we must approach its gates with reverence and should have understanding also for the discipline and even for the ascetic traits that are interwoven with it; we should have understanding even—if one may use this expression—for its disheveled distinction. Understanding and reverence—these are of the very essence of Progressive Judaism."[130]

More than he had in the past, Baeck now stressed to Liberal Jews what he called "the true sense of the presence of God, of a devotional sphere that should continually flow into our life." Without it, he believed, Jewish existence would all too easily become empty, poetry would be squeezed out of the lives of Liberal Jews, and they would be overwhelmed by prose.[131] He continued to believe that ritual laws were not divine commandments in the same sense as moral ones, but he did think that they were essential for making Jews "conscious of the sublime command of the Divine Law," by which Baeck meant the moral law. He went on to suggest that perhaps Liberal Jews should develop their own laws of ritual practice "in a reformed manner"—which is precisely what the next generation of Reform Jews in America undertook when they began to issue "guides" for Jewish observance.[132] Baeck also argued that Conservative Judaism and Reform Judaism in the United States should not oppose each other but should rather assume complementary roles. The more broadly observant form of Judaism could make its more radical counterpart aware of the values in the practice of Jewish ritual traditions while the less traditional form of Judaism could exemplify the spiritual values contained in those same traditions.[133]

If the post-Holocaust Baeck renewed his admonition that Progressive Judaism could not sustain itself without looking inward for continuity and authenticity, he stressed even more the importance of looking outward in the hope of accomplishing something of value that reached beyond its own community. "An egoistic Liberal Judaism, which would only think of itself," he said in that same 1946 address, "which would forget that it has its task for the sake of the greater whole, such a Liberal, Progressive Judaism would be a contradiction in terms. It would be neither Liberal nor Progressive, nor would it be Jewish."[134] The central message of Judaism to the world was "to tell how far still is the way to the messianic days." Perhaps it was because of what the Jews had just suffered that he believed they had a special responsibility to declare the world's moral incompleteness and to oppose all those totalitarian forces that sought to impose a conscience-dominating absolutism upon persons and nations. Jews were required "never to be silent to any wrong, to any lie . . . but to oppose every lulling and manipulation of conscience."[135]

In 1953, in the last address that he was able to deliver personally at a conference of fellow Progressive Jews, Baeck laid out a new direction. In the past, Liberal Jews sought progress through political emancipation, which, for a time, they had gained in Germany and which they fully possessed in America. Further political progress was made for the Jewish people when it established its own state. It was now time for the Jewish citizen and the devotee of the Jewish people and its state to set as a new objective not the person but the Jewish religion, not religious reform but its application to the end that justice and love might reign over such tyranny as had disfigured the recent past. Jews believed, Baeck insisted, "in the constant task, and not in the achievements. With every new generation the problems of the world are born anew. We should not miss the time. Our religion should approach the world. Humanity, it seems, waits for us."[136] Baeck did not speak of specific actions, and the expectations were certainly large for a small people, but they were a challenge to Progressive Jews who in Germany had not succeeded in establishing a strong program of social justice. In new historical environments, their voice, calling for justice from out of their religious tradition, he believed, ought to be raised aloud.

Much as Baeck continued to be focused on the centrality of deeds in Judaism, he now stressed that an awareness of their origin was no less important than the acts themselves. Moral acts, he believed, originated in the realm of divine mystery, which set a border to rational inquiry even as it was the center of piety.[137] Science arrives at the mystery, and religion issues from it.[138] Deeds that did not flow from recognition of the mystery lacked the force that could be supplied only by their divine, if rationally unknowable, source. To his former associate at the Liberal seminary in Berlin, Rabbi Max Wiener, who in a groundbreaking work published as early as 1933, had written of a modern Judaism that goes beyond rational understanding, Baeck wrote in 1947: "Everything rational, after all, is rooted in the irrational and every commandment receives its power and its legitimation because it is rooted there. When the sentence 'Love your neighbor as yourself' [Lev. 19:18] is recited in that form, it is actually amputated. The sentence is not complete until the 'I am the Eternal, your God' is added to it."[139] For Baeck, a secular Judaism was a misunderstanding. He was deeply convinced that "he who does not grasp mystery will never grasp Judaism."[140] Awareness of the mystery, which

Baeck extended to the survival of the Jewish people, lay not in human reason but in the realm of feeling.[141] There could be no adequate Judaism that was purely rational. The war and what was later called the Holocaust only served to deepen the divine mystery. Baeck never attempted a theodicy, a rational explanation of the Jewish tragedy. For him, like the biblical Job, there could be no persuasive answer but only the acceptance of an unknowable and inexplicable Presence.[142] The Holocaust was overwhelming; perhaps in choosing not to dwell on it, Baeck was also fearful lest its traumatic memory overshadow a hoped-for Jewish future.

If it was not possible to provide a theological explanation for the recent past, it nonetheless remained possible, even after so horrendous a catastrophe, to harbor hope for what could lie ahead.[143] As Judaism without the mysterious commanding God was not Judaism, the same was true for a Judaism that abandoned faith in the future, a faith in what Baeck called "the great 'thou shalt hope!,' the messianic patience and the patient messianism."[144] This looking and striving for a better future was a life necessity, and not for Jews alone. "Perhaps," he once said, "a human being does not die until he no longer sees anything but the past and the present moment."[145] But for Baeck, hoping alone was insufficient, since it was ultimately a passive, if worshipful, stance. The messianic vision of justice and peace had to be combined with the commandment, the human task in striving toward it.[146] Judaism was as much a religion of "the way" as it was of the messianic goal. "The phrase 'the chosen people,' so often misunderstood, really means . . . : the people of the chosen way, of the way shown by God and chosen by man—the people of the categorical command and categorical trust, saved from illusion by the steadfastness of the deed, and from despair by the steadfastness of hope."[147]

In addition to his invited lectures in Great Britain, America, Germany, and Israel, Baeck conducted a weekly class in London, "The Monday Seminar." His audience for these lectures comprised refugee rabbis and laypersons who had managed to reach England. Some non-Jews, conversant in German, also came to hear him. Together they formed an intimate circle in which Baeck could feel at home, speak in his native German, and reflect more informally than he did in other settings. He used no text but only a few notes on a tiny sheet of paper. In this company, Baeck felt free to introduce personal experiences and feelings, as he had rarely done in earlier sermons or lectures. The writer Hans Bach, who regularly attended the lectures, remembered that when Baeck lovingly described the nature of childhood, one could sense the delight he felt when playing with his tiny great-grandchild. Conversely, one could note that when Baeck spoke harshly of Luther, his stress on coercion echoed his own experience in Nazi days, when silence had been imposed upon him.[148]

The subjects of the lectures, given in the first half of 1956, dealt principally with the successive epochs of Jewish history. Toward the end of his life, Baeck's thought turned increasingly to the history of the Jews; in these lectures, he approached the issue that all historians seeking to describe a longer stretch of time must consider: periodization. Like earlier historians of the Jews—specifically, the Galician thinker Nahman Krochmal and the German Heinrich Graetz—Baeck noted that, similar to the individual person, a people, as well, has its childhood, its youth, its time of strength and maturity, its increasing weakness, and, finally, its demise. For some peoples, the transformations occur quickly; for others, they require a longer time. What set Jewish history apart was that the Jewish people had gone through not one but several such periods, or, as Baeck prefers to call them, epochs. Whereas other peoples had not been able to recover from eventual decay, the Jewish people experienced repeated rebirth. When one center of Jewish settlement and learning declined, another took its place; the demise of one was replaced by the sprouting and growth of another; death was repeatedly averted by renaissance. "Rebirth is the beginning, the breakthrough," Baeck said, "the epoch is the expanse, the breadth which the reborn then prepares for itself in all the realm of its possibilities."[149] Of Jewish history, Baeck contends that it is a history of epochs, that is to say, it is a history of rebirths: with the Prophets a new epoch with new ideas is born; with the Rabbis an epoch emerges that is characterized by Jewish law even as the central ideas of the Prophetic epoch live on among the Rabbis, as they do in succeeding epochs. The centrality of essence has here given way to the centrality of historical evolution.

Baeck's Monday Seminar lectures, delivered near the end of his life, reveal a naturalistic theological position that is not explicit elsewhere. Of prayer, he says in these lectures that it is not to be understood as a dialogue but rather "when a person speaks with God, it is in the highest sense of the word a monologue. . . . The person speaks, as it were, with his highest self, with the revelation of God that is within him. . . . In the highest sense he is speaking with himself."[150] The implication is that God does not answer prayer, which here becomes not an outward directed petition but the quest for inner transformation.[151]

Figure 12. Leo Baeck engaged in writing, probably in London (undated). Courtesy of Leo Baeck Institute, New York.

These informal lectures remained incomplete and were not published until eight years after his death. While presenting them, Baeck was working assiduously on a more detailed view of the entirety of Jewish history, which would reach completion only with part 2 of his more formal history of the Jewish faith, *Dieses Volk: Jüdische Existenz* (This people: Jewish existence). This second and last major work, in its English translation called *This People Israel: The Meaning of Jewish Existence*, is comparable in scope to Baeck's *The Essence of Judaism*, but it is a very different work. It is not the *essence* of Judaism that concerns Baeck here but the *existence* of the Jewish people as the historical bearers of their religion. It is an attempt to convey the variety and fullness of all the Jewish people's spiritual epochs. Baeck's focus shifts back and forth across the boundary between the religion and the people, making clear that Jewish identity can be fully understood and internalized only by those who do not limit themselves to religion or history alone—that is, only by the individual who has adopted the values of both. Judaism and Jewish history, Baeck is now convinced, stand in a reciprocal relationship that can be fully penetrated only by the historian who also affirms the validity of religion: "One can grasp history only if one has penetrated into faith and one can understand faith only if one also comprehends history."[152]

Baeck had begun to write *Dieses Volk: Jüdische Existenz* while still in Berlin, continued it in the Theresienstadt ghetto whenever a scrap of paper and a quiet moment were at hand, and taken up the task anew in London after the war. The first of two parts appeared in 1955, and the second posthumously, two years later. In accordance with Baeck's wishes, the German text was published in the new Germany, perhaps because Baeck believed that the German nation was most in need of its message.[153] It had been prompted by his days of suffering, a time that he felt imposed a personal reassertion of this oppressed Jewish people in past and present: "In dark days this book was written," he wrote in the preface to the first volume. "At that time, when the destruction of Jewish life had been announced and widely inflicted, there was awakened in the person who then wrote these pages the need to render an account to himself, an account of this Jewish life, of this Jewish people."[154]

Dieses Volk: Jüdische Existenz eludes simple classification. It cannot be defined simply as history, theology, or philosophy, for it encompasses all three. Its tone is at times sober, but it also rises to rhapsody or, to use Baeck's favored German term, *Poesie*. Insofar as it is a history of the Jewish people, it is a history of its spirit and not of its body, a history of affirmations and of heights far more than of depths. It eschews denials and despair in favor of hope and expectation. It speaks of the mystery that requires commandment and of the commandment that requires mystery, and of the rebirths that blot out death. It is the Jewish people's answer, over the course of its history, to God's question: Will it be true to its moral task in the world?

The two volumes are not easy reading. For the most part, Baeck avoids specifics, frustrating the desire for concrete examples and arguments to support contentions. He introduces few dates, marks off Jewish history not by centuries but by millennia that, in turn, encompass the biblical period, the rabbinic, the medieval, and the modern, each an epoch—and each, after the first, launching a new rebirth that brings forth new questions and new responses. The work moves along on the spiritual plane, describing a highly idealized view of the Jewish people. One might call it a paean to the covenant binding Israel to its God from Abraham on through the millennia, a tribute rendered to "an eternal people." It is a deeply religious book, written from within Judaism, not an examination of it from the outside. In midrashic style, Baeck interprets—but more fundamentally, he testifies to—the ongoing relationship between God and the Jewish people. He is little interested in secular history; what matters is how Jews, in generation after generation, responded to God's demand for justice in the world, and how they sought to move forward in history on the path to the messianic goal.

In this work, Baeck shows respect for all the currents in Jewish history. Noting its influence during modern times, designated as the fourth millennium, he singles out the Romm Publishing House, which gained fame for printing the standard text of the Talmud along with its commentaries. He then writes appreciatively of the broad spectrum of modern Jewish thinkers and prominent personalities, in the East and in the West, Zionist and non-Zionist. He writes very little on the November pogrom of 1938 and the Holocaust that followed, and presents no evidence that the tragedy caused him to doubt God's presence. The book's challenge is not to God but to fellow Jews. Will they, in times of new tranquility, continue to harbor the messianic vision? Will they remain the people of the commandment?

For nearly the last twenty years of his life, Leo Baeck was a widower who had to live his life without the emotional support of his beloved Natalie. In 1950, he wrote of "the first great loneliness when, thirteen years ago, my wife was taken from me."[155] Then came the other lonelinesses as friends and associates were murdered. But he could speak a prayer of thanks that his daughter and her family were in London to comfort him. Although he lived with them, they provided a furnished room at an unrevealed location where he could do his scholarly work undisturbed by his many admirers. In quiet moments, his thoughts could turn to the future, inhabited by new generations that included his own progeny. And he could direct his imagination to the furthest horizon, to "the secret of the world beyond, the secret of eternity."[156] His eyes were becoming weaker, forcing him gradually to give up handwritten letters and resort to dictation; his writing grew wobbly and more difficult to read; and his hearing became deficient.[157] He became less formal, even sentimental. In April 1955, Baeck spent a few days in a London hospital after a motorcyclist knocked him down while he was crossing a street near where he lived. An intestinal operation forced a longer hospital stay in June. Yet even in the last months of his life, Baeck continued to be active, lecturing in Frankfurt, Münster, and London. And, of greatest importance to him, he was finishing the second volume of *Dieses Volk: Jüdische Existenz*, still reading the proofs a few days before his death. But to his distress, on Yom Kippur of 1956, he was unable to attend religious services.[158] On November 2 of that year, Leo Baeck died and was buried in the Jewish cemetery on

Hoop Lane. The president of Germany sent a wreath to the funeral; the Israeli ambassador was present.[159] A year later, when his gravestone was unveiled, its text, as ordained by Baeck himself, presented a final example of his self-effacement and humility. It said nothing of his status and achievements but was confined to his name, dates of birth and death, and the simple Hebrew inscription *migeza rabanim*, "from a lineage of rabbis."[160]

Epilogue

The Icon and the Person

Until the end of World War II, the name Leo Baeck remained unfamiliar outside Germany. That changed radically when, after his remarkable survival, the story of his experience received broad attention. Although Baeck had never been a self-aggrandizer, he now became a celebrity and a symbol of Jewish spiritual resistance and personal courage. He was seen as the incarnation of all that was admirable in German Jewry and in Liberal Judaism. Several Jewish institutions desired to preserve his memory.

These institutions were spread broadly across the Jewish world and were of different types, even though all were devoted to Liberal Judaism or Jewish scholarship or both. The first person to want Baeck's name for a synagogue was the refugee Liberal rabbi Fritz Steinthal, who—in 1944, while his teacher at the Lehranstalt was still in Theresienstadt—wrote to Baeck's daughter in London for permission to name his synagogue in Buenos Aires for Leo Baeck. But the response was negative: Ruth feared that it might endanger her father and, moreover, "whoever is familiar with my father knows how averse he is to every such form of esteem."[1] However, during the last years of his life and after his death, one institution after another chose to tie itself to the increasingly venerated name of Leo Baeck: in Israel, the Leo Baeck School in Haifa, founded by Baeck's colleague Max Elk; in London, the Leo Baeck College, a rabbinical seminary for the British Liberal and Reform movements, and also a Leo Baeck Fellowship; in Los Angeles, the newly formed Leo Baeck Temple, whose rabbi, Leonard Beerman, was a radical proponent of social justice and reconciliation among nations; in Canada, a Leo Baeck Day School in Toronto; in Germany, the Leo Baeck Foundation supporting Liberal Judaism, Leo Baeck Street in the Zehlendorf section of Berlin, and the Leo Baeck Prize, the highest award given by the Central

Association of Jews in Germany; and in New York, Jerusalem, and London—and eventually also in Germany—the Leo Baeck Institute, dedicated to the preservation and critical study of the German Jewish legacy.

The LBI, as the institute came to be known, was established in Jerusalem in 1955 by, among others, Gershom Scholem, Martin Buber, and Siegfried Moses, who would be its second international president, following Baeck himself. Leo Baeck was unable to attend the initial meeting, but he wrote a letter of encouragement to the founders, in which he referred to the unbroken tradition of learning and teaching in both Eastern and Western Ashkenazi Jewry: although their institutions of learning had been destroyed, "the spirit cannot and will not be annihilated; it is summoned to live on. Books may be burnt, but what they say remains winged and seeks its [new] location."[2]

During his lifetime and even more so after his survival in Theresienstadt and his death, Baeck's contemporaries described him in words of praise that, in some instances, virtually exceeded the human and jarred with what was Baeck's own sense of self. In an article in the *Atlantic Monthly*, Rabbi Joshua Loth Liebman, who had met Baeck on a few occasions after the war, called him "a saint for our times" and compared his "authentic human greatness" to that of Rabbi Akiba in the Jewish tradition, Francis of Assisi and Albert Schweitzer among Christians, and Gandhi in Hinduism.[3] Accolades only slightly less exuberant came from numerous sources: he was "the greatest Jew I have ever known . . . the most civilized man I have ever encountered"; "a symbol of civilized humanity facing bestiality, the father who would not abandon his children"; "no generation . . . has found a leader of greater stature than Dr. Baeck."[4] The chairman of the Robert Bosch Works, who was a supporter of Baeck's during the Nazi years, declared that he was "one of the very few figures truly worthy of respect in a time so impoverished of authentically spiritual personalities."[5] Selma Stern, the historian and friend of Baeck's, dedicated her biography of Josel of Rosheim, an advocate of Jewish interests in Germany in the sixteenth century, to Leo Baeck, whom she called "the noblest defender of the Jewish people."[6] The historian Peter Gay cited a Berlin Jew who claimed that he knew of only two truly pious men: his father and Leo Baeck.[7] A collection of essays honoring Baeck on his eightieth birthday in 1953 included contributions by such prominent figures as Albert Einstein, Thomas Mann, Jacques Maritain, Karl Jaspers, and Abraham Joshua Heschel.[8]

Of particular interest is what Martin Buber said about Baeck in the Zionist periodical *Jüdische Rundschau*, as early as 1933. Buber recalled that when a representative of the German nobility visited him, they engaged in a long discussion of what constituted genuine nobility. In the midst of the discussion, his visitor exclaimed: "If I want to imagine an embodiment of nobility, I think of Leo Baeck." Ten years later, after Baeck had been deported to Theresienstadt, Buber remembered the incident, noting that it reinforced his belief that nobility was a personal quality of character, not a designation of class, and that Baeck possessed that quality.[9]

The prominent American Jewish writer Cynthia Ozick encountered Baeck's writings a short time after her undergraduate years, when she had become intoxicated by the rapture and ecstasy of the British Romantic poets. At the age of twenty-four, she "stumbled into the majesties of [Baeck's essay] 'Romantic Religion'" and came to realize that her former passion, with "its illusory beauty, anchored in nothing but vapor," concealed self-pride, delusion, and delirium. She chose Rabbi Baeck over the Romantics. Although Ozick later reread the essay with a more critical eye, she declared that Baeck's controversial piece, "with its emphasis on humane conduct over the perils of the loosened imagination remains an essay to live by."[10]

Gershom Scholem and Leo Baeck, who met as early as 1922, were friendly with each other, and, as noted, Scholem hosted Baeck during the latter's visits to Israel.[11] But characteristically for Scholem, in writing of Baeck he mixed admiration with mild critique. He was glad that Baeck would participate in the annual Eranos yearly conferences in Switzerland, but he was glad for *him*—that is, for the opportunity it gave Baeck and apparently not, or less so, for his listeners. "He is a somewhat weak but honest spirit, insofar as spirit can be honest, which is already questionable," Scholem wrote.[12] However, when Hannah Arendt attacked Baeck's leadership of German Jewry in the Nazi period, notoriously writing that "in the eyes of both Jews and Gentiles [Baeck] was the "Jewish Führer," Scholem took her severely to task: "For no one of whom I have heard or read was Leo Baeck, whom we both knew, a Führer in the sense that the reader of your book must associate with it."[13]

Aside from Arendt, who later regretted her use of the unfortunate term,[14] and the political opponents who fought against Baeck's leadership in the 1930s, only one other person publicly called Baeck's personal reputation into question: Recha Freier, founder of Youth Aliyah. A contentious person, she had also clashed with Henrietta Szold, with whom she worked in Hadassah, the women's Zionist organization. According to Freier, Baeck had been grossly unfair when the Reichsvereinigung did not support her illegal efforts for children's emigration, which its staff regarded as dangerous. Her damning evaluation of Baeck (and his associates) and her fulsome praise for Baeck's nemesis Heinrich Stahl, "the noble and revered president of the Berlin Jewish community," is without parallel. Regarding Baeck, she hoped that someday "this man, who was celebrated as a hero," would finally "be divested of his crown of holiness."[15]

It is supremely difficult to probe the true character of the man underneath this "crown of holiness," who was raised on so high a pedestal after the war. He left no diary, wrote no memoir—not only because he would have had difficulty finding time to write one but also because such self-absorption ran counter to his character.[16] He had long been a critic of personality cults.[17] One disciple claimed that it was scarcely possible to comprehend his teacher's personality, given that he withdrew his "I" from the public and that any attempt to unveil it would be tactless.[18] Yet it does seem possible, by following up on a few hints, to draw a portrait, albeit incomplete, of the person behind the icon. Baeck represents the extraordinary phenomenon of a man acclaimed by others, but who never sought acclaim himself. He held an abundance of offices; but as far as we know, he did not seek them—rather, those who knew him insisted that he accede to their wishes. This is explicit with regard to his acceptance of leadership of the Reichsvertretung in 1933 and seems to have been the case in other instances, as well. Unlike rabbinical and scholarly colleagues, Baeck characteristically did not sign "Dr." before his name, or "Rabbi," or even "Leo." It was mostly simply L. Baeck, excluding titles and minimizing his individuality. I do not believe that this was a case of false modesty; rather, it is possible that behind it lay an internal battle with an ego that Baeck had successfully sublimated into useful activity. Ernst Ludwig Ehrlich thought that Baeck's extraordinary politeness not only distanced him from others but also covered up suppressed emotions.[19] As we have seen, Baeck was intent on keeping his own sexuality in check while castigating its unchecked expression in others, especially fellow rabbis. "Maybe you think that I am too stern," he wrote to Lily Montagu. "But I cannot help it. I am a Puritan—perhaps you will think me a hard-boiled one."[20] Unlike his contemporaries, Baeck believed that "religion cannot exist without a certain measure of asceticism, without the capacity, within the desires of daily life, to engage in [self-] prohibition."[21] Although Baeck wrote little about Jewish law, he did affirm its capacity to enable the individual "to master the passions of the moment."[22]

Adolf Leschnitzer, a historian and friend of Baeck's, wrote of him: "He wanted his person to disappear in his achievements and his work; he *wanted* to be inconspicuous."[23] His work was largely his life, his many tasks divinely imposed obligations. And if these obligations demanded risking his life, so be it. Baeck believed martyrdom—which, in Jewish tradition, is the most exalted of the divine commandments—to be a privilege; it was "the consummate commandment of Jewish religiosity, the strongest expression of its being taken seriously."[24] As mentioned earlier, the name "Baeck" may have derived from the Hebrew *ben kedoshim* (son—or descendant—of martyrs).[25] One of his disciples noted that Baeck "constantly wrote of martyrdom."[26] Another disciple thought that he offered himself to it.[27] And a former associate at the Lehranstalt held that Baeck possessed "a human softness that cast its rays even into the readiness and the hardness of martyrdom."[28] One can therefore argue that Baeck's choice to remain with his flock in Nazi Germany was not purely an act of self-sacrifice but the creation of a possibility for fulfilling a mitzvah. Or, at the very least, Baeck's awareness of the historical significance of "sanctifying God's name," as Jewish martyrdom is called, gave him the strength to face peril when it overtook his life.

Whether by personal intention or simply by his demeanor and by the respect he elicited from most everyone with whom he came into contact, Baeck remained distant from others. Intimacy was limited to his wife, whom he genuinely loved even if he was unable to express that love easily in words.[29] Rudolf Callmann, a close acquaintance and a preeminent legal scholar, attested: "As much as we not only honored, but loved him, the word friendship would not have been the appropriate expression to describe our relationship to him; friendship assumes equality of *niveau*."[30] Baeck's dignity, so essential to his character, along with his elevated status, which was imposed on him by others, made truly intimate contact unlikely. The aura that surrounded him, some believed, was difficult to penetrate.[31]

Baeck was a political as well as a religious liberal—not an affiliated socialist but a person with a deep appreciation for non-Marxist egalitarianism as represented especially by the Israeli kibbutz. He was bourgeois in manner, yet an admirer of the nobility. He prized restraint; forced emotion repelled him. He confided to President Heuss that he found it objectionable when photographers in America would order their subjects to "keep smiling," whether they wanted to smile or not. The result, Baeck believed, was that the subject was turned into a caricature.[32] In fact, Baeck's painted and photographed portraits, of which there are a number, almost invariably reveal a reflective, serious countenance.

But was there rebelliousness beneath the restrained demeanor? Max Grünewald, who knew Baeck in Germany, wondered whether "perhaps in this man, noted for his restraint and for his conservative leanings, there was nonetheless something of an unruly dissenter, who, associated in a hundred ways with middle class society, yet remained aloof and apart from it."[33] Baeck's sermons to his fellow Liberal—and very bourgeois—coreligionists, in which he insisted that Jews must be the nonconformists of their time, lend validity to Grünewald's suggestion.

Does the person of Leo Baeck then stand in conflict with the iconic status given him after his emergence from persecution in Nazi Germany and deprivation in Theresienstadt? Was he made into an icon simply because of the felt need for heroes of resistance after the war? No doubt, better than anyone else, Baeck could serve as the living exemplar of what was best in German Jewry and could be the outstanding symbol for its legacy. When he was used for that purpose, he did not object, for he wanted the heritage to live on. But it would be a mistake to say that his admirers shaped his image in a way that was totally out of character with his true self. Baeck's high ideals were not negated by the actuality of his behavior. And that is the most remarkable aspect of Leo Baeck, the person. His person reflected his ideals. It is not an exaggeration to suggest that, in Baeck's case, the credibility of the thought is enhanced by its congruity with the life of the thinker.

Else Meidner, a painter and friend of Baeck's, recognized this extraordinary quality: "If we expect of those individuals who lend their expression to the highest and holiest matters—that is, to religion—that they distinguish themselves by especially noble behavior, then Leo Baeck embodied that ideal to the most consummate degree."[34] An ancient accolade found in the Midrash, *tokho kevaro*, literally translated as "his inside is as his outside," seems applicable to Baeck. To be sure, there was much inside him that was suppressed and that we will never know; but unlike in the case of many others, there is no chasm between what he preached and what he did. The moral life, commanded by God and obligatory on all, was both his burden and his joy.

Finally, one might ask: Has Leo Baeck's thought had a significant influence beyond his lifetime? The empirical answer to this question must be in the negative. As a thinker, Baeck is far less studied and cited than such diverse members of the German Jewish religious elite as Hermann Cohen, Martin Buber, and Franz Rosenzweig. He coined no religious aphorism, established no school of thought, and can be difficult to read. Yet, as I hope this book has shown, that may be an injustice. His work as historian and theologian came together in his self-chosen role as a teacher in the long line of Jewish teachers, each personifying and adding nuance to the traditions of a religious people.[35] His assertion of the powerful connection between a God dwelling in mystery but known to Jews and others through the imperative to act justly and strive toward a messianic horizon seems more relevant than ever in our own time.

Notes

CHAPTER 1

1. S. Bäck, *Die Geschichte des jüdischen Volkes und seiner Literatur vom babylonischen Exil bis auf die Gegenwart*, 3rd ed. (Frankfurt a.M.: J. Kauffmann, 1906), 549. Possibly, this reference was added by his son. For an analysis of Bäck's guardedly favorable attitude toward kabbala, see George Y. Kohler, *Kabbalah Research in the Wissenschaft des Judentums (1820–1880)* (Oldenbourg: De Gruyter, 2019), 240–242.

2. H. Schreiber, "The Birthplace of Dr. Leo Baeck," *Synagogue Review* 27.9 (May 1953): 267.

3. Letter to Robert Beer, 31 October 1948, Leo Baeck Collection AR 66, Leo Baeck Institute Archives, DigiBaeck, Frame 1177.

4. The founders, in 1872, used the term *Hochschule*, indicating an institution of higher learning, instead of *Lehranstalt*. But in 1883, antisemitic influences forced substitution of the academically inferior designation. The term *Hochschule* was restored during the Weimar years, only to be taken away again during the Nazi period.

5. This publication is mentioned by Leo Baeck's granddaughter, Marianne Dreyfus, in an interview that she and her husband gave on 26 March 1974 (transcript in my personal possession). I have not been able to obtain copies of the periodical for the dates when Baeck was a student in Berlin. It is, in any case, likely that he used a pseudonym.

6. "Motive in Spinozas Lehre" (1932), in *Werke* 3: 249.

7. "Romantische Religion" (1922), in *Werke* 4: 62.

8. *Dieses Volk: Jüdische Existenz*, pt. 2, in *Werke* 2: 368.

9. "Gerechte und Engel" (1930), in *Werke* 4: 221.

10. Baeck to Franz Rosenzweig, 5 January 1924, in *Werke* 6: 582.

11. Hermann Cohen, "Die Versöhnungsidee" (1899), in *Hermann Cohens jüdische Schriften* (Berlin: C. A. Schwetschke & Sohn, 1924), 1:134. My thanks to George Kohler for this reference.

12. Cited in Alexander Altmann, "Leo Baeck and the Jewish Mystical Tradition," in idem, *Essays in Jewish Intellectual History* (Hanover, N.H.: Brandeis University Press, 1981), 293.

13. Baeck also developed a lifelong fondness for the German historian Leopold von Ranke, on account of his universal sympathy, which enabled him to understand the human in all its forms, each in direct relationship to God. Fritz Kaufmann, "Baeck and Buber," *Conservative Judaism* 12.2 (Winter 1958): 11.

14. Just before completing his rabbinical studies at the Lehranstalt in Berlin, Hermann Vogelstein served as one of three "opponents" at the oral defense of Baeck's doctoral dissertation. Like Baeck, he studied first in Breslau and then in Berlin; and his father, too, had been a Liberal rabbi.

15. "Gemeindeleben" (1905), in *Werke* 6: 43–46.

16. Michael A. Meyer, ed., *Joachim Prinz, Rebellious Rabbi: An Autobiography—the German and Early American Years* (Bloomington: Indiana University Press, 2008), 19.

17. Eva G. Reichmann, "Die Juden in Oppeln: Kindheitserinnerungen an Rabbiner Leo Baeck" (1968), in idem, *Größe und Verhängnis deutsch-jüdischer Existenz* (Heidelberg: Schneider, 1974), 258–259.

18. Cited in Bastian Fleermann, *Die Düsseldorfer Rabbiner: Von den Anfängen 1706 bis zur Auflösung der Synagogengemeinde 1941* (Düsseldorf: Droste, 2016), 54.

19. A variant version of this episode is related in the interview cited above in n. 5.

20. Michael A. Meyer, "Leo Baeck und Schlesien," *Silesia Nova: Vierteljahresschrift für Kultur und Geschichte* 9.1 (2012): 37–41.

21. Leo Baeck, "Zur Rabbinerausbildung" (1898), in *Werke* 6: 35; Hermann Levin Goldschmidt, "Der junge Leo Baeck," *Tradition und Erneuerung* 14 (December 1962): 201–205.

22. "Orthodox oder ceremoniös?" (1896–1897), in *Werke* 6: 29–35.

23. Letter to Franz Rosenzweig, 17 October 1924, in ibid., 584.

24. "Orthodox oder ceremoniös?," 33.

25. "Gesetzesreligion und Religionsgesetz" (1912), in *Werke* 6: 91–95.

CHAPTER 2

1. "Rezension zu *Der Kalam in der jüdischen Literatur*: Von Martin Schreiner" (1895/1896), in *Werke* 6: 28.

2. Richard Fuchs, "The 'Hochschule für die Wissenschaft des Judentums' in the Period of Nazi Rule," *Leo Baeck Institute Year Book* 12 (1967): 12.

3. "The Character of Judaism," in *The Pharisees and Other Essays by Leo Baeck* (New York: Schocken, 1947), 150.

4. Leo Bäck, "Zur Charakteristik des Levi ben Abraham ben Chajjim," *Monatsschrift für Geschichte und Wissenschaft des Judentums* (*MGWJ*) 44 (1900): 24ff.

5. "Der im Dornbusch Wohnende" (1902), in *Werke* 4: 245–247; "Epochen der jüdischen Geschichte" (published posthumously in 1974), in *Werke* 5: 257. Although the theory was not novel with Baeck, he supplied a fresh linguistic argument.

6. Leopold Zunz, *Zur Geschichte und Literatur* (Berlin: Veit, 1845), 20.

7. Preface to *Wege im Judentum* (1933), in *Werke* 3: 26.

8. *Das Wesen des Judentums* (1922 ed.), in *Werke* 1: 70.

9. *Dieses Volk: Jüdische Existenz*, vol. 1 (1955), in *Werke* 2: 332.

10. "Wissen und Glaube," *C.V.-Zeitung*, 2 June 1938, Beiblatt.

11. Adolf Harnack, *Die Aufgabe der theologischen Facultäten und die allgemeine Religionsgeschichte* (Giessen: J. Ricker, 1901), 11.

12. For Baeck on Christianity, see Reinhold Mayer, *Christentum und Judentum in der Schau Leo Baecks* (Stuttgart: Kohlhammer, 1961), and Walter Homolka, *Jewish Identity in Modern Times: Leo Baeck and German Protestantism* (Providence, R.I.: Berghahn, 1995). That Baeck did not regard Harnack as an antisemite is evident from the letter of condolence that he wrote to Harnack's wife on behalf of the Liberal seminary's faculty, following her husband's death in 1930. It may be found at Signatur: Nachl. Harnack: Baeck Leo, Handschriftenabteilung, Staatsbibliothek zu Berlin.

13. Franz Rosenzweig, "Apologetisches Denken: Bemerkungen zu Brod und Baeck" (1923), in idem, *Kleinere Schriften* (Berlin: Schocken, 1937), 31–42. An English trans. is Franz Rosenzweig, *Philosophical and Theological Writings*, trans. Paul W. Franks and Michael L. Morgan (Indianapolis: Hackett, 2000), 95–108.

14. Leo Baeck to Franz Rosenzweig, 5 August 1923, in *Werke* 6: 581.

15. *Das Wesen des Judentums* (1905 ed.), in *Werke* 1: 337 (Baeck's emphasis). Baeck shared admiration for the Prophets with the cultural Zionist Ahad Ha'am. Although he was not a believer, Ahad Ha'am, like Baeck, saw the Prophets as the source for the ethics that was defining for Judaism.

16. Isaac Heinemann, reviewing a later edition of *Das Wesen des Judentums*, perceptively noted that Baeck, in presenting Judaism, passed over many a matter that, while not "essential" (*wesenhaft*), was nonetheless highly "significant" (*wesentlich*) for its historical effect on Judaism. *MGWJ* 66 (1922): 68.

17. The first part of this citation is already contained in the first edition of *Wesen des Judentums*; the last part was added for the second edition. See *Werke* 1: 65, 332–333.

18. Ibid., 423–424.

19. *Das Wesen des Judentums* (1905 ed.), in ibid., 414.

20. Baeck's book enjoyed positive resonance in the periodicals of both the conservative and the liberal branches of German Jewry. See R. Urbach, "Zwei Bücher über das Wesen des Judentums," *MGWJ* 50 (1906): 129–151; Josel Wohlstein, "Das Wesen des Judentums," *Allgemeine Zeitung des Judentums* 69.29 (21 July 1905): 340–342.

21. Letter to Emil Bernhard Cohn in Berlin, 30 April 1907, in *Werke* 6: 461.

22. "Abschiedspredigt in Oppeln am 1. Oktober 1907," in ibid., 49–52.

23. In a later essay, "And If Not Now, When?" (1932), Buber does speak of divine command: "And if we consult our deep inner knowledge about God's command to mankind, we shall not hesitate an instant to say that it is peace." Martin Buber, *Israel and the World: Essays in a Time of Crisis* (New York: Schocken, 1963), 236–237.

24. Franz Rosenzweig, *The Star of Redemption*, trans. William W. Hallo (New York: Holt, Rinehart and Winston, 1970), 176.

25. "Die Umkehr im Judentum," in *Werke* 6: 67. This article was first printed in a special issue of *Korrespondenz-Blatt des Verbandes der deutschen Juden* 5 (1909): 1–5, devoted to apologetics, and twice reprinted, the second time in the Orthodox publication *Die jüdische Presse* 49 (1918): 386–389.

26. "Englische Frömmigkeit" (1910), in *Werke* 6: 86.

27. "Die Umkehr im Judentum" (1909), in ibid., 68.

28. "Zur Frage der Christusmythe" (1910), in ibid., 78.

29. "Unsere Stellung zu den Religionsgesprächen" (1910), in ibid., 81–82.

30. Ibid., 83.

31. "Das Judentum unter den Religionen" (1912), in ibid., 96. Cf. L. Baeck, "Die jüdische Religionsgemeinschaft," in Joseph Hansen, ed., *Die Rheinprovinz 1815–1915: Hundert Jahre preußischer Herrschaft am Rhein* (Bonn: Marcus & Weber, 1917), 2:235, where Baeck notes that, as nonconformists, the Rhineland Jews did not fit the uniformity demanded by the Napoleonic system.

32. Cited in Bastian Fleermann, *Die Düsseldorfer Rabbiner: Von den Anfängen 1706 bis zur Auflösung der Synagogengemeinde 1941* (Düsseldorf: Droste, 2016), 52.

CHAPTER 3

1. Citations from *Allgemeine Zeitung des Judentums* (*AZJ*), 3 January 1913, supplement.

2. In a sermon for the High Holidays in 1913, Baeck made specific reference to Emerson. See "Der Stil des Lebens" (1913), in *Werke* 6: 110. He also refers to him on other occasions: see ibid., 387, 535.

3. "Griechische und jüdische Predigt" (1913), in *Werke* 4: 151–164.

4. "Die Schöpfung des Mitmenschen" (1914), in *Werke* 6: 112–117.

5. The idea of the *Mitmensch* plays a large role in Hermann Cohen's major work of Jewish philosophy, *Die Religion der Vernunft aus den Quellen des Judentums* (Leipzig: Gustav Fock, 1919), esp. chap. 8. Clearly, there is some mutual influence here between Cohen and Baeck in the prewar years, when both were living in Berlin. My thanks to Professor Michael Morgan for calling this to my attention.

6. "Die Kraft der Wenigen" (1915), in *Werke* 6: 132.

7. Cited in Sabine Hank, Hermann Simon, and Uwe Hank, *Feldrabbiner in den deutschen Streitkräften des Ersten Weltkrieges* (Berlin: Hentrich & Hentrich, 2013), 268.

8. Ulrich Sieg, *Jüdische Intellektuelle im Ersten Weltkrieg* (Berlin: Akademie Verlag, 2001), 129–130.

9. See Hank et al., *Feldrabbiner*, 373, 514.

10. Ibid., 30.

11. Eugen Tannenbaum, ed., *Kriegsbriefe deutscher und österreichischer Juden* (Berlin: Neuer Verlag, 1915), 84.

12. *Israelitisches Familienblatt*, 3 June 1915, 4.

13. Tannenbaum, ed., *Kriegsbriefe*, 87.

14. "Das Drama der Geschichte" (1914), in *Werke* 6: 123. Cf. "Du sollst!" (1915) in ibid., 127.

15. Reichsbund jüdischer Frontsoldaten, *Kriegsbriefe gefallener deutscher Juden* (Berlin: Vortrupp, 1935), 28–29.

16. *AZJ*, 21 May 1915, 244.

17. "Lebensgrund und Lebensgehalt" (1917/1918), in *Werke* 3: 115.

18. *Feldgebetbuch für die jüdischen Mannschaften des Heeres* (Berlin: H. Itzkowski, 1914). A 2nd ed., published in 1916 on the poor-quality paper available at the time, was a bit thicker on account of the addition of the Sabbath afternoon prayer in the Hebrew section. Apparently, the afternoon proved to be a time when Jewish soldiers were freer to attend.

19. *AZJ*, 21 May 1915, 243.

20. Hank et al., *Feldrabbiner*, 558.

21. Ibid., 489.

22. *Gemeindeblatt der jüdischen Gemeinde zu Berlin*, 10 May 1918, 53.

23. "Die jüdische Religionsgemeinschaft," in Joseph Hansen, ed., *Die Rheinprovinz 1815–1915: Hundert Jahre preußischer Herrschaft am Rhein* (Bonn: Marcus & Weber, 1917), 2:234–247. This essay is a rare example of Baeck writing political history and using contemporary documents as well as secondary sources. Although published in 1917, it seems to have been written before the war.

24. Cited in Peter C. Appelbaum, *Loyalty Betrayed: Jewish Chaplains in the German Army During the First World War* (London: Vallentine Mitchell, 2014), 305.

25. "Heimgegangene des Krieges" (1919), in *Werke* 3: 285–296.

26. "Brief an Martin Buber, 24 September 1918," in *Werke* 6: 142.

27. Albert H. Friedlander, *Leo Baeck: Teacher of Theresienstadt* (New York: Holt, Rinehart and Winston, 1968), 263.

28. Leo Baeck, *Von Moses Mendelssohn zu Franz Rosenzweig* (Stuttgart: W. Kohlhammer, 1958), 35–42. The fourth individual, in addition to those in the title and Walther Rathenau, was the socialist and Zionist Moses Hess.

29. Tim Grady, *The German-Jewish Soldiers of the First World War in History and Memory* (Liverpool: Liverpool University Press, 2011), 68–69.

30. "Neutralität" (1929), in *Werke* 3: 167–172.

CHAPTER 4

1. "Gemeinde in der Großstadt" (1929), in *Werke* 3: 218–225.

2. "Mensch und Boden: Gedanken und Soziologie des Großstadtsjuden" (1931), in *Werke* 6: 202.

3. For Prinz's personal reflections, see Michael A. Meyer, ed., *Joachim Prinz, Rebellious Rabbi: An Autobiography—the German and Early American Years* (Bloomington: Indiana University Press, 2008).

4. "Lebensgrund und Lebensgehalt" (1917–1918), in *Werke* 3: 113.

5. Interview cited in Leonard Baker, *Days of Sorrow and Pain: Leo Baeck and the Berlin Jews* (New York: Macmillan, 1978), 169–170.

6. Cited in Albert H. Friedlander, *Leo Baeck: Teacher of Theresienstadt* (New York: Holt, Rinehart and Winston, 1968), 17–18.

7. On this other, specifically Jewish, culture, see Michael Brenner, *The Renaissance of Jewish Culture in Weimar Germany* (New Haven, Conn.: Yale University Press, 1996).

8. Michael A. Meyer, "*Gemeinschaft* Within *Gemeinde*: Religious Ferment in Weimar Liberal Judaism," in Michael Brenner and Derek J. Penslar, eds., *In Search of Jewish Community: Jewish Identities in Germany and Austria, 1918–1933* (Bloomington: Indiana University Press, 1998), 15–35.

9. "Mittelaltlerische Popularphilosophie" (1900), in *Werke* 4: 341.

10. "Die jüdischen Gemeinden" (1928), in *Werke* 6: 200.

11. "Zedakah" (1921), in ibid., 173.

12. See *Verhandlungen der Grossloge für Deutschland VIII U.O.B.B.: 22. ordentliche Sitzung der Grossloge für Deutschland VIII U.O.B.B.* (Berlin: Saling, 1924), and *23. ordentliche Sitzung der Grossloge für Deutschland VIII U.O.B.B.* (Berlin: Saling, 1928).

13. "Antwort auf die von der Schriftleitung der jüdisch-liberalen Zeitung gestellten Frage: Was erwarten Sie von der Londoner Konferenz?" (1926), in *Werke* 6: 498.

14. "The Task of Progressive Judaism in the Post-War World," *Report of the Fifth International Conference of the World Union for Progressive Judaism, July 25–30, 1946*, 55; "The Future of Progressive Judaism," *Liberal Jewish Monthly* 20.7 (July 1949): 88–89.

15. See Jakob J. Petuchowski's translation of Baeck's speech to the Association of German Liberal Rabbis, 22 May 1929, in *Central Conference of American Rabbis Journal* (Spring 1973): 40.

16. "Predigt und Wahrheit" (1928), in *Werke* 3: 234.

17. "Rede auf der Tagung der World Union for Progressive Judaism in London, 1930," in *Werke* 6: 511–512.

18. Ibid., 513.

19. Baeck to Rabbi Caesar Seligmann, 2 September 1926, in *Leo Baeck Institute Year Book* (*LBIYB*) 2 (1957): 45.

20. Dr. S. Moses, "The Impact of Leo Baeck's Personality on His Contemporaries," ibid., 6.

21. See Avraham Barkai, *"Wehr Dich": Der Centralverein deutscher Staatsbürger jüdischen Glaubens (C.V.) 1893–1938* (Munich: C. H. Beck, 2002), 235.

22. "Stellung des religiös-liberalen Judentums zum Zionismus" (1927), in *Werke* 6: 468.

23. Cited in Curt Wilk, "Die zionistische Bewegung und Leo Baeck," in Eva G. Reichmann, ed., *Worte des Gedenkens für Leo Baeck* (Heidelberg: Lambert Schneider, 1959), 69.

24. "'Agency'-Kundgebung" (1929), in *Werke* 6: 470 (Baeck's emphasis).

25. Baeck to Lily Montagu, 26 February 1936, World Union for Progressive Judaism Collection, MSS 16, D12/4, American Jewish Archives.

26. *The Jewish Agency for Palestine: Constituent Meeting of the Council* (London: Jewish Agency for Palestine, 1930), 62.

27. Kurt Blumenfeld to Salman Schocken, 7 June 1921, in Miriam Sambursky and Jochanan Ginat, eds., *Kurt Blumenfeld, im Kampf um den Zionismus: Briefe aus fünf Jahrzehnten* (Stuttgart: Deutsche Verlags-Anstalt, 1976), 71.

28. "Der Aufbau Palästinas und das deutsche Judentum" (1925), in *Werke* 6: 463; "In Memory of Two of Our Dead," *LBIYB* 1 (1956): 53.

29. In a letter to Hermann Keyserling, 23 June 1924, Baeck admitted that the essay was one-sided but that it was only a portion of an intended larger work on both romantic and classical religion. See *Werke* 6: 587.

30. The following analysis of Baeck's essay draws upon my article "The Thought of Leo Baeck: A Religious Philosophy for a Time of Adversity," *Modern Judaism* 19 (1999): 107–117.

31. "Die Auseinandersetzung mit dem entstehenden Christentum" (1929), in *Werke* 6: 159.

32. "Abweichungen der christlichen Religionen vom Judentum in den Grundgedanken: Einleitung" (1929), in ibid., 163.

33. "Romantische Religion" (1938 version), in *Werke* 4: 118.

34. Ibid., 107.

35. *Das Wesen des Judentums* (1926 version), in *Werke* 1: 88 (Baeck's emphasis).

36. Leo Baeck, "Das Judentum," in Carl Clemen, ed., *Die Religionen der Erde: Ihr Wesen und ihre Geschichte* (Munich: F. Bruckmann, 1927), 261–298; "Ursprünge und Anfänge der jüdischen Mystik," in *Entwicklungsstufen der jüdischen Religion* (Giessen: Alfred Töpelmann, 1927), 91–103.

37. For these last two aristocrats, I have drawn especially on Barbara Garthe, *Über Leben und Werk des Grafen Hermann Keyserling* (Nuremberg: Erlangen University, 1976); Ute Gahlings, *Hermann Graf Keyserling: Ein Lebensbild* (Darmstadt: Liebig Verlag, 1996); Karl Klaus Walther, *Hans Hasso von Veltheim: Eine Biographie* (Halle: Mitteldeutscher Verlag, 2004); and Dina Gusejnova, *European Elites and Ideas of Empire, 1917–1957* (Cambridge: Cambridge University Press, 2016).

38. Baeck to Thun-Hohenstein, 9 November 1924, in *Werke* 6: 593.

39. Count Hermann Keyserling, *Europe*, trans. Maurice Samuel (London: Jonathan Cape, 1929), 347.

40. Kurt Tucholsky, "Der Darmstädter Armleuchter," in Tucholsky, *Gesammelte Werke* 6 (Reinbek bei Hamburg: Rowohlt, 1960), 151, 155.

41. Graf Hermann Keyserling, *Wiedergeburt* (Darmstadt: Reichl, 1927), 39 (Keyserling's emphasis).

42. Keyserling to Baeck, 23 June 1924, in *Werke* 6: 589.

43. Keyserling, *Wiedergeburt*, 39.

44. Baeck to Keyserling, 31 December 1932, Keyserling Archive of the Technical University, Darmstadt.

45. Count Hermann Keyserling, *South American Meditations: On Hell and Heaven in the Soul of Man*, trans. Theresa Duerr (New York: Harper, 1932).

46. *Das Wesen des Judentums* (1905 ed.), in *Werke* 1: 338.

47. Kurt Wilhelm, "Leo Baeck and Jewish Mysticism," *Judaism* 11 (1962): 129.

48. Baeck to Ernst G. Lowenthal, 29 November 1949, in *Werke* 6: 662.

49. Rudolf Otto to Birger Forell, 31 January 1930, Rudolf Otto Collection, Bibliothek Religionswissenschaft, University Library, Marburg. I am grateful to Renate Stegerhoff-Raab for excerpts from these letters.

50. *Verhandlungen der Großloge*, 1924, 43.

51. "Okkultismus und Religion" (1925), in *Werke* 6: 187.

52. Zvi Kurzweil, "The Relevance of Leo Baeck's Thought to the Mainstreams of Judaism," *Commentary* 39 (1990): 164.

53. *Das Wesen des Judentums* (1926 ed.), in *Werke* 1: 77–78.

54. Ibid., 45.

55. "Bedeutung der jüdischen Mystik für unsere Zeit" (1923), in *Werke* 3: 87, 89.

56. Ibid., 90.

57. "Geheimnis und Gebot" (1921–22), in ibid., 50

58. Baeck to Rosenzweig, 25 December 1926, in *Werke* 6: 584–585.

59. *Das Wesen des Judentums* (1926 ed.), in *Werke* 1: 150.

60. Abraham Geiger, *Das Judenthum und seine Geschichte* (Breslau: Schlettersche, 1864), 36–37. Trans. of the relevant chap. is in Max Wiener, ed., *Abraham Geiger and Liberal Judaism* (Philadelphia: Jewish Publication Society, 1962), 179–182.

61. Unfortunately, Baeck never wrote a critique of contemporary Jewish religious thinkers, which would have been helpful in defining his own religious philosophy.

62. "Theologie und Geschichte" (1932), in *Werke* 4: 46. An English trans. is in *Judaism* 13 (1964): 274–284.

63. *Werke* 4: 55.

64. *Das Wesen des Judentums* (1926 ed.), in *Werke* 1: 259.

65. Ibid., 266–267.

66. "Das Reich Gottes" (1928), in *Werke* 4: 244.

67. "Das Judentum," 267.

68. Friedlander, *Leo Baeck*, 154.

69. "Amerika," *Liberales Judentum* 3 (1911): 192.

70. "Die religiöse Erziehung" (1930), in *Werke* 4: 369.

71. Although in his extant writings, Baeck does not indicate his personal political loyalty, he hints at it in his 2 September 1926 letter to Caesar Seligmann, in *Werke* 6: 205, wherein he sympathizes with the Social Democrats.

72. *Die erste Konferenz vom Weltverband für religiös-liberales Judentum in Berlin, 18–20 August 1928* (no date or place of publication), 171.

73. Ibid., 172.

74. "Wohlfahrt, Recht und Religion" (1930), in *Werke* 3: 185.

75. Ibid., 188.

76. "Das Geistige im Wohltun" (1926), in ibid., 91–98.

77. Avraham Barkai, "Jüdischer Friedensbund und politische Orientierung," in idem, *Oscar Wassermann und die Deutsche Bank* (Munich: C. H. Beck, 2005), 57–59.

78. "Das Judentum und der Weltfriede," *Arbeitsgemeinschaft der Konfessionen für den Frieden, Religion, und Weltfriede: Überwindung der Kriege* (Leipzig: Gustav Engel, 1930), 9–13. On the league, see Virginia Iris Holmes, "Integrating Diversity, Reconciling Contradiction: The *Jüdischer Friedensbund* in Late Weimar Germany," *LBIYB* 47 (2002): 175–194.

79. "Weltgeschichte" (1929) and "Friedensbahn und Friedensziel" (1930), in *Werke* 3: 149–153, 176–180.

80. "Eine religionssoziologische Linie," *Der Jude*, special issue (1928): 147–152.

81. Baeck in Atlantic City to "Beloved Natalie," 24 April 1925, in *Werke* 6: 536–537.

82. Thus when Fay Hirschberg's husband became the rabbi of Oppeln, Natalie Baeck prepared her for her responsibilities. USC Shoah Foundation, Virtual History Archive.

83. Baeck to Rudolf Jaser, 6 March 1947, in *Werke* 6: 669.

84. "Die Ehe als Geheimnis und Gebot" (1925), in ibid., 179–185. In English; Count Hermann Keyserling, ed., *The Book of Marriage* (New York: Harcourt, Brace, 1926), 464–471.

85. "Die Ehe als Geheimnis und Gebot," 181.

86. Ibid., 183.

87. "Staat, Familie und Individualität" (1932), in *Werke* 3: 173–175.

88. Baeck to Robert Raphael Geis, 13 November 1949, in *Werke* 6: 657.

89. "Frauenbund" (1929), in *Werke* 3: 231.

90. "Das Zusammensitzen von Männern und Frauen in der Synagoge Prinzregentenstraße in Berlin" (1929), in *Werke* 6: 507–511.

91. Baeck to Robert Raphael Geis, 31 October 1949, Leo Baeck Collection AR 66, Leo Baeck Institute Archives, DigiBaeck, Frame 79.

92. "Die religiöse Erziehung" (1930) and "Die Entwicklung zur sittlichen Persönlichkeit" (1931), in *Werke* 4: 357–376, 345–356; "Religion und Erziehung" (1929), in *Werke* 3: 129–138 (citation, 136).

93. "Vorwort zu *Friedhofsschändungen in Deutschland: 1923–1932*" (1932), in *Werke* 6: 207.

94. Letter reproduced in *Freiburger Rundbrief* 6 (1999): 174.

CHAPTER 5

1. *Jüdisches Adressbuch für Gross-Berlin* (Berlin: Goedega Verlags Gesellschaft, 1931), unsigned preface.

2. Memorandum des SD-Amtes IV/2 an Heydrich, 24 May 1934, in Michael Wildt, ed., *Die Judenpolitik des SD 1935 bis 1938: Eine Dokumentation* (Munich: Oldenbourg, 1995), 67; cf. 113.

3. Baeck did not seek minority rights but rather full citizen rights. See Yfaat Weiss, *Etniyut ve-ezrahut: Yehude germanyah ve-yehude polin, 1933–1940* (Jerusalem: Magnes Press, 2000), 256.

4. Gustav Krojanker, cited in Kurt Loewenstein, "Die innerjüdische Reaktion auf die Krise der deutschen Demokratie," in Werner Mosse, ed., *Entscheidungsjahr 1932: Zur Judenfrage in der Endphase der Weimarer Republik* (Tübingen: J. C. B. Mohr, 1965), 387.

5. "Jüdische Zwischenbilanz," *Jüdische Rundschau*, monthly ed. (April/May 1933): 5.

6. "Äußerung der Zionistischen Vereinigung für Deutschland zur Stellung der Juden im neuen deutschen Staat," 21 June 1933, in Hans Tramer, ed., *In zwei Welten: Siegfried Moses zum fünfundsiebzigsten Geburtstag* (Tel Aviv: Bitaon, 1962), 119–122.

7. Jacob Boas, "German-Jewish Internal Politics Under Hitler 1933–1938," *Leo Baeck Institute Year Book* (*LBIYB*) 29 (1984): 20.

8. "Eingliederung," *Jüdische Rundschau* 38 (20 September 1933): 544.

9. Ibid.

10. "Wir 'Juden-Nazis,'" *Der nationaldeutsche Jude*, August 1933.

11. See the Gestapa flow chart of Jewish organized activity, which divided the Jewish community into two major categories: assimilationists and Zionists, in Otto Dov Kulka and Eberhard Jäckel, eds., *Die Juden in den geheimen NS-Stimmungsberichten, 1933–1945* (Düsseldorf: Droste, 2004), 548. ("Gestapa" was the designation for the central office of the Gestapo in Berlin.)

12. Wolfgang Hamburger, "The Reactions of Reform Jews to the Nazi Rule," in Herbert A. Strauss and Kurt R. Grossmann, eds., *Gegenwart im Rückblick: Festgabe für die jüdische Gemeinde zu Berlin 25 Jahre nach dem Neubeginn* (Heidelberg: Lothar Stiehm, 1970), 156, 160.

13. Letter to the editor, *Mitteilungen der jüdischen Reformgemeinde zu Berlin*, 15 August 1934, 5.

14. Bruno Woyda, "Um die künftige Stellung der deutschen Juden: Programmatische Richtlinien," *Jüdisch-liberale Zeitung*, supplement, 31 October 1933. Together with the Orthodox rabbi Esra Munk, Baeck had in the pre-Nazi period worked toward such a concordat with the Prussian government, but nothing came of the effort. See Leo Baeck, "In Memory of Two of Our Dead," *LBIYB* 1 (1956): 52.

15. *Jüdisch-liberale Zeitung*, March 1934.

16. See Michael A. Meyer, "Liberal Judaism in Nazi Germany," in Moshe Zimmermann, ed., *On Germans and Jews Under the Nazi Regime: Essays by Three Generations of Historians* (Jerusalem: Magnes Press, 2006), 281–295.

17. "Aristokratie," *Jüdische Rundschau* 39.8 (26 January 1934): 2.

18. *Jüdische Rundschau* 38.27 (4 April 1933); *Israelitisches Familienblatt*, 35.14 (6 April 1933): 2, repr. in *Werke* 6: 210. My suspicion is that the interview was given before the Nazi boycott of Jewish stores on April 1. I was unable to locate the interview in the French periodical *Intransegeant*.

19. Like Baeck, Ismar Elbogen, a close friend and associate who taught Jewish history at the Hochschule, initially argued for forbearance and continued allegiance to linked loyalties to Judaism and to Germanism. Ismar Elbogen, "Haltung," *C.V.-Zeitung* 12.14 (4 April 1933).

20. "Aufruf!," *C.V.-Zeitung* 12.23 (8 June 1933); *Werke* 6: 285, 288.

21. Schlomo Krolik, ed., *Arthur Ruppin: Briefe, Tagebücher, Erinnerungen* (Königstein/Ts.: Athenäum, 1985), 489.

22. "An die deutschen Juden" (1933), in *Werke* 6: 285.

23. "Saar-Kundgebung der Reichsvertretung" (1935), signed by Baeck, in *Werke* 6: 290.

24. Baeck to Claude Montefiore, 12 April 1932, World Union for Progressive Judaism Collection, MSS 16, D12/3, American Jewish Archives.

25. Baeck's memorial tribute, *Werke* 6: 211–212, was delivered in the newly constructed Prinzregentenstraße Synagogue on 5 August 1934.

26. Kurt Jakob Ball-Kaduri, *Vor der Katastrophe: Juden in Deutschland 1934–1939* (Tel Aviv: Olamenu, 1967), 42.

27. "Der 5. März: Ein Wort an die deutschen Juden," *C.V.-Zeitung* 12.10 (9 March 1933). The meeting took place on March 3, two days before the Nazi party's electoral victory on March 5.

28. H. B. Auerbach, *Die Geschichte des "Bund gesetzestreuer jüdischer Gemeinden Deutschlands," 1919–1938* (Tel Aviv: Olamenu, 1972), 54.

29. *Jewish Daily Bulletin*, 28 June 1933.

30. "Die Reichsvertretung der jüdischen Landesverbände an den Reichskanzler und die Reichsminister, 6 June 1933," in Otto Dov Kulka, ed., *Deutsches Judentum unter dem Nationalsozialismus*, vol. 1: *Dokumente zur Geschichte der Reichsvertretung der deutschen Juden 1933–1939* (Tübingen: Mohr Siebeck, 1997), 48–52.

31. Hugo Hahn, "Die Gründung der Reichsvertretung," in Tramer, ed., *In zwei Welten*, 98.

32. Baeck, "In Memory of Two of Our Dead," 54; Kurt Jakob Ball-Kaduri, *Das Leben der Juden in Deutschland 1933* (Frankfurt a.M.: Europäische Verlagsanstalt, 1963), 137.

33. Shaul Esh, "The Establishment of the 'Reichsvereinigung der Juden in Deutschland' and Its Main Activities," *Yad Vashem Studies* 7 (1968): 19.

34. Heydrich's notice of 26 June 1934 in Kulka, ed., *Deutsches Judentum unter dem Nationalsozialismus*, 151–152.

35. Julius Brodnitz, "Geeint ins neue Jahr: Die neue Vertretung der deutschen Juden," *C.V.-Zeitung* 12.36 (20 September 1933).

36. K. Y. Ball-Kaduri, "The Reichsvertretung of German Jewry: The Basic Problems and the Achievements" [Hebrew], *Yad Vashem Studies* 2 (1958): 153.

37. Günter Plum, "Deutsche Juden oder Juden in Deutschland?," in Wolfgang Benz, ed., *Die Juden in Deutschland 1933–1945* (Munich: C. H. Beck, 1988), 58.

38. Jürgen Matthäus and Mark Roseman, *Jewish Responses to Persecution*, vol. 1, 1933–1938 (Washington, D.C.: AltaMira Press, 2010), 51.

39. Ludwig Freund, "Neugestaltung jüdischen Lebens!," *Der Schild* 12.17 (14 September 1933).

40. "Für Zusammenarbeit der jüdischen Organisationen! . . . Der innerjüdische Burgfrieden," ibid., 13.5 (16 February 1934).

41. "Separatische Tendenzen: Die unabhängige Orthodoxie und der Reichsbund jüdischer Frontsoldaten," in Kulka, ed., *Deutsches Judentum unter dem Nationalsozialismus*, 135.

42. *Der Israelit* 74.38 (20 September 1933).

43. "Der Beitritt der unabhängigen jüdischen Orthodoxie Deutschlands zur Reichsvertretung," in Kulka, ed., *Deutsches Judentum unter dem Nationalsozialismus*, 408n7.

44. Ball-Kaduri, *Vor der Katastrophe*, 37; Herbert A. Strauss, "Jewish Autonomy Within the Limits of National Socialist Policy: The Communities and the Reichsvertretung," in Arnold Paucker, ed., *The Jews of Nazi Germany, 1933–1943* (Tübingen: J. C. B. Mohr, 1986), 133–134.

45. For Baeck's relation to social ethics, see Gerd Stecklina, "Die Sozialethik des Judentums—das Beispiel Leo Baeck," *Medaon* 1 (2007): 1–12.

46. Ernst Herzfeld, "Meine letzten Jahre in Deutschland 1933 bis 1938," in Monika Richarz, ed., *Jüdisches Leben in Deutschland: Selbstzeugnisse zur Sozialgeschichte 1918–1945* (Stuttgart: Deutsche Verlags-Anstalt, 1982), 303–304.

47. Ron Chernow, *The Warburgs: The Twentieth-Century Odyssey of a Remarkable Jewish Family* (New York: Random House, 1993), 403.

48. R. W., "Forderung als Glückwunsch," *Jüdische Rundschau* 38.41 (23 May 1933): 213.

49. "Die neue Reichsvertretung: Einigung über die Leitung," ibid., 38.75–76 (20 September 1933): 544.

50. Hahn, "Die Gründung der Reichsvertretung," 102.

51. On Hirsch, see Baeck, "In Memory of Two of Our Dead," 51–56; Friedrich S. Brodnitz, "Memories of the Reichsvertretung: A Personal Report," *LBIYB* 31 (1986): 268–269; and Paul Sauer, "Otto Hirsch (1885–1941): Director of the Reichsvertretung," *LBIYB* 32 (1987): 341–368.

52. Nathan Stein, "Lebenserinnerungen," in Richarz, ed., *Jüdisches Leben in Deutschland*, 211.

53. Baeck, "In Memory of Two of Our Dead," 56.

54. "Kundgebung der neuen Reichsvertretung der deutschen Juden," in Kulka, ed., *Deutsches Judentum unter dem Nationalsozialismus*, 71–72 (Baeck's emphasis).

55. Kulka, introduction, in ibid., 269.

56. Brodnitz, "Memories of the Reichsvertretung," 270. Brodnitz was the press officer of the Reichsvertretung.

57. Hans Reichmann, "Centralverein deutscher Staatsbürger jüdischen Glaubens," in Eva G. Reichmann, ed., *Festschrift zum 80. Geburtstag von Leo Baeck am 23. Mai 1953* (London: Council for the Protection of the Rights and Interests of Jews from Germany, 1953), 72; Ball-Kaduri, *Das Leben der Juden in Deutschland*, 212; Arnold Paucker, *Deutsche Juden im Kampf um Recht und Freiheit* (Teetz: Hentrich & Hentrich, 2003), 318.

58. The pessimism of the remark is not isolated. A few months later, in a documented speech to the council of the Reichsvertretung, Baeck said: "The fate of the German Jews will one day become the fate of all the Jews of Europe, perhaps also of Palestine." "Reichsvertretung mahnt zur Einigkeit: Erste Sitzung des Beirates," *Jüdische Rundschau* 39.13 (13 February 1934), 3.

59. *Der Schild* 5.13 (18 February 1934): 1.

60. S. Adler-Rudel, *Jüdische Selbsthilfe unter dem Naziregime 1933–1939* (Tübingen: J. C. B. Mohr, 1974), 163.

61. Wolf Gruner, "Poverty and Persecution: The Reichsvereinigung, the Jewish Population, and Anti-Jewish Policy in the Nazi State, 1939–1945," *Yad Vashem Studies* 27 (1999): 34.

62. Kurt Alexander, "Die Reichsvertretung der deutschen Juden," in E. Reichmann, ed., *Festschrift zum 80. Geburtstag von Leo Baeck*, 79.

63. Ibid., 80.

64. Baeck, letter of September 1933 to Anglo-Jewish leaders, cited in Naomi Shepherd, *A Refuge from Darkness: Wilfrid Israel and the Rescue of the Jews* (New York: Pantheon, 1984), 81.

65. "Ansprache zur Eröffnung der jüdischen Winterhilfe" (1935), in *Werke* 6: 292. Baeck spoke without a manuscript; hence, there are variant versions of what he said. For a version that stresses "faith in the commandment," see Georg Heuberger and Paul Spiegel, eds., *Zedaka: Jüdische Sozialarbeit im Wandel der Zeit* (Frankfurt a.M.: Jüdisches Museum, 1992), 307.

66. *C.V.-Zeitung* 14.43 (24 October 1935): 1.

67. "Die jüdische Sozialarbeit umspannt die Welt" (1936), in *Werke* 6: 294–295.

68. For example, the Reform Temple in Hamburg enjoyed extraordinary participation. See Jacob Borut, *Jewish Religious Practice Under Nazi Rule (1933–1938) and Its Reflection in the German Jewish Press* [Hebrew] (Jerusalem: Yad Vashem, 2017), 272.

69. Document 21, in Wildt, ed., *Die Judenpolitik*, 149.

70. Martin Buber, *Briefwechsel aus sieben Jahrzehnten* (Heidelberg: Lambert Schneider, 1972–1975), 2:486, 515–516.

71. "Lehrhaus eröffnet," *Jüdische allgemeine Zeitung* 14.85 (7 November 1934).

72. "Bildungsenge" (1935), in *Werke* 6: 271–272.

73. Cited in Wildt, ed., *Die Judenpolitik*, 106.

74. "Kulturbund—Sache der Gemeinschaft," *C.V.-Zeitung* 16.33 (19 August 1937).

75. "Für den Kulturbund deutscher Juden" (1934), in *Werke* 6: 268.

76. "Europa" (1937), in *Werke* 6: 275, 280.

77. "Zum Sportereignis des Jahres im Sportbund des Reichsbundes jüdischer Frontsoldaten" (1936), in *Werke* 6: 273.

78. Avraham Barkai, "Im Schatten der Verfolgung und Vernichtung: Leo Baeck in den Jahren des NS-Regimes," in Georg Heuberger and Fritz Backhaus, eds., *Leo Baeck 1873–1956: Aus dem Stamme von Rabbinen* (Frankfurt a.M.: Jüdischer Verlag, 2001), 83.

79. "Das Sabbatliche," in Friedrich Thieberger, ed., *Jüdisches Fest: Jüdischer Brauch* (Berlin: Jüdischer Verlag, 1936), 93–94.

80. Esriel Hildesheimer, *Jüdische Selbstverwaltung unter dem NS-Regime: Der Existenzkampf der Reichsvertretung und Reichsvereinigung der Juden in Deutschland* (Tübingen: J. C. B. Mohr, 1994), 42.

81. K. Y. Ball-Kaduri, "The National Representation of Jews in Germany—Obstacles and Accomplishments at Its Establishment," *Yad Vashem Studies* 2 (1958): 175.

82. It is mentioned in Kulka, ed., *Deutsches Judentum unter dem Nationalsozialismus*, 135–136, 161n4.

83. "Erklärung der Reichsvertretung," *Jüdische Rundschau* 39.53 (3 July 1934): 6.

84. "Reichsvertretung der deutschen Juden: Gegen innerjüdische Polemik," *Informationsblätter* 5 (16 July 1934): 55.

85. Michael A. Meyer, ed., *Joachim Prinz, Rebellious Rabbi: An Autobiography—the German and Early American Years* (Bloomington: Indiana University Press, 2008), 89.

86. For a sympathetic treatment of Stahl, see Hermann Simon, *Heinrich Stahl (13 April 1868–4 November 1942)* (Berlin: Hentrich, 1993).

87. The comparison was first made by Strauss, "Jewish Autonomy Within the Limits of National Socialist Policy," 139n25.

88. See the *Lagebericht* dated 6 July 1937, in Wildt, ed., *Die Judenpolitik*, 122.

89. Document 21, in ibid., 149

90. Abraham Margaliot, "The Dispute over the Leadership of German Jewry (1933–1938)," *Yad Vashem Studies* 10 (1974): 144–145.

91. Hans-Erich Fabian, "Zur Entstehung der 'Reichsvereinigung der Juden in Deutschland,'" in Strauss and Grossmann, eds., *Gegenwart im Rückblick*, 179n22.

92. Yehoyakim Cochavi, "Georg Kareski's Nomination as Head of the Kulturbund: The Gestapo's First Attempt—and Last Failure—to Impose a Jewish Leadership," *LBIYB* 34 (1989): 244. Cf. Francis R. Nicosia, "Revisionist Zionism in Germany (II): Georg Kareski and the Staatszionistische Organisation, 1933–1938," *LBIYB* 32 (1987): 231–267.

93. Cited in Lucy Dawidowicz, *The War Against the Jews 1933–1945* (New York: Holt, Rinehart and Winston, 1975), 195.

94. The text of the letter is contained in Kulka, ed., *Deutsches Judentum unter dem Nationalsozialismus*, 334–335.

95. "Protokoll der Sitzung des Präsidialausschusses und des Rats der Reichsvertretung der Juden in Deutschland vom 15. Juni 1937," in Kulka, ed., *Deutsches Judentum unter dem Nationalsozialismus*, 340.

96. For claims regarding weakness of the RV at this time, see Wildt, ed., *Die Judenpolitik*, 167–168. Regarding Stahl's failed efforts, see Ball-Kaduri, "The National Representation of Jews in Germany," 173.

97. The vote of confidence, tendered on 7 July 1937, is noted in Kulka, ed., *Deutsches Judentum unter dem Nationalsozialismus*, 345, and in *Informationsblätter* 5.6/7 (June/July 1937).

98. "Religionen," *Jüdische Rundschau* 39.36 (4 May 1934): 9, in *Werke* 6: 223.

99. "Chukkat haggoj," *Jüdische Rundschau* 39.96, Hanukkah supplement (30 November 1934): 5, in *Werke* 6: 226–227.

100. "Zurückhaltung," *C.V.-Zeitung* 13.5 (1 February 1934): 1, in *Werke* 6: 303–304.

101. "Festrede des Großpräsidenten zum 50. Stiftungsfest der Lessing-Loge des Bne Briss" (1935), in *Werke* 6: 306.

102. The German text is in Kulka, ed., *Deutsches Judentum unter dem Nationalsozialismus*, 226–227.

103. Israelitischer Tempel-Verband, Hamburg, "Rundschreiben Nr. 1 (mimeo), dated Hamburg, Elul 5695 [August/September, 1935], 1.

104. The complete German text is in Kulka, ed., *Deutsches Judentum unter dem Nationalsozialismus*, 245–246.

105. Leo Baeck, "A People Stands Before Its God," in Eric H. Boehm, *We Survived: The Stories of Fourteen of the Hidden and the Hunted of Nazi Germany* (New Haven, Conn.: Yale University Press, 1949), 286.

106. Chernow, *The Warburgs*, 435.

107. A photo of the telegram is in Barkai, "Im Schatten der Verfolgung und Vernichtung," 84.

108. Ball-Kaduri, *Vor der Katastrophe*, 54–55.

109. Hans Reichmann, *Deutscher Bürger und verfolgter Jude: Novemberpogrom und KZ Sachsenhausen 1937 bis 1939* (Munich: R. Oldenbourg, 1998), 47–48.

110. Kulka, ed., *Deutsches Judentum unter dem Nationalsozialismus*, 430.

CHAPTER 6

1. Alexander Guttmann, "The Kristallnacht: Personal Recollections," talk given at Hebrew Union College, Cincinnati, 9 November 1983. Manuscript in SC Box A-2014-90, Klau Library, Hebrew Union College, Cincinnati. Guttmann's recollection may be faulty: what he believes that Baeck said does not match other statements by Baeck or his intensified efforts to expedite emigration.

2. Cited in "Ansprache Max Brauer anlässlich der Grundsteinlegung der Synagoge an der Hohen Weide, 9.1.1958," *Hamburger Schlüsseldokumente zur deutsch-jüdischen Geschichte: Eine Online-Quellenedition* (http://juedische-geschichte-online.net/quelle/jgo:source-146), accessed 12 March 2017.

3. Recollection of Ernst Herzfeld in Otto Dov Kulka, ed., *Deutsches Judentum unter dem Nationalsozialismus*, vol. 1: *Dokumente zur Geschichte der Reichsvertretung der deutschen Juden 1933–1939* (Tübingen: Mohr Siebeck, 1997), 439.

4. Reiner Burger, *Von Goebbels Gnaden: Jüdisches Nachrichtenblatt (1938–1943)* (Münster: LIT Verlag, 2001), 53, 55.

5. Letter of 25 January 1939, in *Werke* 6: 567–568.

6. "Reichsvertretung der Juden in Deutschland: Umgestaltung zum Reichsverband der Juden in Deutschland," *Informationsblätter* 6.7/8 (July/August 1938).

7. Shaul Esh, "The Establishment of the Reichsvereinigung der Juden in Deutschland and Its Main Activities," *Yad Vashem Studies* 7 (1968): 25.

8. A thorough and richly documented recent study of the Reichsvereinigung is Beate Meyer, *A Fatal Balancing Act: The Dilemma of the Reich Association of Jews in Germany, 1939–1945*, trans. William Templer (New York: Berghahn, 2013).

9. Hans-Erich Fabian, "Zur Entstehung der Reichsvereinigung der Juden in Deutschland," in Herbert A. Strauss and Kurt R. Grossmann, eds., *Gegenwart im Rückblick: Festgabe für die Jüdische Gemeinde zu Berlin 25 Jahre nach dem Neubeginn* (Heidelberg: Lothar Stiehm, 1970), 178.

10. Ibid., 172.

11. "Prayer for Natalie Baeck," 7 March 1937, Leo Baeck Family Collection, AR 25449, Leo Baeck Institute Archives (LBIA), DigiBaeck, Frame 396.

12. Hans-Hasso von Veltheim-Ostrau to Edith Andreae, 5 March 1937, cited in Karl Klaus Walther, *Hans Hasso von Veltheim: Eine Biographie* (Halle: Mitteldeutscher Verlag, 2004), 259.

13. Eric H. Boehm, "A People Stands Before Its God: Leo Baeck," in idem, *We Survived: The Stories of Fourteen of the Hidden and Hunted of Nazi Germany* (New Haven, Conn.: Yale University Press, 1949), 282–283.

14. Letter to Ismar Elbogen, 25 April 1939, in *Werke* 6: 569.

15. Letter of 20 December 1939, in ibid., 609.

16. In a note to Leo Israel Baeck, dated 25 January 1941, from the Inland Revenue Office of Schöneberg, the district of Berlin in which Baeck lived, regarding the *Reichsfluchtsteuer*, the tax that Jewish emigrants were required to pay, the official concludes: "Further, I would ask you to communicate whether the date of your giving up your domestic residence has been set or when you anticipate your emigration." Records of the Reichsvereinigung der Juden in Deutschland, LBIJER 556, LBIA.

17. Letter to Hans Hirsch in Ithaca, N.Y., 8 July 1941, in *Werke* 6: 331.

18. Gudrun Maierhof, *Selbstbehauptung im Chaos: Frauen in der jüdischen Selbsthilfe 1933–1945* (Frankfurt: Campus Verlag, 2002), 211.

19. Letter to Hans Schäffer, former state secretary in the ministry of finance, at that time in neutral Sweden, 27 November 1942, in *Leo Baeck Institute Year Book* (*LBIYB*) 2 (1957): 313, and in *Werke* 6: 333–334.

20. Esriel Hildesheimer, *Jüdische Selbstverwaltung unter dem NS-Regime* (Tübingen: J. C. B. Mohr, 1994), 102–103, 122; Yehuda Bauer, *My Brother's Keeper: A History of the American Jewish Joint Distribution Committee 1929–1939* (Philadelphia: Jewish Publication Society, 1974), 258.

21. Letter of 10 June 1942, in Hermann Simon, *Heinrich Stahl (13 April 1868–4 November 1942)* (Berlin: Hentrich, 1993), 35. Stahl was highly regarded by Recha Freier, another severe critic of Leo Baeck and his closest associates. But she was a contentious person, who, in their common work for Youth Aliyah, also had a very poor relationship with Henrietta Szold, its principal leader. See her praise of Stahl in Recha Freier, *Let the Children Come: The Early History of Youth Aliyah* (London: Weidenfeld and Nicolson, 1961), 66; and on the conflict, B. Meyer, *A Fatal Balancing Act*, 385–388.

22. See the strong words he is reported as having addressed to Eichmann, in Hildesheimer, *Jüdische Selbstverwaltung unter dem NS-Regime*, 88.

23. Herbert A. Strauss, *In the Eye of the Storm: Growing Up Jewish in Germany, 1918–1943: A Memoir* (New York: Fordham University Press, 1999), 64, 99.

24. Letter to Immanuel Löw, 21 April 1940, in *Werke* 6: 330.

25. See Baeck's "Looking Forward," *Progressive Judaism: Bulletin of the World Union for Progressive Judaism*, November 1940.

26. "Die Wüste" (1936/1937), in *Werke* 6: 262–264.

27. "Die Reichsvertretung zu Rosch Haschana" (1938), in Kulka, ed., *Deutsches Judentum unter dem Nationalsozialismus*, 430.

28. "Die Existenz des Juden" (1935), in *Werke* 6: 245–253.

29. "Die Freien und die Unfreien" (1933), in ibid., 301–302.

30. "Zeiten und Tage" (1938/1939), in ibid., 266.

31. "Recht und Pflicht," *C.V.-Zeitung* 12.16 (2 May 1933): 71.

32. "Umwälzung und Umwandlung" (1933), in *Werke* 6: 220–223.

33. Introduction to *Aus alter und neuer Zeit: Illustrierte Beilage zum Israelitischen Familienblatt* 21 (6 September 1934): 1.

34. "Schöpfungsordnungen," *Jüdische allgemeine Zeitung* 16.22 (27 May 1936), supplement.

35. "Tag des Mutes" (1933), in *Werke* 6: 300–301.

36. Letter to Hans-Hasso von Veltheim-Ostrau, 28 February 1933, in ibid., 603.

37. Letter to Hans-Hasso von Veltheim-Ostrau, 30 April 1941, in ibid., 612.

38. Letter to Ismar Elbogen, 26 October 1940, in ibid., 573.

39. "Wissen und Glaube," *C.V.-Zeitung*, 2 June 1938, 2nd supplement.

40. Letter to Simon Rawidowicz, 24 December 1933. Copy received from Benjamin Ravid, son of Simon Rawidowicz.

41. Preface to *Das Evangelium als Urkunde der jüdischen Glaubensgeschichte*, in *Werke* 4: 403.

42. Ibid., 447.

43. *Wege im Judentum* (Berlin: Schocken, 1933). Fully contained in *Werke* 3.

44. *Aus drei Jahrtausenden: Wissenschaftliche Untersuchungen und Abhandlungen zur Geschichte des jüdischen Glaubens* (Berlin: Schocken—Jüdischer Buchverlag, 1938). It was reprinted with an introduction by Hans Liebeschütz (Tübingen: J. C. B. Mohr, 1958) and is contained in *Werke* 4: 27–399.

45. "Drei alte Lieder" (1937), in ibid., 211–216.

46. "Glauben" (1935), in ibid., 239.

47. "Sefer ha-Bahir," in ibid., 291.

48. "Israel und die Schechina: Zwei Midraschim," *Almanach des Schocken Verlags auf das Jahr 5697* (Berlin: Schocken, 1936/1937), 11.

49. Letter to Ismar Elbogen, 26 October 1940, in *Werke* 6: 573.

50. Letter to Max Grünewald, 3 March 1939, in ibid., 327. Baeck uses the Hebrew words from Exod. 13:18, *hamushim alu*, referring to the Israelites' armed departure from Egypt.

51. Letter to Ismar Elbogen, 19 February 1941, in ibid., 573.

52. The volume (no. 83) is dated 1939, the year in which it was supposed to appear. As with *Aus drei Jahrtausenden*, it was reprinted after the war from one of the few surviving copies.

53. "Gründung einer Rabbiner-Ausbildungskommission," in Kulka, ed., *Deutsches Judentum unter dem Nationalsozialismus*, 302–307.

54. Edward K. Kaplan and Samuel H. Dresner, *Abraham Joshua Heschel: Prophetic Witness* (New Haven, Conn.: Yale University Press, 1998), 116.

55. Ernst Simon, *Aufbau im Untergang: Jüdische Erwachsenenbildung im nationalsozialistischen Deutschland als geistiger Widerstand* (Tübingen: J. C. B. Mohr, 1959), 64.

56. Nathan Peter Levinson, *Ein Ort ist, mit wem du bist: Lebensstationen eines Rabbiners* (Berlin: Hentrich, 1996), 46.

57. Strauss, *In the Eye of the Storm*, 140.

58. Ibid., 121.

59. Beate Meyer, "Gratwanderung zwischen Verantwortung und Verstrickung: Die Reichsvereinigung der Juden in Deutschland und die jüdische Gemeinde zu Berlin

1938–1945," in idem and Hermann Simon, eds., *Juden in Berlin 1938–1945* (Berlin: Philo, 2000), 293.

60. Cited in Elisa Klapheck, ed., *Fräulein Rabbiner Jonas: Kann die Frau das rabbinische Amt bekleiden?* (Teetz: Hentrich & Hentrich, 1999), 43.

61. Elena Makarova, Sergei Makarov, and Victor Kuperman, *University over the Abyss: The Story Behind 520 Lecturers and 2,430 Lectures in KZ Theresienstadt 1942–1944* (Jerusalem: Verba, 2004), 109.

62. Wolfgang Hamburger, "Leo Baeck: The Last Teacher of the Lehranstalt," in Schlomo F. Rülf, ed., *Paul Lazarus Gedenkbuch* (Jerusalem: Jerusalem Post Press, 1961), 126–127. See also *Werke* 6: 322, 606.

63. Christhard Hoffmann and Daniel R. Schwartz, "Early but Opposed—Supported but Late: Two Berlin Seminaries Which Attempted to Move Abroad," *LBIYB* 36 (1991): 288–296.

64. Hamburger, "Leo Baeck: The Last Teacher of the Lehranstalt," 130.

65. Cited in G. Salzberger, "Dr. Leo Baeck: 70th Birthday," *World Union for Progressive Judaism Bulletin* 15 (December 1943): 6.

66. "Die Existenz des Juden" (1935), in *Werke* 6: 252.

67. Joachim Prinz, "Bilanz der Erneuerung," *Israelitisches Familienblatt*, 11 March 1937.

68. Document 28 in Michael Wildt, ed., *Die Judenpolitik des SD 1935 bis 1938* (Munich: R. Oldenbourg, 1995), 180.

69. Document 21 in ibid., 150.

70. Kulka, ed., *Deutsches Judentum unter dem Nationalsozialismus*, 377–378.

71. "Arbeitsbericht der Reichsvereinigung der Juden in Deutschland für das Jahr 1939," Reichsvereinigung der deutschen Juden Collection AR 221, box 1, folder 10, LBIA.

72. *Informationsblätter* 6.3/4 (March/April 1938): 23.

73. Herbert A. Strauss, "Jewish Emigration from Germany: Nazi Policies and Jewish Responses (1)," *LBIYB* 25 (1980): 317.

74. Konrad Kwiet, "The Ultimate Refuge: Suicide in the Jewish Community Under the Nazis," *LBIYB* 29 (1984): 135–167.

75. Marion Freyer Wolff, *The Shrinking Circle: Memories of Nazi Berlin, 1933–1939* (New York: UAHC Press, 1989), 65.

76. "Rede von Ehren-Grosspräsident Rabbiner Dr. Leo Baeck: Anlässlich der Installation der Districts-Gross-Loge Kontinental-Europa XIX in Basel (4 September 1955)," in *Werke* 5: 469–470. Baeck said in his speech to B'nai B'rith that Gandhi made that suggestion to a friend belonging to the old German nobility. The friend was Baron Hans-Hasso von Veltheim-Ostrau. See Hans-Hasso von Veltheim-Ostrau, *Der Atem Indiens: Tagebücher aus Asien* (Hamburg: Claasen, 1954), 15–16.

77. "Hilfe und Aufbau" (5696 [1935–1936]), in Kulka, ed., *Deutsches Judentum unter dem Nationalsozialismus*, 241.

78. "In Memory of Two of Our Dead," *LBIYB* 1 (1956): 53.

79. Juliane Wetzel, "Auswanderung aus Deutschland," in Wolfgang Benz, ed., *Die Juden in Deutschland, 1933–1945* (Munich: C. H. Beck, 1988), 486; "Die Reichsvertretung an die Juden in Deutschland," *C.V.-Zeitung* 17.38 (22 September 1938).

80. Letter to Isaac Max Rubinow in Cincinnati, secretary of the Independent Order of B'nai B'rith, 29 January 1934, in *Werke* 6: 320.

81. Naomi Shepherd, *A Refugee from Darkness: Wilfrid Israel and the Rescue of the Jews* (New York: Pantheon, 1984), 176.

82. *Werke* 6: 475.

83. Ibid., 472.

84. An example of Baeck's continuing interest in Jewish settlement in Palestine is his letter to Franz Meyer in Tel Aviv, 31 May 1939, Leo Baeck Collection AR 66, LBIA, DigiBaeck, Frames 1132–1133.

85. Kulka, ed., *Deutsches Judentum unter dem Nationalsozialismus*, 251.

86. Letter to Chaim Weizmann, 23 May 1939, in Werke 6: 626.

87. "Die Ferne," *Der Morgen* 14 (August 1938): 181–182, and in *Werke* 6: 281–282.

88. "Die Reichsvertretung an die Juden in Deutschland," *C.V.-Zeitung* 17.38 (22 September 1938): 1, and in *Werke* 6: 314.

89. Herbert Strauss, ed., *Jewish Immigrants of the Nazi Period in the U.S.A.*, vol. 4.2 (Munich: K. G. Saur, 1992), 579.

90. S. Adler-Rudel, *Jüdische Selbsthilfe unter dem Naziregime, 1933–1939* (Tübingen: J. C. B. Mohr, 1974), 157; Strauss, *In the Eye of the Storm*, 124; Hans Reichmann, *Deutscher Bürger und verfolgter Jude: Novemberpogrom und KZ Sachsenhausen, 1937 bis 1939* (Munich: R. Oldenbourg, 1998), 264.

91. Letter to Chief Rabbi J. H. Hertz, 23 January 1939, in *Werke* 6: 325–326.

92. Letter to Ismar Elbogen, 25 April 1939, in ibid., 569.

93. Letter to Lily Montagu, 5 January 1939, in ibid., 323–325. Joachim Prinz emigrated to America in 1937, when he was expelled from Germany. He later questionably claimed that the expulsion was motivated by a desire expressed to him that he act as a Nazi spy in the United States. See Michael A. Meyer, ed., *Joachim Prinz, Rebellious Rabbi: An Autobiography—the German and Early American Years* (Bloomington: Indiana University Press, 2008), 166.

94. H. G. Adler, *Der verwaltete Mensch: Studien zur Deportation der Juden aus Deutschland* (Tübingen: J. C. B. Mohr, 1974), 180; Fritz Backhaus and Martin Liepach, "Leo Baecks Manuskript über die 'Rechtsstellung der Juden in Europa,'" *Zeitschrift für Geschichtswissenschaft* 50 (2002): 61. See also B. Meyer, "Gratwanderung zwischen Verantwortung und Verstrickung," 307–312. The sources do not fully agree.

95. Arnold Paucker and Konrad Kwiet, "Jewish Leadership and Jewish Resistance," in David Bankier, ed., *Probing the Depths of German Antisemitism: German Society and the Persecution of the Jews, 1933–1941* (New York: Berghahn, 2000), 388.

96. "An den Herrn Reichskanzler Adolf Hitler" (1934), in *Werke* 6: 213–214.

97. Kulka, ed., *Deutsches Judentum unter dem Nationalsozialismus*, 141.

98. Ibid., 189–190.

99. Jewish Telegraphic Agency, *News*, 21 April 1937; Reichsvertretung to Reichsminister für Volksaufklärung und Propaganda, 15 May 1934, in Klaus J. Hermann, *Das Dritte Reich und die deutsch-jüdischen Organisationen 1933–1934* (Cologne: Carl Heymanns, 1969), 131.

100. A statement by the German Zionists, dated 21 June 1933, declared that "the boycott propaganda, now frequently directed against Germany, is by its nature un-Zionist since Zionism wants to convince and construct, not engage in battle." Hans Tramer, ed., *In zwei Welten: Siegfried Moses zum fünfundsiebzigsten Geburtstag* (Tel Aviv: Bitaon, 1962), 123.

101. Abba Hillel Silver, "Remove Jews from Germany," *Jewish Advocate*, 10 March 1936.

102. Jacob Jacobson, "Bruchstücke, 1939–1945" (1945), manuscript in Jacobson Collection, LBIA, DigiBaeck, ME329, p. 6.

103. Strauss, *In the Eye of the Storm*, 123–124.

104. Ernst Herzfeld, "Meine letzten Jahre in Deutschland, 1933–1938," undated manuscript, LBIA, DigiBaeck, ME287b, 27–28.

105. Cited in Konrad Kwiet, "Nach dem Pogrom: Stufen der Ausgrenzung," in Benz, ed., *Die Juden in Deutschland*, 567. Had the recipient of the radio been an officer of the Gestapo and not a local police officer, it is unlikely that he would have made such a statement.

106. Hans-Joachim Schoeps, *Ja-Nein-und Trotzdem: Erinnerungen-Begegnungen-Erfahrungen* (Mainz: Hase & Koehler, 1974), 26.

107. Eva G. Reichmann, "Symbol des deutschen Judentums," in idem, ed., *Worte des Gedenkens für Leo Baeck* (Heidelberg: Lambert Schneider, 1959), 44–45.

108. Letter from Leo Baeck, written while briefly outside the country on 29 April 1938, to Friedrich Brodnitz in New York, in Jürgen Matthäus and Mark Roseman, eds., *Jewish Responses to Persecution*, vol. 1: 1933–1938 (Lanham, Md.: AltaMira Press, 2010), 277.

109. Letter to Rudolf Jaser, 17 August 1950, in *Werke* 6: 675.

110. Walther, *Hans Hasso von Veltheim*, 261–262. This correspondent, Charles-Victor von Lüttischau, is likely the soldier referred to in Jacobson, "Bruchstücke, 1939–1945," 14.

111. Boehm, "A People Stands Before Its God," 288.

112. Letter to Rudolf Jaser, 18 January 1953, in *Werke* 6: 679.

113. Jacobson, "Bruchstücke, 1939–1945," excerpted in Monika Richarz, ed., *Jüdisches Leben in Deutschland: Selbstzeugnisse zur Sozialgeschichte 1918–1945* (Stuttgart: Deutsche Verlagsanstalt, 1982), 407.

114. Esh, "The Establishment of the Reichsvereinigung der Juden," 37.

115. Cited by Joachim Scholtyseck, "Die Firma Robert Bosch und ihre Hilfe für Juden," in Michael Kißener, ed., *Widerstand gegen die Judenverfolgung* (Konstanz: Universitätsverlag, 1996), 184.

116. Backhaus and Liepach, "Leo Baecks Manuskript über die 'Rechtsstellung der Juden in Europa,'" 64–65.

117. Letter of 4 January 1955 to Albrecht Fischer, cited in Peter Hoffmann, *Carl Goerdeler and the Jewish Question, 1933–1942* (Cambridge: Cambridge University Press, 2011), 113.

118. Arnold Paucker, *Standhalten und Widerstehen: Der Widerstand deutscher und österreichischer Juden gegen die nationalsozialistische Diktatur* (Essen: Klartext, 1995), 16–20.

119. E.g., Konrad Kwiet, "Leo Baeck und der deutsch-jüdische Widerstand," in Michael Brocke et al., eds., *Neuer Anbruch: Zur deutsch-jüdischen Geschichte und Kultur* (Berlin: Metropol, 2001), 90.

120. See excerpt from her October 2001 letter to Paucker, in Arnold Paucker, *German Jews in the Resistance 1933–1945: The Facts and the Problems* (Berlin: Gedenkstätte Deutscher Widerstand, 2005), 49n115.

121. Hans Reichmann, "Foreword: The Fate of a Manuscript," *LBIYB* 3 (1958): 362–363. Reichmann based his recollection on what he had heard from Baeck himself.

122. The two scholarly collaborators were Rabbi Leopold Lucas and the historian Hilde Ottenheimer; the secretaries were Paula Glück and Johanna Nathan. One of the manuscripts also mentions an otherwise unknown Peter Freund. See Backhaus and Liepach, "Leo Baecks Manuskript über die 'Rechtsstellung der Juden in Europa,'" 58.

123. This is the title as it appears on the title page of the copy held by the Leo Baeck Institute in New York.

124. See Hermann Simon, "Bislang unbekannte Quellen zur Entstehungsgeschichte des Werkes 'Die Entwicklung der Rechtsstellung der Juden in Europa, vornehmlich in Deutschland,'" in Georg Heuberger and Fritz Backhaus, eds., *Leo Baeck 1873–1956: Aus dem Stamme von Rabbinern* (Frankfurt: Jüdischer Verlag im Suhrkamp Verlag, 2001), 103–110. After the war, Baeck told another interviewer that "an official of the Ministry of the Interior suggested

to me in 1941 that we might strengthen the hand of the lenient group [within the Party] by preparing a history of German Judaism which would indicate its cultural contribution to European civilization"; see Boehm, "A People Stands Before Its God," 289. There is no written text by Baeck to support this possibility. Baeck's words, as presented by Boehm, may not always be precise. When Baeck begged off writing the memoir himself, Boehm came to Cincinnati to interview him. In a letter to Baeck of 30 March 1949, Boehm admitted that there were "a few points on which I had to interpolate." Erik H. Boehm Collection, AR 2229, LBIA.

125. This theoretical possibility is suggested in a detailed study of the subject: Backhaus and Liepach, "Leo Baecks Manuskript über die 'Rechtsstellung der Juden in Europa,'" 67; also in Arnold Paucker, *Deutsche Juden im Kampf um Recht und Freiheit* (Teetz: Hentrich und Hentrich, 2003), 249–250.

126. An analysis of the document and two brief excerpts are given in Albert Friedlander, "A Muted Protest in War-Time Berlin: Writing on the Legal Position of German Jewry Throughout the Centuries—Leo Baeck—Leopold Lucas—Hilde Ottenheimer," *LBIYB* 37 (1992): 363–380.

127. Boehm, "A People Stands Before Its God," 289–290.

128. Strauss, *In the Eye of the Storm*, 132.

129. Hildesheimer, *Jüdische Selbstverwaltung unter dem NS-Regime*, 216.

130. Jacobson, "Bruchstücke, 1939–1945," 8; also in Richarz, ed., *Jüdisches Leben in Deutschland*, 403.

131. Ernst Ludwig Ehrlich, "Leo Baeck—Rabbiner in schwerster Zeit," *Theresienstädter Studien und Dokumente* (1996): 132–133.

132. Boehm, "A People Stands Before Its God," 288. After a while, the Nazis could no longer tolerate considerate behavior displayed toward Jews about to be transported to their deaths and gave the task of collecting the potential victims to Gestapo officials or members of the police. See B. Meyer, "Gratwanderung zwischen Verantwortung und Verstrickung," 305.

133. O. D. Kulka, "The "Reichsvereinigung" of the Jews in Germany," in Yisrael Gutman and Cynthia Haft, eds., *Patterns of Jewish Leadership in Nazi Europe* (Jerusalem: Yad Vashem, 1979), 54–55.

134. Walther, *Hans Hasso von Veltheim*, 260.

135. Appeal in the *Jüdisches Nachrichtenblatt Berlin*, 12 June 1942, in *Werke* 6: 295–296 (Baeck's emphasis).

136. Letter to Max Grünewald, 3 March 1939, in ibid., 326.

137. Letter to Rudolfo Löb, 18 November 1942, in ibid., 333.

138. Letter to Ilse Blumenthal-Weiss, 12 December 1942, in ibid., 336.

139. Boehm, "A People Stands Before Its God," 290.

140. In Ruth Klüger's book of recollections, *Weiter Leben: Eine Jugend* (Göttingen: Wallstein, 1992), 100–101, she mistakenly considers that Baeck may have wanted to make a good impression on the Gestapo officers or make them less antisemitic. Nothing could be further from the truth.

CHAPTER 7

1. Before Baeck arrived, the number had been even greater, more than 53,000 in September 1942. See Zdenek Lederer, *Ghetto Theresienstadt*, trans. K. Weisskopf (London: Edward Goldston & Son, 1953), 247.

2. "Vision und Geduld" (1945), in *Werke* 6: 362. An English version, "Life in a Concentration Camp," appeared in *Jewish Forum* 3.6 (March 1946): 29–32, and in *Jewish Spectator* (July 1946): 12–13.

3. Various sources give differing statistics. These are taken from *Jerusalem Report* (22 January 2018): 27.

4. Leo Baeck, foreword to H. G. Adler, *Theresienstadt 1941–1945: The Face of a Coerced Community*, trans. Belinda Cooper (New York: Cambridge University Press, 2017), xi; original German version in *Werke* 6: 366.

5. Cited by Hermann Levin Goldschmidt, "Leo Baeck," in Eva G. Reichmann, ed., *Worte des Gedenkens für Leo Baeck* (Heidelberg: Lambert Schneider, 1959), 193.

6. Elsa Bernstein, *Das Leben als Drama: Erinnerungen an Theresienstadt*, ed. Rita Bake and Birgit Kiupel (Dortmund: Ebersbach, 1999), 91, 175.

7. Ilse Blumenthal-Weiss, *Begegnungen mit Else Lasker-Schueler, Nelly Sachs, Leo Baeck, Martin Buber* (New York: Leo Baeck Institute, 1977), 22.

8. Letter to W. Gunther Plaut, a former student then in the United States, 6 June 1943, Leo Baeck Collection AR 66, Leo Baeck Institute Archives (LBIA), DigiBaeck, Frame 708.

9. Heinrich F. Liebrecht, *"Nicht mitzuhassen, mitzulieben bin ich da": Mein Weg durch die Hölle des Dritten Reiches* (Freiburg im Breisgau: Herder, 1990), 105–106.

10. Bernstein, *Das Leben als Drama*, 32–35; Beate Meyer, "'Altersghetto,' 'Vorzugslager' und Tätigkeitsfeld: Die Repräsentanten der Reichsvereinigung der Juden in Deutschland und Theresienstadt," in *Theresienstädter Studien und Dokumente* (Prague: Academia, 2005), 140.

11. Richard Feder, *Jüdische Tragödie—Letzter Akt: Theresienstadt, 1941–1945, Bericht eines Rabbiners* (Potsdam: Verlag für Berlin-Brandenburg, 2004), 68.

12. Emil Fackenheim, *An Epitaph for German Judaism: From Halle to Jerusalem* (Madison: University of Wisconsin Press, 2007), 45.

13. H. G. Adler, "Leo Baeck in Theresienstadt," *AJR* supplement (December 1956): 7.

14. Liebrecht, *"Nicht mitzuhassen, mitzulieben bin ich da,"* 90.

15. Feder, *Jüdische Tragödie—Letzter Akt*, 69.

16. Jindrich Flusser, "Ein Rückblick," in *Theresienstädter Studien und Dokumente* (Prague: Academia, 1999), 56.

17. Cited in Leonard Baker, *Days of Sorrow and Pain: Leo Baeck and the Berlin Jews* (New York: Macmillan, 1978), 304.

18. Elena Makarova, Sergei Makarov, and Victor Kuperman, *University over the Abyss: The Story Behind 520 Lecturers and 2,430 Lectures in KZ Theresienstadt, 1942–1944* (Jerusalem: Verba, 2004), 43; Adler, *Theresienstadt, 1941–1945*, 540.

19. "Vision und Geduld" (1945), in *Werke* 6: 363.

20. Jacob Jacobson, *Terezin: The Daily Life, 1943–1945* (London: Jewish Central Information Service, 1946), 3.

21. Letter to Albert Einstein, 3 August 1945, in *Werke* 6: 633.

22. Jacob Jacobson, "Bruchstücke, 1939–1945" (1945), manuscript in Jacobson Collection, LBIA, DigiBaeck, ME329, pp. 32–33.

23. Adler, *Theresienstadt, 1941–1945*, 215. A 1978 recorded discussion among four Czech inmates of Theresienstadt, Rudolf Bunzel and his wife [name not given] and Leonard and Edith Ehrlich, minimizes Baeck's activity for others. But this may simply be a lack of awareness. United States Holocaust Memorial Museum Collection, RG-50.862.0002.

24. Blumenthal-Weiss, *Begegnungen*, 22–23.

25. Kramer is cited in Makarova et al., *University over the Abyss*, 189.

26. "Vision und Geduld" (1945), in *Werke* 6: 361–362.

27. Paul Eppstein to Franz Meyer in Tel Aviv, 4 July 1939, Yad Vashem Archives, Record Group 0.8—Germany Collection, file 11, item ID 3687979. Eppstein reports that, with the exception of the innermost circle of the Reichsvereinigung, an ever swifter substitution of emigrated personnel was taking place.

28. Adler, *Theresienstadt, 1941–1945*, xix, 304–306. For a day-by-day chart of the food items distributed by the central kitchens, see the document in Käthe Starke, *Der Führer schenkt den Juden eine Stadt* (Berlin: Haude & Spenersche, 1975), 238–247.

29. Vera Schiff, *Theresienstadt: The Town the Nazis Gave to the Jews* (Toronto: Lugus, 1996), 74.

30. Jacobson, "Bruchstücke, 1939–1945," 35–36.

31. Details of Eppstein's arrest and murder are given in Lederer, *Ghetto Theresienstadt*, 149–151. See also the account of the relationship in Wolfgang Benz, *Theresienstadt: Eine Geschichte von Täuschung und Vernichtung* (Munich: C. H. Beck, 2013), 50–54, and Fritz Backhaus, "'Ein Experiment des Willens zum Bösen'—Überleben in Theresienstadt," in Georg Heuberger and Fritz Backhaus, eds., *Leo Baeck 1873–1956: Aus dem Stamme von Rabbinern* (Frankfurt a.M.: Jüdischer Verlag, 2001), 121. Benz presents a sympathetic view of Eppstein in his *The Holocaust: A German Historian Examines the Genocide*, trans. Jane Sydenham Kwiet (New York: Columbia University Press, 1999), 112–116.

32. Told to the author when the survivor accompanied him on a visit to Theresienstadt in September 1979.

33. Norbert Troller, *Theresienstadt: Hitler's Gift to the Jews* (Chapel Hill: University of North Carolina Press, 1991), 89.

34. Lederer, *Ghetto Theresienstadt*, 123.

35. Jacobson, "Bruchstücke, 1939–1945," 30–31.

36. Makarova et al., *University over the Abyss*, title page.

37. Baeck later recalled that Jewish sentries were posted every hundred or so feet to warn of the approach of SS guards. See Murray Frank, "Leo Baeck: Prophetic Spirit," *Liberal Judaism* (January 1948): 16.

38. Maurice N. Eisendrath, "Our Inescapable Responsibility," *Liberal Judaism* (February 1948): 14.

39. Makarova et al., *University over the Abyss*, 187.

40. "Das Vortragswesen zu Theresienstadt," document printed in Starke, *Der Führer schenkt den Juden eine Stadt*, 231.

41. Troller, *Theresienstadt*, 47.

42. Philip Manes, *As if It Were Life: A WWII Diary from the Theresienstadt Ghetto*, ed. Ben Barkow and Klaus Leist, trans. Janet Foster et al. (New York: Palgrave Macmillan, 2009), 91.

43. Ibid., 108.

44. A copy of the required ticket is in Miriam Intrator, "Storytelling and Lecturing During the Holocaust: The Nature and Role of Oral Exchanges in Theresienstadt, 1941–1945," *Leo Baeck Institute Year Book* 51 (2006): 222.

45. See, e.g., Baeck's "Die Entwicklung zur sittlichen Persönlichkeit" (1931), in *Werke* 4: 345–356.

46. Manes, *As if It Were Life*, 201.

47. Interview of Trude Simonsohn by Minka Pradelski, in Frank Kind and Esther Alexander-Ihme, eds., *Zedaka: Jüdische Sozialarbeit im Wandel der Zeit* (Frankfurt a.M.: Jüdisches Museum, 1992), 136.

48. Jacobson, "Bruchstücke, 1939–1945," 33.

49. Ruth Klüger, *Weiter Leben: Eine Jugend* (Göttingen: Wallstein, 1992), 100.

50. Jacobson, *Terezin*, 13.

51. Cited in Makarova et al., *University over the Abyss*, 191.

52. A list of all thirty-eight topics can be found in English trans. in ibid., 434–435, and an abbreviated version with the original German titles in *Werke* 6: 341–342.

53. The original German text is in *Werke* 6: 342–358. An English trans. is in *Synagogue Review* 37 (September 1962): 51–59.

54. *Werke* 6: 353.

55. Ibid., 358.

56. On the activity of Regina Jonas in Theresienstadt, see Makarova et al., *University over the Abyss*, 108–111, 473. Baeck does not mention Jonas in his own very limited writing about Theresienstadt or in recollections of conversations with him by others. One cannot be certain about the reason: Did he have a grudge against her on account of an affair that she had after ordination with a much older rabbi? Or would he have mentioned her, had he written more about his experience in the ghetto?

57. See the report of the delegation at a meeting of the Danish Legation in Stockholm on 19 July 1944, in the World Jewish Congress Collection, MSS 361, H132/28, American Jewish Archives.

58. Eric H. Boehm, "A People Stands Before Its God: Leo Baeck," in idem, *We Survived: The Stories of Fourteen of the Hidden and Hunted of Nazi Germany* (New Haven, Conn.: Yale University Press, 1949), 294.

59. Interview with Margot Friedlander, USC Shoah Foundation, Virtual History Archive.

60. For the notion that the delegation may not have been totally deceived, as well as for the film, see Jacobson, *Terezin*, 16.

61. Jacobson, "Bruchstücke, 1939–1945," 40–41. However, one survivor recalled that Baeck used the Nazi rule specifying that only complete families should be deported in order to save members of a family where the husband was temporarily outside the ghetto. Supposedly, he told the guards: *streichen*, i.e., cross the names off the list. Interview with Joel Fabian, USC Shoah Foundation, Virtual History Archive.

62. Letter to undesignated recipient, 18 April 1946, in *Werke* 6: 359.

63. Cited in Boehm, "A People Stands Before Its God," 295–296. A German text is in Hans Erich Fabian, "Die letzte Etappe," in Eva G. Reichmann, ed., *Festschrift zum 80. Geburtstag von Rabbiner Dr. Leo Baeck am 23. Mai 1953* (London: Council for the Protection of the Rights and Interests of the Jews from Germany, 1953), 96n25.

64. Frank, "Leo Baeck: Prophetic Spirit," 16.

65. Liebrecht, *"Nicht mitzuhassen, mitzulieben bin ich da,"* 119.

66. This is the subject in Joshua Franklin, "Tell No One: Leo Baeck and the Terrible Secret" (master's thesis, Clark University, 2007).

67. Liebrecht, *"Nicht mitzuhassen, mitzulieben bin ich da,"* 186.

68. Ibid., 187.

69. Miroslav Karny, "Die Flucht des Auschwitzer Häftlings Vítězslav Lederer und der tschechische Widerstand," in *Theresienstädter Studien und Dokumente* (Prague: Academia, 1997), 168–169.

70. Interview with Charlotte Opfermann, USC Shoah Foundation, Virtual History Archive.

71. Ruth Bondy, *"Elder of the Jews": Jakob Edelstein of Theresienstadt*, trans. Evelyn Abel (New York: Grove Press, 1989), 375.

72. Cited from a personal conversation with Tillich by Albert H. Friedlander in his *Leo Baeck: Teacher of Theresienstadt* (New York: Holt, Rinehart and Winston, 1968), 47. In his personal life, Tillich behaved far differently from Baeck. He was a womanizer and, especially late in life, a lover of wealth and fame. See Wilhelm Pauck and Marion Pauck, *Paul Tillich: His Life and Thought* (New York: Harper & Row, 1976), vol. 1.

73. Lederer, *Ghetto Theresienstadt*, 169.

74. Letter to an unknown recipient, 18 April 1946, in *Werke* 6: 359.

75. Cited in Ron Chernow, *The Warburgs: The 20th-Century Odyssey of a Remarkable Jewish Family* (New York: Random House, 1993), 537.

76. Manfred E. Swarsensky, "Out of the Root of Rabbis," in Herbert A. Strauss and Kurt R. Grossmann, eds., *Gegenwart im Rückblick: Festgabe für die jüdische Gemeinde zu Berlin, 25 Jahre nach dem Neubeginn* (Heidelberg: Lothar Stiehm, 1970), 225. The words are from Rom. 12:19.

77. Letter to an unknown recipient, 18 February 1947, in *Werke* 6: 360.

CHAPTER 8

1. Letter to undisclosed recipient, 23 June 1947, in *Werke* 6: 360–361.

2. Letter to Fritz Steinthal in Buenos Aires, 30 July 1945, Leo Baeck Collection MF 145, Leo Baeck Institute Archives (LBIA), microfilm. Rabbi Steinthal repeatedly invited Baeck to visit Argentina, but the visit did not come about.

3. "Gespräch mit Leo Baeck," *Aufbau* 11.51 (21 December 1945): 2; *Werke* 6: 370–371.

4. Article from *New York Times*, 11 July 1945, in World Jewish Congress Collection MSS 361, H133/1, American Jewish Archives.

5. "A Message from Rabbi Leo Baeck," *National Jewish Monthly* 6.5 (January 1946): 158; *Werke* 6: 371–372.

6. Gershom Scholem to Aniela Jaffé, 7 May 1963, in Thomas Sparr, ed., *Gershom Scholem Briefe II, 1948–1970* (Munich: C. H. Beck, 1995), 94–95; David Biale, *Gershom Scholem: Master of the Kabbalah* (New Haven, Conn.: Yale University Press, 2018), 160–161.

7. "Gespräch mit Leo Baeck," 1–2.

8. Cited in Murray Frank, "Leo Baeck: Prophetic Spirit," *Liberal Judaism* (January 1948): 17.

9. Letters to Ernst Ludwig Ehrlich, 10 November 1946 and 17 December 1946, in *Werke* 6: 637–639. Also noted in Michael A. Meyer, "Toward a 'Culture of Humanity': Leo Baeck," in Zeev Mankowitz et al., eds., *Europe in the Eyes of Survivors of the Holocaust* (Jerusalem: Yad Vashem, 2014), 68–69.

10. Letter to Rabbi and Mrs. Robert Raphael Geis, 10 March 1950, in *Werke* 6: 658–659.

11. Letter to Gershom Scholem, 22 August 1950, in ibid., 650–651.

12. Letter to Mrs. M. Dienemann, 14 June 1946, in *Leo Baeck Institute Year Book* 10 (1965): 238.

13. Letter to Mally Dienemann, 2 March 1949, Leo Baeck Collection AR 66, LBIA, DigiBaeck, Frame 1241.

14. Letter to Frau Scheinmann-Rosenzweig, 31 August 1945, Leo Baeck Collection AR 66, LBIA, DigiBaeck, Frame 731.

15. Letter to Rabbi Dagobert Nellhaus in Roxbury, Mass., 24 September 1945, ibid., Frame 609.

16. Letter to Marija Bogicevic von Hollitscher, 18 April 1946, cited in Fritz Backhaus, "'Ein Experiment des Willens zum Bösen'—Überleben in Theresienstadt," in Georg Heuberger and Fritz Backhaus, eds., *Leo Baeck 1873–1956: Aus dem Stamme von Rabbinern* (Frankfurt a.M.: Jüdischer Verlag, 2001), 111.

17. Letter "To Whom It May Concern," 3 July 1946, in *Werke* 6: 375.

18. Hans-Hasso von Veltheim-Ostrau to Leo Baeck, 30 April 1946, in ibid., 618–621.

19. "Vom Gewissen," *Aufbau* 11.48 (30 November 1945): 1–2.

20. "Judaism in the World of Tomorrow," *Jewish Spectator*, January 1946, 9.

21. "Leo Baeck's Message," *AJR Information* 3.2 (October 1948): 3; "Staat und Kultur" (1946), in *Werke* 6: 417–421.

22. *Dieses Volk: Jüdische Existenz*, pt. 2 (1957), in *Werke* 2: 359, and in English trans., *This People Israel: The Meaning of Jewish Existence*, trans. Albert H. Friedlander (Philadelphia: Jewish Publication Society, 1965), 386. Cf. M. Meyer, "Toward a Culture of Humanity," 72. The main title is taken from Isa. 43:21—"This people that I formed for Myself."

23. "Gerechtigkeit" (1948), in *Werke* 6: 442.

24. "Menschlichkeit" (1948), in ibid., 445.

25. Ibid., 446–447.

26. "Frieden" (1948), in ibid., 451. See also Leo Baeck, *Der Sinn der Geschichte* (Berlin: Carl Habel, 1946), 42. Only the first part of this volume is reprinted in *Werke* 5: 25–34, and in English trans. in *Reform Jewish Quarterly* (Fall 2018): 109–125.

27. "Individuum Ineffabile" (1947), in *Werke* 5: 72–108.

28. "The New Jew," *World Union for Progressive Judaism Bulletin* (*WUPJB*) (March 1946): 5.

29. "Vom Gewissen," 2.

30. "The Task of Progressive Judaism in the Post-War World," *Report of the Fifth International Conference, Held in London July 25 to July 30, 1946* (London: WUPJ, 1946), 56.

31. *WUPJB* 20 (September 1948): 35. Baeck would have pronounced the phrase using the Ashkenazi pronunciation of Hebrew, which in German transliteration becomes: *l'saken olam b'malchus Schaddai.*

32. "Die Idee bleibt" (1946), in *Werke* 6: 387–389. Leo Baeck's son-in-law, Hermann Berlak, was a member of the K.C. fraternity. When survivors from the fraternity met in Chicago in 1956, one of them, Fritz Rosenthal, who had been a guest in Baeck's home in Berlin, delivered a lengthy lecture on what Baeck had meant for German Jewry: "Leo Baeck, der Repräsentant des deutschen Judentums unserer Zeit," *K.C. Blaetter Festschrift*, October 1956, 36–38.

33. *Von Moses Mendelssohn zu Franz Rosenzweig: Typen jüdischen Selbstverständnisses in den letzen beiden Jahrzehnten* (Stuttgart: Kohlhammer, 1958); also in *Werke* 5: 158–204.

34. Letter to Ottilie Schönewald, 16 December 1953, Leo Baeck Collection AR 66, LBIA, DigiBaeck, Frames 738–739.

35. "Bewährung des deutschen Judentums" (1953), in *Werke* 6: 396.

36. Ibid., 397.

37. "London Session of Leo Baeck Institute," *AJR Information* 10.11 (November 1955): 6.

38. Letter to American Jewish Joint Distribution Committee, 7 September 1950, Joint Distribution Committee Archives, within Joint Distribution Committee Digitized Archives, accessed 23 March 2018.

39. Letter to the board of directors of the Jewish Restitution Successor Organization in New York, 20 July 1950, in ibid.

40. Monroe Goldwater to Leo Baeck, 13 April 1954, in ibid.

41. Letter to the Jewish Restitution Successor Organization, att. Mr. Monroe Goldwater, President, n.d. but presumably 1954, in ibid.

42. The letter of withdrawal, dated 12 March 1954, is in *Werke* 6: 385–386.

43. Gershom Scholem to Leo Baeck, 2 June 1946, in Itta Shedletzky, ed., *Gershom Scholem Briefe I, 1914–1947* (Munich: C. H. Beck, 1994), 315.

44. Baeck to Georg Landauer, 7 February 1950, in *Werke* 6: 383–384.

45. Letter to Salo Baron, 12 April 1949, cited in Adi Livny, "Who Is the Successor of European Jewry? A Dispute Between Gershom Scholem and Leo Baeck in 1949," at www.daat-hamakom.com/wp-content/uploads/2015/08/Adi-Livni-Essay.pdf, accessed 23 August 2018.

46. Letter to Ernst G. Lowenthal, 3 January 1947, in *Werke* 6: 661–662.

47. Arthur Loewenstamm, "The Society for Jewish Study," in *Festschrift zum 80. Geburtstag von Rabbiner Dr. Leo Baeck am 23. Mai 1953* (London: Council for the Protection of the Rights and Interests of Jews from Germany, 1953), 98–101.

48. "Juden und Deutsche," *Aufbau* (19 November 1948): 3; in *Werke* 6: 377.

49. Ibid.

50. Ibid.

51. Letter to Robert Raphael Geis, 5 April 1950, Leo Baeck Collection AR 66, LBIA, DigiBaeck, Frame 71.

52. "Israel und das deutsche Volk," *Merkur* 10 (1952): 901–911; in *Werke* 5: 49–61.

53. Interview with Alexander Schindler, USC Shoah Foundation, Virtual History Archive.

54. This account is based on Ernst G. Lowenthal, "1948: Leo Baecks erstes Wiedersehen mit Deutschland. Erinnerungen seines Reisebegleiters," *Tradition und Erneuerung* 37 (March 1974): 16–19.

55. "Maimonides—der Mann, sein Werk und seine Wirkung" (1954), in *Werke* 5: 139–157.

56. Cited in Hans Lamm, ed., *Theodor Heuss an und über Juden* (Düsseldorf: Econ-Verlag, 1964), 10.

57. Letter to Ludwig Meidner, 8 January 1953, in *Werke* 6: 630.

58. "Seelisches Schicksal: Zu Theodor Heuss' 70 Geburtstag" (1954), in *Werke* 6: 689–692.

59. "Theodor Heuss zu Leo Baecks 80. Geburtstag am 23 Mai 1953," in ibid., 687.

60. "German Order for Dr. Baeck," London *Jewish Chronicle*, 29 May 1953.

61. After a 1950 lecture in New York, Baeck clearly displays ambivalence when asked about the reestablishment of a Jewish community in Germany. He calls it "impracticable and impossible" because of what occurred before 1945 and the ongoing failure to make reparations. Yet, even though he reiterates that the history of the Jews of Germany has come to an end, analogously to Spanish Jewry in 1492, "some Jews did stay there, and others did or do go back. And living there, they must—and should—be helped to have their congregations"; see "Judaism: The Religious Character and the Historical Situation," in *Two Series of Lectures by Dr. Leo Baeck* (New York: Congregation Emanu-El, 1950), 28.

62. Letter to Siegfried Guggenheim in Flushing, N.Y., 6 January 1955, Leo Baeck Collection AR 66, LBIA, DigiBaeck, Frame 184.

63. See the letters in *Werke* 6: 401–405, 654–655.

64. Letter to Robert Raphael Geis, 31 October 1949, in ibid., 657.

65. Letter to Steven S. Schwarzschild, 11 May 1949, Leo Baeck Collection AR 66, LBIA, DigiBaeck, Frames 742–743.

66. Letter to Abraham Joshua Heschel, 11 March 1947, received from Susannah Heschel.

67. Frank, "Leo Baeck: Prophetic Spirit," 12.

68. Maurice N. Eisendrath, "Our Inescapable Responsibility," *Liberal Judaism* (February 1948): 12; letter to Gertrud Luckner, 27 February 1948, in *Werke* 6: 644.

69. *Aufbau* 14.2 (9 January 1948): 19.

70. Letter to Rudolf Jaser, 11 December 1952, in *Werke* 6: 678–679.

71. Daniel L. Davis, "Baeck Comes to America," *Liberal Judaism* (January 1948): 44. However, for family reasons, it was Great Britain that became Baeck's new home. In 1950, he received British citizenship and, in a short piece, "The Crown," wrote of the deep sense of "unity through all diversity" that that symbol inspired. See *Synagogue Review* 27.10 (June 1953): 1.

72. "Rede von Ehren-Grosspräsident Rabbiner Dr. Leo Baeck anlässlich der Installation der Districts-Gross-Loge Kontinental-Europa XIX in Basel" (4 September 1955), in *Werke* 5: 465.

73. Letter to Rudolf Jaser, 17 August 1950, in *Werke* 6: 674–675.

74. Cited in Frank, "Leo Baeck: Prophetic Spirit," 12.

75. See Howard Mortman, *When Rabbis Bless Congress: The Great American Story of Jewish Prayers on Capitol Hill* (Boston: Academic Studies Press, forthcoming, 2020). Thanks to Gary Zola for calling this work to my attention.

76. Letter to Hans-Hasso von Veltheim-Ostrau, 31 December 1940, in *Werke* 6: 611.

77. *Congressional Record—House* (1948): 1275; also in *Werke* 6: 549.

78. *Das Wesen des Judentums*, in *Werke* 1: 258.

79. Letters to Rudolf Jaser, 3 February 1949, and 14 January 1951, in *Werke* 6: 671, 677.

80. Michael A. Meyer, "The Refugee Scholars Project of the Hebrew Union College," in idem, *Judaism Within Modernity: Essays on Jewish History and Religion* (Detroit: Wayne State University Press, 2001), 345–361. Although deeply grateful to Julian Morgenstern for bringing him to America, Heschel soon moved to the Jewish Theological Seminary in New York, which was more in keeping with his religious orientation.

81. Letter to Franz Landsberger, 17 May 1949, Franz Landsberger Collection AR 2318, Box 1/3, LBIA.

82. Cited in Marina Sassenberg, *Selma Stern (1890–1981): Das Eigene in der Geschichte. Selbstentwürfe und Geschichtsentwürfe einer Historikerin* (Tübingen: Mohr Siebeck, 2004), 137. A short-term visitor to Cincinnati was another old acquaintance, the psychologist and psychiatrist Erich Fromm, whom Baeck hadn't seen for fifty years and with whom he was glad to spend a few hours daily during his visit. Letter to Rudolf Jaser, 18 January 1953, in *Werke* 6: 679.

83. One of Marianne and Stanley Dreyfus's sons, James (Jimmy), a physician, married Ellen Weinberg, one of the earliest American female rabbis and the one carrying on the succession of rabbis in the Baeck family.

84. "Religious Education of Children in Palestine" (1948), in *Werke* 6: 484–485.

85. "Das Judentum auf alten und neuen Wegen" (1950), in *Werke* 5: 45. English trans. as "Judaism on Old and New Paths," *International Review of Missions* 39.154 (April 1950): 197–198.

86. "Presidential Address by Rabbi Dr. Leo Baeck Given at the 25th Anniversary Conference of the World Union for Progressive Judaism in London, July 1951" (printed as a pamphlet without indication of place or date), 7.

87. Letter to Lily Montagu, 12 February 1952, MSS 16, D12/4, American Jewish Archives.

88. "The Present Contribution of Judaism to Civilization," *Report of the Seventh International and Twenty-Fifth Anniversary Conference, July 12 to July 18, 1951* (London: WUPJ, 1951), 66. The

transfer of the World Union headquarters to Israel did occur, but not until 1973, when it was prompted by its then-president, Rabbi Richard Hirsch.

89. "Gutachten vom Oktober 1951," in *Werke* 6: 488–490.

90. Letter to Fritz Steinthal in Buenos Aires, 29 December 1947, Leo Baeck Collection MF 145, LBIA, microfilm.

91. Letter to David Werner Senator in Jerusalem, 12 December 1952, in *Werke* 6: 491.

92. Letter to Rudolf Jaser, 12 October 1947, in ibid., 669.

93. "Judaism and Zionism: A Liberal Jewish View" (1947), in ibid., 477.

94. Davis, "Baeck Comes to America," 8.

95. Letter to Hans Paeschke in Munich, 4 November 1949, in *Werke* 6: 488; interview in *Aufbau* 14.2 (9 January 1948): 19; Maurice N. Eisendrath, "Leo Baeck Meets the Jewish Press," *Liberal Judaism* (January 1948): 20.

96. "World Religion and National Religion" (1953), in *Werke* 5: 557.

97. Frank, "Leo Baeck: Prophetic Spirit," 18.

98. Letter to Ernst Ludwig Ehrlich, 24 December 1946, in *Werke* 6: 639–640. Baeck was welcomed at the Zionist Congress held in London in July 1945.

99. Davis, "Baeck Comes to America," 8.

100. "Palestine Cooperation: Appeal Made to Jews to Work for Goal of Common Welfare (18 April 1948)," in *Werke* 6: 480–482.

101. Letter to Ernst Ludwig Ehrlich, 22 October 1947, in ibid., 641–642.

102. "Das Judentum auf alten und neuen Wegen," 45.

103. Letter to George Manasse, 20 November 1952, Leo Baeck Collection MF 145, LBIA, microfilm.

104. The Jewish Society for Human Service, GB152, MSS.157/3/JS, undated pamphlet, copy received from the Modern Records Center, University of Warwick Library.

105. Cited in Norman Bentwich, *My 77 Years: An Account of My Life and Times, 1883–1960* (Philadelphia: Jewish Publication Society, 1961), 226. On the Jewish Society for Human Service, see also Ruth Dudley Edwards, *Victor Gollancz: A Biography* (London: Victor Gollancz, 1987), 473–490.

106. In the issues of 11 June 1948 and 6 August 1948.

107. Letter to Gershom Scholem and his wife, 24 May 1951, in *Werke* 6: 652.

108. Most easily accessible in *Werke* 5: 526–532.

109. See Benjamin C. I. Ravid, ed., *Israel: The Ever-Dying People and Other Essays* [*by*] *Simon Rawidowicz* (London: Associated University Presses, 1986), 151.

110. "The State of Israel: The Social Character and the Historical Situation," in *Two Series of Lectures*. Three years later, wanting to give Europe, as well, a central role, Baeck wrote: "There is a three-fold sphere of Jewish life today: that of historic achievement, Europe; that of solid reality, America; that of faithful adventure, Israel. Each is an entity in its own right. Israel is not to be Americanized or Europeanized, nor is America to be Israelized." Hebrew Union College–Jewish Institute of Religion, *Founders' Day Services . . . Honoring the Eightieth Birthday of Dr. Leo Baeck* (Cincinnati: HUC-JIR, 1953), [2].

111. "Judaism in the World of Tomorrow," 9.

112. Yet Baeck was convinced that his "Romantic Religion" should not appear in English translation immediately following the war. To his editor at Schocken Books, Nahum Glatzer, he wrote: "I must confess today that a short time ago, after a conversation with an American acquaintance, the question arose whether 'Romantic Religion' should already now, that is to say as the first literary introduction, be presented to the American reader. So I can

agree with you [on that subject]. . . . The time for 'Romantic Religion' will only then have arrived when the author, so I hope, will have won the trust of his readers, so much so that they will follow him, not all too reluctantly and perhaps even readily, along the new and for them untrodden paths that 'Romantic Religion' wants to point out." See letter to Nahum Glatzer, 28 March 1947, in Nahum Glatzer Collection, Vanderbilt University Special Collections. An English translation of "Romantic Religion" did not appear until 1958, following publication of a revised English edition of *The Essence of Judaism* that had been undertaken by the American social and literary critic Irving Howe, and two years after Baeck's death.

113. Letter to Gertrud Luckner, 28 June 1950, in *Werke* 6: 645.

114. See the photo of the three men in conversation in *Allgemeine Wochenzeitung der Juden in Deutschland* 6.20 (24 August 1951): 1.

115. "Cardinal Dr. Michael von Faulhaber, Archbishop of Munich," *Common Ground* 6.5 (August–October 1952): 14–16. For Faulhaber's negative views on Judaism, see his *Judaism, Christianity and Germany*, trans George D. Smith (New York: Macmillan, 1934).

116. See Baeck's letters to Clara Urquhart, 15 December 1955, 8 April 1956, and 30 August 1956, Leo Baeck Collection AR 66, LBIA, DigiBaeck, Frames 794–797.

117. "Some Questions to the Christian Church from the Jewish Point of View" (1954), in *Werke* 5: 462.

118. "The Profile—Rabbi Baeck," *Observer*, 17 May 1953.

119. "Judaism on Old and New Paths," 199.

120. "The Pharisees," in *The Pharisees and Other Essays by Leo Baeck* (New York: Schocken, 1947), 12. The original German version appeared in *Publikation der Lehranstalt für die Wissenschaft des Judentums* 44 (1927): 34–71, and is reprinted in *Werke* 5: 367–410.

121. "The Pharisees," 44.

122. "The Faith of Paul," in Walter Kaufmann, ed., *Judaism and Christianity: Essays by Leo Baeck* (Philadelphia: Jewish Publication Society, 1958), 160.

123. Ibid., 164.

124. "Judentum, Christentum und Islam: Rede gehalten von Ehren-Grosspräsident Dr. Leo Baeck anlässlich der Studientagung der Districts-Gross-Loge Kontinental-Europa XIX in Bruxelles (22 April 1956)," in *Werke* 5: 488.

125. On 11 February 1912, when still a rabbi in Düsseldorf, Baeck wrote to an unnamed colleague that missionizing was "for us a commandment of self-preservation, since recognition by others will awaken pride of possession in our own ranks." Leo Baeck Collection AR 66, LBIA.

126. "Some Questions to the Christian Church from the Jewish Point of View," in *Werke* 5: 455–456.

127. "The Mission of Judaism: Its Later Development and Its Significance for World Judaism Today" (1949), in *Werke* 6: 528.

128. Letter to Robert Raphael Geis, 19 February 1954, Leo Baeck Collection AR 66, DigiBaeck, Frame 25.

129. Lily Montagu, who did the day-to-day work for the World Union, urged Baeck to persist in the position, claiming that his scholarship, his personality, and the broad respect that he commanded were essential for keeping the union together. See Lily Montagu to Leo Baeck, 31 October 1950, MSS 16, D12/4, American Jewish Archives.

130. "The Task of Progressive Judaism in the Post-War World," 57.

131. On one occasion, Baeck spoke of the poetic attitude in language that recalls Martin Buber's concept of "I and Thou." In an address at the West London Synagogue, he said:

"Standing before an oak or a pine, one can speak with it. To hear this tree speaking and, as it were, to be able to answer the question of this tree, this horse, this dog—this is poetry." "Judaism as a Life-Force," *Synagogue Review* (June 1951): 293.

132. "The Law in Judaism," *Synagogue Review* (July 1950): 284–285. For an example of a current guide to Reform Jewish practice, see Mark Washofsky, *Jewish Living* (New York: URJ Press, 2010).

133. Letter to Louis H. Epstein in Brookline, Mass., 11 November 1951, SC-627, American Jewish Archives.

134. "The Task of Progressive Judaism in the Post-War World," 55.

135. "Presidential Address," *Report of the Sixth International Conference [of the World Union for Progressive Judaism], Held in London July 14 to July 19, 1949* (London: WUPJ, 1949), 24.

136. "The Religious Approach to World Problems," *Report of the Eighth International Conference, Held in London July 2 to July 9, 1953* (London: WUPJ, 1953), 69.

137. "Individuum Ineffabile," 107.

138. "The Interrelation of Judaism and Science" (1949), in ibid., 116.

139. Letter to Max Wiener, 21 November 1947, Leo Baeck Collection AR 66, LBIA, DigiBaeck, Frames 853–854. The volume by Wiener is *Jüdische Religion im Zeitalter der Emanzipation* (Berlin: Philo, 1933).

140. "Presidential Address," *Report of the Sixth International Conference*, 25.

141. Baeck uses the term *ahnen* to describe apprehension of the mystery, e.g., in "Das Judentum auf alten und neuen Wegen," 47.

142. This concept of a transcendent, mysterious God must have created problems for Baeck in praying the Jewish liturgy, which, even in its non-Orthodox form, speaks of a personal God who not only commands but also loves. In Baeck's extant writings, there is little attention to liturgy.

143. Surely, Baeck's knowledge of Jewish suffering in the distant past and his "and nevertheless" faith in the future helped to diminish for him the significance of the Holocaust, which, unlike for the theologian Emil Fackenheim, does not become a major category in his writing. However, I find it difficult to believe, as Eliezer Schweid twice suggests, that he related to the catastrophe "as a passing episode." That would have been psychologically impossible. See Schweid, "From *The Essence of Judaism* to *This People Israel*: Leo Baeck's Theological Confrontation with the Period of Nazism and the Holocaust," in his *Wrestling Until Daybreak: Searching for Meaning in the Thinking on the Holocaust* (Lanham, Md.: University Press of America, 1994), 7, 9.

144. "Jewish Mysticism" (1950), in *Werke* 5: 550.

145. Anonymous editor's introduction to *The Pharisees and Other Essays*, vii.

146. "Peace," *WUPJB* 19 (January 1948): 9–10.

147. "Judaism: The Religious Character and the Historical Situation," 25.

148. See Hans I. Bach, ed., *Epochen der jüdischen Geschichte von Leo Baeck* (Stuttgart: Kohlhammer, 1974), introduction. The introduction and text are reprinted in *Werke* 5: 209–263.

149. "End of an Epoch" (1956), in *Werke* 6: 695.

150. *Epochen der jüdischen Geschichte*, in *Werke* 5: 325.

151. In an earlier reflection on prayer, Baeck noted that it is not by chance that biblical language uses reflexive verbs (*hitpalel* and *hithanen*) to indicate that the very act of prayer affects the individual who prays. "Gebet im Judentum," *B'ne Briss* (September/October 1935): 82.

152. *Dieses Volk: Jüdische Existenz* 2 (1957), in *Werke* 2: 332.

153. Manfred E. Swarsensky, "Out of the Root of Rabbis," in Herbert A. Strauss and Kurt R. Grossmann, eds., *Gegenwart im Rückblick: Festgabe für die jüdische Gemeinde zu Berlin 25 Jahre nach dem Neubeginn* (Heidelberg: Lothar Stiehm, 1970), 224.

154. *Werke* 2: 33.

155. Letter to Graf Thun-Hohenstein, 16 March 1950, in *Werke* 6: 596.

156. "Die vier Stationen des Lebens" (1946), in ibid., 434–435. Although Baeck is speaking in general terms of old age, it seems obvious that he was also speaking of himself.

157. Letter to Ludwig Meidner, 24 November 1954, in ibid., 631.

158. Ruth Berlak to Stanley Dreyfus, 21 September 1956, Leo Baeck Family Collection AR 25449, DigiBaeck, Frame 218.

159. Hans Reichmann to Theodor Heuss, 2 and 6 November 1956, Theodor Heuss Nachlass, Bestand N 1221, Bundesarchiv Koblenz.

160. Hans Reichmann, "Bericht über die letzte Krankheit und den Tod Dr. Leo Baecks," in Eva G. Reichmann, ed., *Worte des Gedenkens für Leo Baeck* (Heidelberg: Lambert Schneider, 1959), 241–244.

EPILOGUE

1. Ruth Berlak-Baeck to Fritz Steinthal, 14 May 1944, Leo Baeck Collection MF145, LBIA, microfilm. The synagogue was called Culto Israelita de Belgrano.

2. *LBI Information* 10 (2003): 8.

3. Joshua Loth Liebman, "A Living Saint: Rabbi Leo Baeck," *Atlantic Monthly*, June 1948, 40–43.

4. Manfred E. Swarsensky, "Out of the Root of Rabbis," in Herbert A. Strauss and Kurt R. Grossmann, eds., *Gegenwart im Rückblick: Festgabe für die jüdische Gemeinde zu Berlin 25 Jahre nach dem Neubeginn* (Heidelberg: Lothar Stiehm, 1970), 226; Marion Freyer Wolff, *The Shrinking Circle: Memories of Nazi Berlin, 1933–1939* (New York: UAHC Press, 1989), 29; Judah Magnes, in *World Union for Progressive Judaism Bulletin* 20 (September 1948): 37.

5. Cited in Eva G. Reichmann, ed., *Worte des Gedenkens für Leo Baeck* (Heidelberg: Lambert Schneider, 1959), 233.

6. Selma Stern, *Josel of Rosheim: Commander of Jewry in the Holy Roman Empire of the German Nation*, trans. Gertrude Hirschler (Philadelphia: Jewish Publication Society, 1965).

7. Peter Gay, "In Deutschland zu Hause . . . Die Juden in der Weimarer Zeit," in Arnold Paucker, ed., *Die Juden im Nationalsozialistischen Deutschland, 1933–1943* (Tübingen: J. C. B. Mohr, 1986), 38.

8. N. Bentwich et al., eds., *Essays Presented to Leo Baeck on the Occasion of His Eightieth Birthday* (London: East and West Library, 1954).

9. Martin Buber, "Adel," *Jüdische Rundschau* 41 (23 May 1933): 213; idem, "In Theresienstadt," *Mitteilungsblatt der Hitachduth Olej Germania we Olej Austria* 7.21 (21 May 1943): 1.

10. Cynthia Ozick, "A Youthful Intoxication," *New York Times Book Review* (10 December 2006): 35. I am grateful to Nancy Weaver Durka for calling this item to my attention.

11. According to Steven M. Wasserstrom, *Religion After Religion: Gershom Scholem, Mircea Eliade, and Henry Corbin at Eranos* (Princeton, N.J.: Princeton University Press, 1999), 54, 275, Scholem borrowed the notion of romantic religion from Baeck but used it in a positive sense for the stage of mysticism that followed the classical stage in the formation of Judaism.

Wasserstrom also noted that Baeck was responsible for Scholem being invited to the Eranos conferences.

12. Gershom Scholem to Siegmund Hurwitz, 24 October 1947, in Itta Shedletzky, ed., *Gershom Scholem Briefe I, 1914–1947* (Munich: C. H. Beck, 1994), 327–328.

13. Gershom Scholem to Hannah Arendt, 23 June 1963, in Thomas Sparr, ed., *Gershom Scholem Briefe II, 1948–1970* (Munich: C. H. Beck, 1995), 97.

14. Arendt first used the epithet regarding Baeck in "A Reporter at Large: Eichmann in Jerusalem—III," *New Yorker*, 2 March 1963, 42; it appeared as well in the first book version, *Eichmann in Jerusalem: A Report on the Banality of Evil* (New York: Viking Press, 1963), 105. It had appeared slightly earlier in Raul Hilberg, *The Destruction of the European Jews* (New York: Harper & Row, 1961), 292. Hilberg noted that the epithet was coined by a Nazi official, but he nevertheless adopted it into his own text. For later editions of her book, Arendt deleted the unfavorable designation and, in an interview with Albert Friedlander, commended Baeck for his "unquestionable courage and disregard for personal danger." Albert H. Friedlander, *Leo Baeck: Teacher of Theresienstadt* (New York: Holt, Rinehart and Winston, 1968), 12n1. However, Arendt continued to refer to Baeck erroneously as the former "Chief Rabbi of Berlin." That title did not exist in the Berlin Jewish community.

15. Recha Freier, *Let the Children Come: The Early History of Youth Aliyah* (London: Weidenfeld and Nicolson, 1961), 66; Konrad Kwiet, "Leo Baeck und der deutsch-jüdische Widerstand," in Michael Brocke et al., eds., *Neuer Anbruch: Zur deutsch-jüdischen Geschichte und Kultur* (Berlin: Metropol, 2001), 84.

16. According to the minutes of the meeting of the international Leo Baeck Institute, held in Jerusalem, 1 December 1955, and as reported there by Robert Weltsch, head of the London LBI, Baeck had promised to write memoirs, especially for the period when he headed the Reichsvertretung. But he did not undertake that task during the remaining months of his life, when he was eager to complete vol. 2 of *Dieses Volk: Jüdische Existenz.*

17. "Lebensgrund und Lebensgehalt" (1917/1918), in *Werke* 3: 113.

18. E. L. Ehrlich, "Leo Baeck—Leben und Lehre," *Freiburger Rundbrief* 25 (1973): 78.

19. Ernst Ludwig Ehrlich, "Leo Baeck—Rabbiner in schwerster Zeit," *Theresienstädter Studien und Dokumente* 3 (1996): 130.

20. Letter to Lily Montagu, 9 January 1952, MSS Col No 16, D/R/4, American Jewish Archives.

21. *Wesen des Judentums*, 2nd ed. (1922), in *Werke* 1: 291.

22. "Die religiöse Erziehung" (1930), in *Werke* 4: 374. However, the Orthodox Israeli educator Zvi Kurzweil, himself of German Jewish origin, thought that Baeck wrote lovingly on halakha and—questionably, in my opinion—regarded him as standing very close to Orthodox Judaism. He hoped that Baeck's thought might counteract the extremism in contemporary Orthodoxy. Zvi Kurzweil, "The Relevance of Leo Baeck's Thought to the Mainstreams of Judaism," *Judaism* 39.2 (Spring 1990): 170.

23. Adolf Leschnitzer, "The Unknown Leo Baeck," *Commentary* 23.5 (May 1957): 420 (Leschnitzer's emphasis).

24. *Wesen des Judentums*, 2nd ed. (1922), in *Werke* 1: 202.

25. Noted in Leonard Baker, *Days of Sorrow and Pain: Leo Baeck and the Berlin Jews* (New York: Macmillan, 1978), 11.

26. For his references to martyrdom in the 1st ed. of *Wesen des Judentums*, see *Werke* 1: 366, 383.

27. Robert Rafael Geis, "Leo Baeck," in Geis et al., eds., *Männer des Glaubens im deutschen Widerstand* (Munich: Ner Tamid, 1959), 16–17; Eva Reichmann, "Ansprache bei der Gedenkkundgebung für Dr. Leo Baeck," Eva Reichmann Collection, Leo Baeck Institute Archives, DigiBaeck, Frame 1149.

28. Fritz Kaufmann to Martin Buber, 19 December 1956, in Grete Schaeder, ed., *Martin Buber Briefwechsel aus sieben Jahrzehnten*, *Vol. III: 1938–1965* (Heidelberg: Lambert Schneider, 1975), 425.

29. Recall Baeck's letter to his wife cited in Chap. 4.

30. Rudolf Callmann, "Ein grosser Mensch," *AJR* supplement (December 1956): 10.

31. Among those who used the word "aura" regarding Baeck was W. Gunther Plaut, Baeck's student in Germany who later became a prominent Canadian rabbi. See the interview with Plaut at the Virtual History Archive, USC Shoah Foundation.

32. Letter to Theodor Heuss, 3 March 1954, Heuss Collection, Deutsches Literaturarchiv/Schiller-Nationalmuseum, Marbach am Neckar.

33. Max Grünewald, "Leo Baeck," *American Jewish Yearbook* 59 (1958): 482. See also Ehrlich, "Leo Baeck—Leben und Lehre," 76: "Baeck won over the German Jewish bourgeoisie, without its really understanding him. It respected his personality, but did not penetrate to the core of his work, which was decidedly averse to the bourgeoisie."

34. Else Meidner, "Ein Wort des Dankes," in E. Reichmann, ed., *Worte des Gedenkens für Leo Baeck*, 199.

35. "Theologie und Geschichte" (1932), in *Werke* 4: 56–57.

Bibliographic Essay

In 1954, two years before Leo Baeck's death, Theodore Wiener, a librarian at Hebrew Union College in Cincinnati, compiled a chronological bibliography of Baeck's writings, containing 408 entries, with an appended alphabetical index of the items arranged according to the venues in which they were published. It appeared as "The Writings of Leo Baeck: A Bibliography," *Studies in Bibliography and Booklore* 1.3 (June 1954): 108–144. A second bibliography arranges Baeck's works alphabetically. Unlike Wiener's bibliography, it covers the entire span of Baeck's life and includes secondary literature as well as selected reviews. It was compiled by a student, Tom Schutter, for the course "The Theology of Leo Baeck," taught by Morton C. Fierman at California State College, Fullerton. It appeared in manuscript form in 1974 as "The Serial Literature of Leo Baeck: A Bibliography" and is available at the Hebrew Union College–Jewish Institute of Religion Library in Cincinnati.

Although it does not include all of Leo Baeck's publications, the six-volume *Leo Baeck Werke*, ed. Albert H. Friedlander, Berthold Klappert, Werner Licharz, and Michael A. Meyer (Gütersloh: Gütersloher Verlagshaus, 1996–2003), includes all his major works as well as nearly all his significant articles and lectures, along with a selection of his extant letters. All items are presented in their original language—German or English—and are provided with introductions. English translations of Baeck's German works are *The Pharisees and Other Essays* (New York: Schocken, 1947); *The Essence of Judaism*, rev. ed., trans. Irving Howe (New York: Schocken, 1948); *Judaism and Christianity*, trans. Walter Kaufmann (Philadelphia: Jewish Publication Society, 1958); and *This People Israel: The Meaning of Jewish Existence*, trans. Albert H. Friedlander (Philadelphia: Jewish Publication Society, 1965). There is also a Hebrew translation of *The Essence of Judaism*, by Lea Zagagi, with an introduction by Akiba Ernst Simon (Jerusalem: Mosad Bialik, 1968).

The first biographical work to appear was Albert H. Friedlander, *Leo Baeck: Teacher of Theresienstadt* (New York: Holt, Rinehart and Winston,

1968). Friedlander, a disciple of Baeck's from the time that Friedlander was a student at the Hebrew Union College, focuses on Baeck's theology, which he integrates with Jewish and non-Jewish thinkers of Baeck's time, and locates him between the philosophical idealism of Hermann Cohen and the existentialism of Martin Buber and Franz Rosenzweig. The second major work on Baeck, focusing on the other side of the subject—Baeck's practical activity—is Leonard Baker's *Days of Sorrow and Pain: Leo Baeck and the Berlin Jews* (New York: Macmillan, 1978), which is a popular book by a writer on political history. At the time of his writing, Baker was able to conduct numerous interviews with people who knew Baeck personally, thereby enriching his account. However, his fondness for the poignant occasionally led him to dramatizing events excessively, and his lack of familiarity with Jewish history produced some misunderstandings. Fortunately, however, when Baker's book won a Pulitzer Prize, it brought Baeck's life to the attention of a wider circle of American readers, and, like Friedlander's book, it was translated into German.

In 2001, the Frankfurt Jewish Museum mounted an exhibition on Leo Baeck, accompanied by a large catalog comprising eleven essays by several authors: Georg Heuberger and Fritz Backhaus, eds., *Leo Baeck 1873–1956: Aus dem Stamme von Rabbinern* (Frankfurt: Jüdischer Verlag im Suhrkamp Verlag, 2001). The essays, though unable to provide an integrated presentation, incorporated newly discovered material, and the volume was supplemented by selected personal recollections. The most recent full-length biography is by Maurice-Ruben Hayoun: it appeared first in French as *Léo Baeck: Conscience du judaïsme moderne* (Paris: Armand Colin, 2011) and then in German as *Leo Baeck: Repräsentant des liberalen Judentums*, trans. Alexandra Maria Linder (Darmstadt: WBG, 2015). This large volume contains valuable material, but much of it is only tangentially, or not at all, related to Leo Baeck, and some important works and views are not considered. Since the book does not follow a strict chronology, the reader cannot easily assess the development of the person or the thought. That it was initially oriented toward a French readership is indicated by the author's introduction of such French figures as Ernest Renan, Edmond Fleg, and Emmanuel Levinas.

Walter Homolka has written a variety of works on Leo Baeck. His special interest has been to relate Baeck to Christian thought. On this subject, he has published *Jewish Identity in Modern Times: Leo Baeck and German Protestantism* (Providence, R.I.: Berghahn, 1995), which appeared the previous year in a German translation. His later short book on Baeck's thought, *Leo Baeck: Jüdisches Denken—Perspektiven für heute* (Freiburg: Herder, 2006), likewise concentrates on Baeck and Christianity. His two brief illustrated and highly sympathetic biographies of Baeck, coauthored with a Christian friend, Elias H. Füllenbach—*Leo Baeck: Eine Skizze seines Lebens* (Gütersloh: Gütersloher Verlagshaus, 2006) and *Rabbiner Leo Baeck: Ein Lebensbild* (Berlin: Hentrich & Hentrich, 2009)—provide basic facts of Baeck's life. Collections of secondary literature on Baeck include Werner Licharz, ed., *Leo Baeck—Lehrer und Helfer in schwerer Zeit* (Frankfurt: Haag + Herchen, 1983); Verena Mühlstein, ed., *Leo Baeck—Zwischen Geheimnis und Gebot: Auf dem Weg zu einem progressiven Judentum der Moderne* (Karlsruhe: Bertelsmann, 1997); and one such collection in Hebrew, Avraham Barkai, ed., *Leo Baeck: Leadership and Thought, 1933–1945* (Jerusalem: Zalman Shazar Center and Leo Baeck Institute, 2000). The recent Spanish biography by Juan Agustín Blasco Carbó, *Rabino Leo Baeck* (Valencia: Drassana, 2016), draws almost exclusively on the earlier secondary literature.

There is even an imaginatively enhanced historical novel on Leo Baeck, by the German writer Waldtraut Lewin, *Leo Baeck, Geschichte eines deutschen Juden: Eine Romanbiografie* (Gütersloh: Gütersloher Verlagshaus, 2012); and a radio play by Erwin Sylvanus, trans. David Dowdey and Robert Wolfgang Rhée, *Leo Baeck: A Radio Play Based on Authentic Texts* (New York: Peter Lang, 1996).

Finally, among the numerous articles and chapters that deal with Leo Baeck in a variety of books and periodicals, especially worth mentioning for its unusual insight is Eliezer Schweid, "From *The Essence of Judaism* to *This People Israel*: Leo Baeck's Theological Confrontation with the Period of Nazism and the Holocaust," in Schweid, *Wrestling Until Day-Break: Searching for Meaning in the Thinking on the Holocaust* (Lanham, Md.: University Press of America, 1994), 3–84.

Index

Page numbers in italics indicate illustrations.

Acknowledgments

Many individuals and institutions have generously assisted me in my work. I am most grateful to Michael Morgan, Michael Brenner, and my wife, Margie, who all read the entire manuscript and provided helpful comments. At the Klau Library of the Hebrew Union College–Jewish Institute of Religion in Cincinnati, Allan Satin was always available to help me track down rare books and articles, and Marilyn Krider helped obtain volumes from elsewhere. Similarly, at the Leo Baeck Institute in New York, I was assisted by Frank Mecklenburg Michael Simonson, and Hermann Teifer. At the American Jewish Archives, my research was advanced by Kevin Proffitt and Dana Herman. And at the United States Holocaust Memorial Museum, Scott Miller and Liviu Carare were of welcome assistance. Others to whom I am grateful for their interest and help in various ways include Inka Bertz, Andreas Brämer and his assistant Jonas Stier, Ellen and James Dreyfus, Joshua Franklin, Susannah Heschel, George Kohler, Michael Marmur, Ann Millin, Benjamin Ravid, and Erik Riedel. I am also appreciative of comments by the two anonymous readers of the University of Pennsylvania Press, its copy editor, and other members of its staff. All had a share in my being able to bring this study to publication.

Lightning Source UK Ltd.
Milton Keynes UK
UKHW010712020322
399416UK00002B/73

9 780812 252569